LINCOLN CHRISTIAN COLLEGE AND SEMINARY

OLDER PEOPLE AND THE CHURCH

D0881985

T&T CLARK LTD

A Continuum imprint

59 George Street
Edinburgh EH2 2LQ
Scotland
www.tandtclark.co.uk

370 Lexington Avenue
New York 10017–6503
USA
www.continuumbooks.com

Copyright © T&T Clark Ltd, 2002

All rights reserved. No part of this publication may be reproduced, stored in a retrieval system, or transmitted, in any form or by any means, electronic, mechanical, photocopying, recording or otherwise, without the prior permission of T&T Clark Ltd.

First published 2002

ISBN 0 567 08882 0 (Paperback)
ISBN 0 567 08916 9 (Hardback)

British Library Cataloguing-in-Publication Data
A catalogue record for this book is available from the British Library

Typeset by Fakenham Photosetting Ltd, Fakenham, Norfolk NR21 8NN
Printed and bound in Great Britain by Biddles Ltd, Guildford and King's Lynn

Acknowledgements

This book could not have been written without a great deal of help and advice, permission to use material, hard work from others and general encouragement. In particular my thanks go to the following:

- The Rev. Albert Jewell and The Methodist Homes for the Aged.
- Gillian Crosby at the Centre for Policy on Ageing.
- The Christian Council on Ageing.
- Research into Ageing.
- Rhena Taylor and *Outlook.*
- The staff of the 40:3 Trust, in particular Darren Burgess, Sue Pratt and Julie Mottershead.
- Prof. John Copas, University of Warwick Professor of Statistics.
- Most of all:

Prof. Margaret Archer: Department of Sociology, University of Warwick.
My wife, Ruth, my main typist and encourager.

Scripture quotations taken from the HOLY BIBLE, NEW INTERNATIONAL VERSION copyright © 1973, 1978, 1984 by International Bible Society. Used by permission of Hodder and Stoughton Ltd, a member of the Hodder Headline plc group. All rights reserved. 'NIV' is a registered trademark of International Bible Society. UK Trademark number 1448790. Unless otherwise stated, all Scripture quotations taken from the Holy Bible, New International Version are referred to in the text as NIV.

Extracts from the Authorized Version of the Bible (referred to in the text as AV), the rights in which are vested in the Crown, are reproduced by permission of the Crown's Patentee, Cambridge University Press.

Extracts from the Jerusalem Bible (referred to in the text as JB)

104633

taken from the Jerusalem Bible, copyright © 1966, 1967 and 1968 by Darton Longman and Todd Ltd and Doubleday Co. Inc., and used by permission of the publishers.

Extracts from the Amplified Bible (referred to in the text as Amplified) copyright © 1954, 1958 The Lockman Foundation, are reproduced by permission of the publishers, HarperCollins Publishers Ltd.

Extracts from The Book of Common Prayer, the rights in which are vested in the Crown, are reproduced by permission of the Crown's Patentee, Cambridge University Press.

Contents

1

An Overview

It is possible to say something very simple, which can be evocative and even provocative, which is also universally true. Three words will demonstrate this: 'I am ageing.'

Whoever says that sentence will receive a reaction, as well as feeling one inside themselves. Most people seem to react negatively. This book seeks to deal with these three words in the context of the church, and its attitude to an ageing population.

Why the Book?

In seeking to explore the relationship between the Christian church in England and older people, four factors combined to persuade me to go forward. Firstly, this is a subject which theoretically involves everyone, as all are ageing. Secondly, this therefore has an important place in overall sociological research. Thirdly, there have been great changes in society, in the church, and for older people in recent years, which deserve exploration. Finally, I have a personal interest in this subject, as I will seek to show. Let me deal with each of these in turn.

Everyone's involvement

The question of old age is one for the whole of society (Tournier, 1972, p.36). 'To be concerned with gerontology is to be pragmatically selfish' as it is our own future (Blech, 1981, p.4). Growing old has been described as everyone's 'terminal illness' from birth (Botting, 1986, p.2), an 'inescapable part of the human existence' (Dulin, 1988, p.7). Not only is growing older a factor for everyone, but we would all like to know how to do it well and what we should make of our older lives (Yoder, 1996, p.417).

Even for the young, 'It is never too early to begin getting ready to be old' (Stagg, 1981, p.8), so all might achieve 'successful ageing' (Hunt, 1988, p.215). By this I would take the term to include a sense of fulfilment of life, happiness and well-being. This is one of the greatest challenges at the beginning of this new millennium for the simple reason that most people live longer (Greengross, 1997, p.1). If people are to continue in any relationship with the church, as I found many seemed minded so to do, then this research could play a part in the overall need to understand their position.

Here I have drawn on several reliable sources, both in literature and from official figures, for statistical assistance, with particular help from the research of Dr Peter Brierley (1991, 1999a, b, c). When looking at ageing, it is sobering to realize that life expectancy in the Roman Empire averaged 26 years (Boote, 1994). William Hutton, the Birmingham historian who died in 1815, estimated that only one in a thousand reached the age of 90 in 1812 (Hutton, 1998, p.117). In Japan today, average life expectation is 80 (Weiss, 1997, p.12). In the United Kingdom, it is estimated that between 1950 and 2050 the number of over 80's will increase sixfold to nearly five million (Gaunt, 1998). Today, one writer asserts that half of Great Britain is over 50 (Beasley-Murray, 1995, p.180). Nineteen out of every twenty people in Britain now reach 50 (*World Health Report*, 1998). The biblical three-score years and ten has been reached for the first time in history as a social norm (Brown, 1982, p.5). Those over 75 and 85 are the fastest growing age groups in America (Daniels, 1988, p.3).

In Britain, there were 350,000 people aged over 85 in 1961, but this had risen to 1.1 million in 1996 (Office for National Statistics, 1998). In 1951, 300 men and women were over 100 years old: the estimate for 2031 is 34,000 (Age Concern, 1997, p.2), by which time 6 million will be over 80 (Appleton, 1998). The over 80's will have risen from 0.7 per cent of the population in 1951 to 3.2 per cent in 2025 (*Social Trends*, 1994). Yet of all those over 65, only 4 per cent live in residential care: the same as in 1900 (*An Ageing Population*, 1988, p.22). This puts a great burden on an estimated 6.8 million informal carers, who 'provide a staggering 92 per cent of all care' (Harris, 1998, p.3).

As far as gender is concerned, in 1981 there were 3.3 women aged 85 plus for every man of the same age (Johnson and Falkingham, 1992, p.19). In the 75 to 84 age group, women outnumber men two to one (*Population Trends*, 1998). In 1996 men's life expectancy was 74.4 but for women it was 79.7, whereas in 1901 it was 45.5 (men) and 49 (women) (Tinker, 1999). Such is the improvement in life expectancy (Coleman *et al.*, 1993, pp.1–18). All these figures are typical of the developed world.

With these remarkable statistics, others of which will be quoted throughout the book, the churches in general should be asking serious questions about their relationship with this section of society.

A place in sociological research

In recent years there has been a growing interest in gerontology, but little in its relationship with the church and how the church and older people interact. The deep social evil of ageism has been all but ignored until comparatively recently, compared with much debate on the allied subjects of feminism, sexism and racism. Hardly anything on the specific relationship between older people and religion appeared before Pollak's *Social Adjustment in Old Age* (Pollak, 1948), and Moberg's *Religion and Personal Adjustment* (1951), which led to the key work *The Church and the Older Person* (Gray and Moberg, 1962) and Moberg's article 'Religion and the ageing family' (Moberg, 1972).

The United Kingdom, by comparison, has few studies or empirical research on the religious concerns and practices of older people (Howse, 1999, pp.6, 101). 'Studying the lives of older people has become a central concern for those involved in sociological as well as gerontological research and investigation ... [yet] much work must be done in respect of developing a sociology of old age' (Phillipson, 1998, pp.138–40). It seemed necessary, therefore, to conduct some 'sociological ... research and investigation' not only to develop this 'sociology of old age' but, in particular, to look at these religious concerns and practicalities of older people. I wanted to understand whether the church in general was contributing to the life and welfare of the older person, whether it was sociologically as well as spiritually aware of the specific needs of the growing number within this category. Could there be a greater care shown, and more opportunities given?

Changes

'The times ...' according to Bob Dylan, 'are a-changin'' (Dylan, 1964). The world known by our parents is very different from ours (Handy, 1995, p.5). *The Harvard Business Review* put it very dramatically:

> Every few hundred years throughout western history a sharp transformation has occurred. In a matter of decades society altogether rearranges itself – its world view, its basic values, its social and political structures, its arts, its key institutions. Fifty years later a new world exists and the people born into that world cannot even imagine the world in which their grandparents lived and into which their own parents were born. Our age is such a transformation. (Drucker, 1992)

I will address my understanding of this 'transformation' at the end of this chapter when dealing with the book's main themes. However, among the societal changes implied by Drucker have been key reforms within the church, too. I will consider in further detail under that latter heading parts of Vatican II, new liturgies in several denominations, new styles of worship and music, new movements such as the Charismatic movement and the establishment of New Churches (capitalized as they are now seen as a specific denomination). How have these impacted the older generation? With the abandonment in many quarters of older styles (the *Authorized Version* of the Bible and the 1662 *Prayer Book* in the Church of England, for example), many feel the church has adopted a youth culture (Beasley-Murray, 1995, p.180). Do older people need to be treated as a 'special case' by the church (Howse, 1999, p.84)? Despite all the changes, the older age group is the only one to see a rise in its numbers of church attenders in the last few years (Brierley, 1999c). As I will seek to show, some older people feel there is now no place for them in the church and they are not needed, now they are (as the Beatles sang) 'sixty-four' (Lennon and McCartney, 1967). I intend to explore whether there is a marginalization of older people by the church (Guillemard, 1983, p.6).

Personal interest

As members of Parliament have to do in another context, I must declare a personal interest in this whole subject. As a Senior Solicitor in Local Government, I had major dealings with older people as the lawyer responsible for the legal advice to a major Social Services Department. I now work as the Director of a charity which helps churches in their sharing the Christian faith with others, including a considerable emphasis on those who are older in years. This experience and the contacts already established were expected to be of utility in conducting the research. It has encouraged a deliberate attempt to be as unbiased as possible. Everyone must have some view on their particular subject of research and others have declared similar interests (as Hornsby-Smith, 1987, pp.17–18, referring to his support of Vatican II as set out in Abbott, 1966). The bringing of personal interests into a book of this nature is inescapable. I was further propelled to this subject of the church and older people after researching for my own book *Bereaved* (Knox, 1994). I had met so many older people who felt the need of the church's help in their loss and loneliness: some were encouraged by the church's attitude, but others felt more could have been done. I was thus motivated to explore this further. By way of explanation, when I refer to 'the church', I mean all Christian churches: it is used as a collective noun in lower case, not implying any one particular denomination.

Help Along the Way

Literature

In a book relating to the church, older people and their relationship with each other, there had to be three areas for research. The only problem relating to the church was selection: whole library shelves deal with this. However, I was looking for two specifics: the definition of 'church', and what the Bible and Christian literature had to say about older people. This latter theme necessitated exploring a number of commentaries, from Matthew Henry onwards through to the *Tyndale Commentaries* and the *New Bible Dictionary*, together with commentaries on specific books of the Bible, such as *Acts and Letters of the Apostles* (Lattimore, 1982). For definitions of 'church' it seemed wise to go right back to Hus, working through sociologists such as Weber and Troeltsch to modern-day researchers such as Hornsby-Smith and Gill, for example. This enabled me to have a wider overview across the centuries to give as composite a definition as possible.

There is also a wealth of literature on the subject of older people, ageing and ageism. Classic works by Simone de Beauvoir and Paul Tournier gave a good starting point, followed by Bytheway's *Ageism* (Bytheway, 1995) and Guillemard's edited book *Old Age and the Welfare State* (Guillemard, 1983).

However, there are gaps in the literature concerning the links between older people and the church. Despite the 40-year-old *The Church and the Older Person* (Gray and Moberg, 1962), based largely on research ten years earlier in the United States, few have written on this specific relationship. Further publications have emanated from the States, up to and including Moberg's latest edited work *Aging and Spirituality* (Moberg, 2001) and the anthology of papers *Religion and Aging* (Watkins, 2001), but not solely on the church's role. I was helped by two reports already produced by leading denominations: *Respecting the Gift of Years* (Appleton, 1998) for the United Reformed Church, and *Ageing* (Report of the Social Policy Committee of the Board of Social Responsibility, 1990) for the Church of England. As my research progressed, I realized I was delving into an area that needed much more work.

People

I wanted to explore whether there might be different attitudes or approaches by the various churches: would the newer churches and denominations consider older people in a more or less favourable way from those churches of long standing? Would town and city churches prove less helpful than those in the countryside – or the other way round? How would the Church of England and Roman Catholic Churches compare with the more eclectic Free Churches? In relation to the leaders, I visited four different denominational Theological

Colleges (Appendix 2). When it came to who could help me in researching for this book, it became clear that I needed to meet many leaders or spokespersons if I were to get a proper cross-sectional view. Full details of those I saw are in Appendix 4. To obtain an overview, representatives of at least ten denominations were seen, including some at their headquarters and senior leaders of each church. Clergy and laity in various churches and ordinary members who were young and in mid-life were interviewed (again, detailed in Appendix 4).

In particular, I interviewed over 50 older churchgoers and 60 older non-attenders. Certain questions seem paramount. For those who do not attend church, why do they not now go, assuming they once did? If I were to find a fall-off in religious attitudes, would this be because of a national secularization process, or would the factors be more complicated and personal? As for those older people who attend church, would their attitude towards church be affected by their denomination, and by whether they lived in an urban or rural setting? For these older people, I included eight residential homes (Appendix 3). These were in addition to the individual sample, and enabled those who cared for older people to express their views.

To make the book have as much balance as possible, people were seen on as random a basis as could be managed, in an area which was geographically viable. The Church of England Diocese of Coventry (see Figure 1.1) is made up of the County of Warwickshire and is an excellent microcosm of the whole country. It includes a major industrial city (Coventry), a number of towns (Rugby, Stratford-upon-Avon, Nuneaton, Meriden) and many large and small villages. It lies at the very heart of England.

Having detailed the geographical area, I wish to explain my choice of denominations. Representatives of every major denomination in England were seen, including Roman Catholic, Church of England, several Free Churches, Black Churches and New Churches. This gave me as broad a cross-section as possible for my research, and individuals as well as leaders, ordained and lay, came from this range. To enable me to describe the church's approach, the voice of the leadership of several churches was crucial, as was the 'voice from the pew'. When it came to the older people, they were chosen as

Figure 1.1 The Diocese of Coventry, divided into Deaneries: each sub-division was visited, with several denominations in each

randomly as possible, until the numbers detailed in Appendix 4 had been seen from a particular denomination. Significantly, every older non church attender wished to be identified with a church, however long ago their previous attendance was. Regarding gender, I saw 30 female and 22 male older attenders, with 35 and 25 being the respective numbers for non attenders, which roughly coincides with their proportional representation in the population of those over the age of 65.

Figure 1.2 Figure 1.1 in the national context. The whole area has a population of 810,000: an approximation derived from the Coventry City Council and Warwickshire County Council official figures. Coventry itself has the third highest proportion of over-65's in the country (Hall, 1998).

Research methods

This sub-section, in which I explain in more detail my research methods, will only be of interest to fellow researchers. My overall aim, as I have stated, was to get as good a cross-section of opinions as possible. To help achieve this, I sought to be as random as possible, though I accept that there is no way of checking this, compared with the specific 'lottery' and 'random numbers' methods (Moser and Kalton, 1979, p.82).

The leaders of denominations were inevitably self-selected (a Roman Catholic bishop is the only one in an area, for example). For everyone else, various sampling styles were adopted. Ministers of churches were chosen to represent a variety of areas in town, city and country. Older people were easier to find on a door-to-door basis in a village, whereas in a town or city I located respondents in a sheltered housing complex, flats where older people tended to live, or in a club. I went quite deliberately to one Ex-Servicemens' Club because I knew that each older man there would have been affected by the Second World War in some way. As a bonus, I realized immediately that there were a number of women there from a similar background.

With this random approach, there was also a certain amount of 'snowball' sampling. 'Have you seen Mr X next door-but-one?' I would be asked. 'He used to go to the Methodists.' Occasionally I might ask for help, such as, 'Are there any other older Catholics near here?' I felt this was a legitimate way of finding those I needed to see without having to visit homes where no-one would be in the 'older' category.

As I progressed, some 'stratified sampling' was inevitable (Moser and Kalton, 1979, pp.85–99). I wanted not only a cross-section of opinion, but also as balanced a representation as I could obtain from members of different denominations and those who did not attend church. I tried to reproduce the national ratios of churchgoers and the various figures in Appendix 4 give an exact breakdown. These ratios are based on a national annual census of church attendance. I accept the imperfection of this as a guide to beliefs, as there are many reasons for attendance. However, this is a justified guide to proportional representation because it is the same for all denominations, and is better than individual statistics generated by particular churches which are not denominationally comparable. For example, as the baptism of infants in the Church of England or the Roman Catholic Church is very different from adult baptism for the Baptists, comparisons in such terms would not be helpful.

This meant having to move on from one village to another, for example, when I had exhausted a particular category. In all cases I saw my interviewees *in situ*, opening with the words, 'I need your help!' Whenever stratified cells were nearing completion or were complete, I asked if potential subjects came into the categories I still needed, apologizing for troubling them if they did not. The interviews were conducted in as relaxed a manner as possible, with no sense of pressure to answer, or constraints on time. Although most people were seen on their own, I was happy to see a couple together, or even (once or twice) a small group of younger or older people, as they then encouraged each other to add thoughts to ones already given, producing an accumulative response. I have tried to indicate in the text these infrequent group encounters. I felt it strengthened the individual interviews, as more than one person present enabled views to be debated and exchanged on these occasions. Answers given were noted in detail, being transcribed into typescript immediately I returned home.

Regarding other faiths, I decided that, as with the geographical area, restrictive parameters had to be drawn. I was encouraged to believe that numerically I had got it about right by two other major research projects: Gray and Moberg (1962) is partially based on Moberg's earlier research among 219 persons in an American city (Moberg, 1951). *Habits of the Heart, Individualism and Commitment in American Life* (Bellah *et al.*, 1985) uses just over 200 interviews to survey how Americans live, with the whole of the first chapter based on four people.

I obtained specific permission to quote certain interviewees; I have referred to others only by Christian names or titles. However, I have sought not to breach any confidentiality.

Main Themes

The book begins by asking two seminal questions: who are 'older people'? and what is 'church'? Would these definitions be easy, or would there be variations, contradictions and disagreements? I proceed to a further question about the church: has it changed? If it has, has any change been radical, and has this affected the relationship between the church and older people? I probe the problem of ageism, and whether the last decades of life are to be 'deterioration and decline, or development and growth' (Coggan, 1997, p.1). Is ageism a problem within the church itself as well as in society? How does the church view older people, and would there be contradictions between what is said and what is done? Would the Bible challenge or endorse the church's view?

As the book proceeded, I wanted to discover how older people viewed the church. Would there be differences between attenders and non attenders? Would non attenders want to return – and why did they leave in the first place? Would the church be able to get older people to return: and would it want to? Does the church want the presence and help of older people? If it does, what can older people do for the church? What is their potential? Conversely, what could (and, perhaps, should) the church be doing for older people, whether they attend or not? Should this help be of an exclusively spiritual nature, or should there be a caring, sharing and practical side as well?

There are so many questions, and my aim is to approach them and address them sequentially, to give a cumulative response. The order of chapters seeks to reflect this: from who are 'older' and the question of ageism to what is 'church' and its changes. What the church says about older people is then compared and contrasted with the Bible's approach. How older people view the church leads to what they can do, and finally to how the church can respond positively to an ageing population. What follows is a brief summary of the approach taken to these questions.

Who is an older person?

Chapter 2 asks this first basic question, and makes some surprising discoveries. Answers were given, especially by older people themselves, with frankness and not a little humour. That chapter will demonstrate the delights and frustrations of qualitative interviewing, and shows great divergences of opinion. Writers' research was extensive, but writers were much more willing than respondents to be specific (even dogmatic) as to what constitutes an 'older person'. The interviewees, however, gave much more attention to matters of health, attitude and circumstances, with a frequent reluctance to categorize themselves. However, in a book entitled 'Older people and the church', this question was a *sine qua non.*

Ageism

Once a working definition of 'older people' had been established, it was thought necessary to explore the inherent dangers of people getting older and receiving negative reactions to so doing. Only in very recent years has ageism been recognized as a social evil akin to racism and sexism. I wanted to explore whether this was perceived as a difficulty for older people. Was it possible that the church had an ageist attitude? There was good literature to draw on here.

What is 'church'?

This is the other half of the equation in the book title. Upon the answer to this will depend how a relationship between the church and older people can be conducted. Do church leaders and older people see the church as the same thing? Is this answer affected by whether a person attends church or not? It is remarkable that over 70 different answers are given in Chapter 4 to the question 'What is "church"?' I have attempted to group these into such definitions as 'the building', 'the people', 'what happens' and 'feelings'. One is left with the view that the church will have to be many things to satisfy the hopes and needs of those both on the inside and outside of it.

The changing church

Part of the problem within chapter 4 is that the church is not static, and several denominations have made great changes in the last 40 to 50 years: hence this chapter. Under Pope John XXIII the Roman Catholic Church underwent a near revolution as a Council, colloquially known as 'Vatican II', allowed major reforms, including use of the vernacular rather than Latin for services, lay involvement on an unprecedented scale and encouragement of the use of the Bible by all. As stated above, other denominations also saw major changes. The Church of England welcomed many new forms of services, the Free Churches saw different forms of worship, and the New Churches sprang up to challenge the existing regimes. All these changes were to bring the church into the modern era, with the intention of encouraging the faithful and of winning back the lapsed. Again, over 70 perceived changes were detailed in my research: a vital component in the emerging relationship between the church and older people.

What does the church say?

How does the church, meaning both its official representatives and younger attenders, feel about older people? This is the question explored in Chapter 6. A paradox is discovered here. On the one hand, older people are spoken of in glowing terms – with some exceptions. On the other hand, provisions for older people are often sadly (and badly) lacking, it appears. I quoted from Guillemard, speaking of the marginalization of older people: this chapter asks the question as to whether, in its pursuit of younger congregations and new, unfamiliar forms of worship, the church is implicitly aiding and abetting this. However, despite some poor provisions, there does appear to be a refreshingly caring approach, as Chapter 6 seems to show.

Older people – and God

Chapter 7 goes 'back to basics'. All denominations within the church regard the Bible as a foundation for belief and practice. As much research draws on its original literature sources, I have devoted one chapter to the Bible's view on older people and ageing. This enables a relevant contrast to be made with the church's attitude. The chapter shows how, from cover to cover, the Bible commends a positive attitude to ageing, whilst not glossing over the failures of some older people. The implications for how the church approaches older people, and their care and their involvement, are great.

What older people think of the church

As one would possibly suspect, Chapter 8 is revealing. Older people are well prepared to speak their minds, and did so enthusiastically when asked how they felt about the church. Comments ranged from the highly positive to the extremely negative. Some older people spoke of help and care, others of rejection and even cruelty. In viewing whether the church and older people are together or apart, this is a highly significant chapter, giving cause for both hope and concern. Suggestions are proffered as to how perceived wrongs can be righted, and also how the goodwill on both sides could be harnessed.

What can older people do for the church?

Statistics quoted in this chapter and the next show that the population is not only ageing but contains a rapidly increasing number of 'young-old', active older people ready and willing to be involved in many forms of voluntary activities, including those associated with the church. There is much which not only they *could* do but *wish* to do. Far from being a threat to those who are younger, they can provide time, stability, encouragement and guidance. Chapter 9 sets out what could be accomplished. It makes the interesting discovery that a number of non church attenders would like to be involved, given the invitation.

The caring church, and the Conclusion

The final chapters seek to suggest ways in which the church can be a positive, practical and spiritual partner for older people. There are needs to be met, people to whom the church can reach out and ways to give help in many areas of life. Buildings often need intelligent adaptation, transport would be valued, and clubs could be run. At a deeper level, help with bereavement, loneliness, visiting and spiritual counselling can be opportunities for service. These chapters seek to bring out a positive way forward on the basis of the research contained in this book. 'Much future research is needed to improve the understanding of the relationship between religiosity, coping and well-being in the later life' (Koenig *et al.*, 1988, p.28). This book seeks to help in that research.

2

Who is an 'Older Person'?

What do we mean by 'elderly', 'old', 'older person'? In this chapter I will attempt to define these terms. When does 'old age' start according to those who have written on the subject, and what sorts of 'elderly' are there? What statistics are available and what causes ageing? Most of all, what do older people say? We will look at the results of the interviews I have conducted (detailed in Appendix 4, 'Assistance received'), and only then attempt some sort of answer to this vital and complex problem.

The depth of these problems is well described by Robert Katz, looking at the sociopsychological perspectives of ageing from a Jewish viewpoint:

> Despite vast medical progress we know relatively little about the phenomenon of aging. The term itself is imprecise and ambiguous. We do know some things about the processes of aging, one of these being that we begin to 'age' while we are still in our late teens. We age at different rates; aging has different meanings for different people; to be aged may be a chronological variable because Picasso at ninety-plus had more vigor than some of us who would be loosely categorized as being of 'middle-age'. Medical researchers only recently discovered that the arteries of young men can be 'aged', while some people attain a 'ripe old age' with cardiovascular systems resembling those associated with much younger people. Are we 'aged' if we choose to retire at the age of forty-five or fifty, or are we 'aged' when we first become eligible for social security? Do we become 'aged' when we leave our own apartment and move into a residence complex where our fellow residents are classified as being 'elderly'? There simply is no unequivocal meaning for the 'aging' or 'aged'; moreover, we cannot be sure when we are speaking in the language of physiology, psychology, economic status, athletic ability and physical co-ordination, medicine and health status,

> political influence, familial role, or something else. More than most of us realize, aging is a state of mind; we are what *we* think we are, the ways we perceive ourselves, and the ways we imagine our family and our community to perceive us. Aging is, at the very least, a relative term. (Katz, 1975, p.136)

There are several strands to be drawn out of the quotation from Katz. All of these point to the fact that terms like 'old', 'aged' and their cognates are fundamentally contested. There is a fundamental divide between objective and subjective definitions. However, there are variations within each and no method of resolving these. Basically their use is a matter of the purpose in hand. Thus, in relation to objective definitions, we could consider the following. Ageing is a physiological process, which occurs at different chronological ages. Therefore such a classification could span a range from 25 to 100 years.

Secondly, for certain purposes, the statutory retirement age seems to provide a dividing line. The problem here is that 'retirement' itself increasingly departs from these statutory limits. In Europe, more and more people take early retirement and in some countries only the minority of the active population is still working then. Thus a category of 'the retired' could straddle chronological ages beginning at under 50.

On the other hand, subjective definitions are equally diverse. For example, whose subjectivity is to count: that of the subjects themselves, or of their peers, their children or of the investigator? Again we would find vastly different definitions which assigned people to conflicting categories.

Even the word 'old' itself can be used as the opposite of 'new' as well as 'young', giving it 'dread connotations of decline and decay' (Midwinter, 1991). No one wants that, not least because it reflects on each of our lives. 'It is we and not just the "elderly population" who compromise the ageing society' (Johnson and Slater, 1993). Jon Rainbow retells the old American folk-tale about a wooden bowl, from Sharon Curtlin's *Nobody Ever Died of Old Age*:

> It seems that Grandmother, with her trembling hands, was guilty of occasionally breaking a dish. Her daughter angrily handed her a wooden bowl, and told her that she must eat out of it from now on. The young grand-daughter, observing this, asked her mother why Grandmother must eat from a

> wooden bowl when the rest of the family was given china plates. 'Because she is old!' answered her mother. The child thought for a moment then told her mother, 'You must save the wooden bowl when Grandma dies.' Her mother asked why, and the child replied, 'For when you are old.' (Rainbow, 1991, pp.195–204)

Simone de Beauvoir, in her classic sociological treatise, *Old Age*, speaks of how we try to delude ourselves about the truth seen by others:

> People have said to me, 'So long as you feel young, you are young.' This shows a complete misunderstanding of the complex truth of old age: for the outsider it is a dialectic relationship between my being as he defines it objectively and the awareness of myself that I acquire by means of him. Within me it is the Other – that is to say the person I am for the outsider – who is old: and that Other is myself. (de Beauvoir, 1972a, p.284)

This is further shown in the following:

> Few admit to being old. I was talking with my Gran when she was ninety-eight – 'You know, Ian, there are some old people in our church.' She said it in a rather pitying way, and it was quite clear she did not include herself in their number. I wanted to look round her church and see these folk who topped ninety-eight years old. However, despite her implied denial, my Gran *was* old, and death was to meet her three years later. (Knox, 1994, p.30)

What is 'Old Age'?

By the very asking of the question, 'What is "old age"?' we enter a veritable minefield of definitions and contradictions. Many people, be they sociologists, gerontologists or so-called 'older people', are unwilling to commit themselves, or alternatively give suggestions which are then immediately criticized by others. This may be inevitable in an emerging area of study, where hardly any literature is found before the 1950s. There is a great difference between the existence of older people and studies about them. There do not appear to be any social policies specifically for the elderly in Britain until the 1890s (Victor, 1994, p.26). ' "Retirees" have only emerged in recent times, especially since the Second World War, as people who have left work in advance of physiological decline' (Guillemard, 1983, p.6).

With this emerging specific social group, definitions have been attempted. These quickly became negative, linking old age with the process of ageing. *The Fullness of Time* (Regan and Smith, 1977), quotes (p.24) Bromley's (1988) *Human Ageing* thus: 'Bromley's definition of ageing as "a complex, cumulative, time-related process of psycho-biological deterioration" sounds pessimistic but is difficult to fault'. With such a poor image of getting older, who would then define themselves as being old aged? 'Ageing' and 'elderly' are terms best avoided if possible. 'It is better to speak of "older people", or "elderly people" than "The Elderly" ', Anthea Tinker said in a presentation on growing older (Tinker, 1999). Her book on the subject published in 1980 was entitled *Elderly People in Modern Society*, but the 1997 edition is renamed *Older People in Modern Society*. Tinker says that 'This is because of a growing recognition that the term "elderly people" gives the impression of a clearly defined group' (Tinker, 1997, p. xiii). But could it also be because the word 'elderly' now creates disagreeable feelings?

Is there a better term for what Guillemard calls 'a new naturality of old age'? She prefers the French expression 'troisième age' (Guillemard, 1983, p.82). Within six years this term was queried as having limitations, as Laslett comments, 'The Third Age is not to be defined wholly by the calendar, nor are its true limits to be reckoned by birthdays' (Laslett, 1989, p.77). The danger of this unwillingness is that we are left with saying that old age is only an idea, a way of thinking, albeit reflecting 'enormously powerful cultural forces' (Bytheway, 1995, p.43). Writers are being subjective about something objective, though this is hard to pin down in definitions.

A further factor is the way old age is changing between generations. 'We cannot expect the current sixty-year-old cohort, when they reach the age of eighty, to behave like the current eighty-year-old cohort; nor can we assume that current eighty-year-olds behaved like the current cohort of sixty-year-olds when they themselves were sixty' (Askham *et al.*, 1992, p.13). It often boils down to this: How do *I* see it? How does the term 'old age' affect *me*? It depends who one is, and one's personal perception of old age. If one is young, old age may start a great deal earlier than if one is, say, 50 (Age Concern, 1993, p.1). It becomes almost a thing to joke about: 'Do you ever notice that the older we get the later old age starts?' (*Readers Digest*, 1997, p.54). The American comedian, Bill Cosby, asks, 'What, after all, is old? To a child of seven, ten is old, and to a child of ten, twenty-five is middle-aged; and fifty is an archaeological exhibit' (Cosby, 1987, p.31). If there were initiation ceremonies to confirm that old age had started, perhaps that would help (de Beauvoir, 1972a). But is it chronological, or functional, or a matter of retirement (Bray, 1991, p.5).

Older adulthood leads to old age as a process (Lyon, 1985, p.121), a process which may lead to people becoming elderly sooner, rather than later, as work is either rejected or unavailable (Guillemard, 1983b, p.82). If we are to define 'old age', it must be in the context of the whole of life (Report of the Social Policy Committee of the Board for Social Responsibility, 1990). All this leads one to the conclusion that 'old age' is almost impossible to define, and it would be folly to put any date for its beginning. But many have and, as we shall now see, their diversity may confuse us even further in our search for the elusive definition of an 'older person'.

When is 'Old Age'?

Is there a starting point for being old? Let me say at the outset, there is plenty of choice! Simone de Beauvoir trawls through history to show the diversity, going back to Hippocrates, for whom old age starts at 56. Aristotle (384–322 BC) thought there were two points of perfection – the body's at 35 and the soul's at 50, after which life lapsed or declined. Dante picked 45 instead. With modern industrial societies retiring their workers at 65, de Beauvoir herself, in the early 1970s, says that she uses 'the words old, elderly and aged for people of sixty-five and over' (de Beauvoir, 1972a, p.13).

The age for the start of being old does seem to have advanced considerably over the centuries, with one notable exception, which I will detail later. Apart from the thoughts of Aristotle, with his 35, Shakespeare takes the earliest time at 40:

> When forty winters shall besiege thy brow
> And dig deep trenches in thy beauty's fold.
> (Shakespeare, c.1600)

Perhaps with tongue in cheek, Daisy Ashford refers at one place to 'Mr Salteena', who was an 'elderly man of forty-two' (Ashford, 1919, p.1). My office calendar, not quoting a source, informed me one day that 'Forty is the old age of youth, fifty the youth of old age.' Moving through the fifties (as an age), McFadyen defines 'older people' as 'those aged fifty-five or older' (McFadyen, 1997, p.11). However, the majority seem to go for the sixties as their chosen starting point for getting old.

Minois has a whole book devoted to the *History of Old Age*, and shows that, despite Plutarch starting old age at 50 (along with the references to ancient Greece already cited), even Pythagoras spoke of 60, while Mimnermus, in the seventh century, is quoted as saying:

> Happy they who die at the age of sixty, since once painful old age has arrived, which renders man ugly and useless, his heart is no longer free of evil cares, and the sun's rays bear him no comfort.

As Minois points out, 60 as a beginning for old age has been around for a long time (Minois, 1989, p.47). Henri Nouwen agrees with this, in his breakdown of life's stages. He gives 20 to 40 to young adults, 40 to 60 to middle age, and 'from sixty on you are considered to be "elder"' (Nouwen, 1995, pp.1–8). There does seem to be a broad consensus today that 60 to 65 is the modern start of being old, even though people over these ages reject the label (Ward, 1984, p.74). In my research, and in the writing of others, even the eighty-plus group still occasionally say they are middle-aged (Victor, 1994, p.74).

Sometimes an arbitrary line has to be drawn – for example, in research questionnaires. Sixty-five seems the most popular here (McCreadie *et al.*, 1997). This age is used for statistical data bases (Report of the Social Policy Committee of the Board for Social Responsibility, 1990, p.15), or even as a bald, sweeping generalization: 'The elderly are an age group ... over age sixty-five' (Daniels, 1988). The reason is clear: 'The age of sixty-five as the standard retirement age for men within the UK may still seem a convenient age limit for defining "old age"' (Coleman *et al.*, 1993, pp.1–18). Conversely, 60 seems to be accepted across Europe and the USA (Tinker, 1997, p.6). A survey across Europe showed that a third of over-60's liked to be called 'senior citizens', and a similar percentage 'older people' (Walker, 1993). Sixty-five is the age at which statistics refer to 'elderly people' in England, according to an OPCS study (Bone, 1996, p.1). Writers on both sides of the Atlantic see retirement as a watershed, leading to people being 'old' (Whitehead and Whitehead, 1981, p.128), or 'aged' (Jewell, 1999, p.1). This 'relatively recent phenomenon' of a retirement date (Hannah, 1986) has given 65 a particular significance. The question is, if the date for retirement moves, will the onset of 'old age' have to change, too, or is 65 the age older people themselves prefer? In Queensland, Australia, a telephone survey found that 65 was the age the majority of the respondents saw as the beginning of old age. But when people were asked when *they* would be old, they chose 70! (Howe, 1993, pp.3–11).

But there is an exception, to which I said I would refer. The 1999 report, *Social Focus on Older People*, refers throughout to 'older people' as those of 50 plus (Matheson and Summerfield, 1999). Not unexpectedly, such a backtrack caused a stir, and Carol Summerfield, co-author of the report, had to give this explanation when interviewed in *The Times* by Helen Rumbelow:

> The idea of when you are 'old' is very much a blur now – when we rang up people in their fifties they were affronted if you called them old, we had to say, no, not old, 'older'. (Rumbelow, 1999, p.11)

The lesson seems to be, tread carefully, for you tread on my life. Having looked at all the figures, I would venture to suggest that the Beatles were not a million miles away. In their youthfulness during the 1960s (which I shared), they spoke of getting older, losing hair, and wondered if they would still be needed and fed at the age of 64. I could live with that.

Who is 'Old Aged'?

Here I consider two matters germane to the question posed by this chapter, 'Who is an "older person"?' These are: the huge diversity in those who are older people, and the numbers involved.

Diversity

> The elderly population is highly diverse. The 20-year age difference between a 40-year-old and a 60-year-old person is often given great significance whilst the similar gap in age between a person of 70 and 90 is usually overlooked. (Victor, 1994, p.48)

Victor is right: a large part of the problem of defining older people is because those who may come within this category naturally resent an arbitrary lumping together of those aged (say) 55 or 65 with those in their 90's. Attempts have therefore been made to subdivide 'old' into 'the younger senior years' of 65 to 74, and 'the later adult years' of 75 to 84, 'and especially age 85 and beyond' (Jordan, 1996, pp.43–54) such a division, or convention, being 'widely recognised' (Johnson and Falkingham, 1992, p.25). Terms vary: 'young–old' (65–74), 'middle old' (75–84) and the 'frail elderly' or 'old old' from 85 upwards (Stafford, 1989, p.27). An Irish division takes 80 as the break point, with those from 65 upwards between 'young-old' and 'old old' (Patterson, n.d.).

As expected, these fixed divisions lead to immediate criticism, which is quite justified unless large caveats are inbuilt. For example:

> The danger of using chronological definitions is that they 'distance' us from people; we begin to think of groups of people in terms of the categories we fix. Looked at with other spectacles people over 75 years need not be 'aged' any more than those between 60–74 years need be 'elderly'. ... Chronological definitions are only useful for establishing demographic trends. (Creber, 1990, p.4)

Mannes Tidmarsh points out that 'It is as unjust and as unrealistic to lump together everyone in the last 25 years of life as it would be to lump together all those in the first 25 years' (Tidmarsh, 1998, p.A1). Continuing in similar vein, 'Given the minute age-specific groups into which the young have been subdivided in developmental psychology, it is remarkable how much tolerance we have for crudely lumping together "the aged" as though they formed one homogenous mass. The category of "the aged" may span as many as four or five whole decades!' (Pruyser, 1975, p.115). Anthea Tinker would thus divide people into cohorts, where 'A five-year cohort is reasonable: ten years is too big' (Tinker, 1999), which all but makes the two- or three-fold division meaningless. Tidmarsh (1988, p.A1) helps to explain the problem:

> Gerontologists generally agree on 60–65 as marking the 'threshold range' for ageing because by then no one can deny the demonstrable physical and physiological changes that have taken place in themselves. However, it is important to remember that chronological age by itself is a very imperfect measure: as has been remarked, 'Your birthday only tells you when you were born, not how old you are'.

We must beware of seeing older people as a uniform group: they differ as much as any other group in such basics as health, wealth, character and needs (Lampen, 1989, pp.9–10). Even when two people are exactly the same age, one may be a young (say) 70 and the other old (Board for Social Responsibility, 1990). We ignore class, gender, race and personal history to our and their detriment (Bray, 1991, p.9). To these one could add family support, physical and mental disability and religion (Tinker, 1997). 'For the healthy individual, normal ageing could be just a state of mind' (Hunt, 1988, p.121). Who, then *is* 'old aged'? I corresponded with Age Concern about this, and was helped by a reply from their Assistant Director, Jeremy Fennell:

> I have not answered directly your question about how Age Concern regards someone as 'elderly'. This is partly because there is no straightforward answer we can give to questions like this. Ageing is a process that affects different people in different ways, and different people of the same chronological age would not regard themselves as elderly .... People who would have been regarded as 'elderly' a few generations ago are now young compared to a growing group of 80 and 90 year olds. (Fennell, 1997)

For the purpose of this book, I am driven to look at this whole question, ultimately, from a pragmatic viewpoint rather than just a theoretical one. As a book title says, this is *Our Future Selves* (Roberts, 1970). Those who helped in qualitative interviews may give us a clearer answer as to who is an older person, rather than general statistics. The 1999 *Social Focus on Older People* picks out

John Glenn going into space at 77, and an 89 year old completing the London marathon as two examples of those pushing the boundaries of 'too old' (Matheson and Summerfield, 1999, p.7). To one person we could say, 'You haven't aged a bit since I saw you years ago', while another has said of them (rather than *to* them), 'They've aged a lot' (Report of the Social Policy Committee of the Board for Social Responsibility, 1990, p.28). Who is old? 'Not a homogenous human group', whether they face old age well or badly (Pontificium Concilium pro Laicis, 1999, p.13), but different people at different times.

A medical definition would look at a person's physique in answering a question such as, 'is X fit to drive a motor vehicle?' A carer would look at a sufferer from Parkinson's Disease and define 'old age' at 74 or 84, or even 50. An employment agency may or may not see someone aged 66, being over the statutory retirement age. An insurance company may look at the actuarial tables for premiums which depend on certain ages, whether a person be healthy or not. The age for 'old' can thus vary depending on purpose.

My purpose is to *include* as many as possible, because often people are excluded, or exclude themselves. There has to be some pure arbitrariness, and I admit to choosing a lower limit than some others, because of this desire for inclusiveness. Having said that, it is also worth realizing that we are talking of very many people, as we shall now see.

Quantity

Here is a sobering thought: 'Of all the people in the world who have ever lived beyond 65, half of them are alive today' (Hacker, 1999, p.14). The reason is simple: until very recently, most people failed to reach even halfway to the 'three-score years and ten' of the Psalms, whereas today, for the first time, the population of advanced societies has the opportunity to reach that age and beyond almost universally (Laslett, 1989, p.1). 'Scientific advances and the consequent progress in medicine have made a decisive contribution in recent decades to prolonging the average duration of human life' (Pontificium Concilium pro Laicis, 1999, p.11).

Those aged 65 and over are increasing worldwide by 800,000 each month, with a projected growth of 1.1 million each month by 2010 (Yoder, 1996, pp.417–37). The growth, both in numbers and percentages this century, is enormous. In 1901 in Britain, only 6 per cent of the population were over 60 (Creber, 1990, p.3); now it is over 20 per cent. Those over 70 have gone up from 1.5 per cent in 1901 to 7 per cent in 1991. By 2021, the over 60's will be 25 per cent of the population (Office of Population Censuses and Surveys, 1991). If we drop the age to 50 plus, the official figures show 18.8 million in Britain in 1997, more than three times as many as in 1901. As a proportion of the population, those over 50 were one in seven in 1901, and in 1997 were one in three (Matheson and Summerfield, 1999).

These figures have massive implications for life today, with 32 per cent of all those over 60 living alone (Askham *et al.*, 1992, p.17). Many who are older suffer from dementia: 6 per cent of those 65 plus do, with nearly two in every five over 90 doing so. With the huge numbers aged over 65, this alone is an enormous challenge. To these figures must be added the projections for the early part of the twenty-first century, the most startling of which is that for those reaching 100. When Queen Elizabeth became queen in 1952, 134 people received a congratulatory telegram. In 1996, 6,325 (only 655 men) were 100 plus. By 2021 it is estimated that 22,500 women and 4,300 men will be aged 100 and over (National Population Projections, 1996, Table 6). The implications for successive Governments in Britain are enormous. By 2010, 50 per cent of all voters will be 50 plus. Those over the current pensionable age (now 60 for women and 65 for men) will rise from 10.7 million in 1996 to 11.8 million in 2010, and 14 million by 2021, peaking at 17 million (National Population Projections, 1996, Table 6). Of course, this depends on what changes are made to the 'pensionable age': whether the Government moves it up, or down, or keeps it as it is.

The Mortality Tables show that age at death is rising even more rapidly than expected even a few years ago. A man of 35 in 1999 can expect to live to 85 years 1 month, compared with a 60-year-old man, who is projected to live to 83 years 9 months. For the 35-year-old, this is five years more than predicted in 1980. For a woman, life expectancy is now 88 years 1 month, having climbed from 84 years 7 months (Nowell, 1999). Most couples marrying in their twenties can thus expect (barring divorce) to celebrate their golden wedding (until now a comparative rarity) (Gill, 1997, pp.81–2).

This explosion in numbers and percentages of older people must make young and old alike sit up and take notice, and the caring agencies – not least the church – take positive steps to face the challenge, and grasp the opportunity. But that pre-empts what follows in later chapters. More immediately, and to keep focused on our question, 'Who is an Older Person?' I intend to deal briefly with the 'Why?' of ageing.

Why 'Old Age'?

In an article in the *Sociological Review,* Jerrome describes her research into older people in specific churches, one of which was a Methodist church. She recounts a brief exchange between four people at the Worship Committee to illustrate the various meanings attached to old age, and then comments on each person's words:

> 'R: Is she (the proposed speaker) an old person?
> S: Oh quite young.
> G: Careful (mind who you're calling old!)
> O: People can be old at 20 or 60.
> The earlier speakers refer to chronological age and seek to establish that of the visitor in relation to their own: age is relative. The third comment implies that 'old' is an insult. The fourth suggests that 'old' describes a kind of behaviour of which anyone is capable (Jerrome, 1989, pp.761–84).

In trying to answer the question of 'why old age?' no single answer can be given, because people view the term differently, as Jerrome shows. Further, there are different sorts of ageing, which give different reasons for why ageing occurs. Creber draws on research done by Birren to give three ways in which people age, answering this 'Why?' in each:

1. Biological. We age physiologically, as biological processes work in us and in our environment.
2. Psychological. We are affected by cultural and educational influences, personal emotions and temperament and social behaviour. We age because of our attitude and response to these.

3. Social. We also age because we adopt certain behaviour according to the social roles and expectations of the society in which we live.

These three reasons for ageing interact and overlap, giving a complex answer as to why we age (Creber, 1990, pp.4–5; Birren, 1960, pp.176–86).

Other writers have chosen to deal with one or more of these. Weiss briefly mentions biology, life history, genes and environment, but emphasizes that 'it is also a matter of sociology – of how a person shares the experience of old age with others' (Weiss, 1997, p.30). The Church of England Report agrees: 'Much more important than arbitrary chronological distinctions were life events – retiring from paid employment, becoming a grandparent, experiencing unexpected redundancy, or the death of a partner' (Report of the Social Policy Committee of the Board for Social Responsibility, 1990, p.9). Hubbell includes retirement and biological indicators, but then adds 'the sensory system'. Hearing and sight problems, in particular, both contribute to ageing (Hubbell, 1996, pp.56–7). Victor also goes with the biological and chronological factors, but adds two more of her own. The first is 'lifecycle', which is her word for the social definition of stages, including old age, 'via the operation of social cues and norms'. Her main approach to why old age occurs is 'the development of a political economy of old age'. This approach rejects the individualistic perspective to the study of ageing and seeks to examine the social construction of old age and dependency within the wider arenas of the economic and political structures and interests of society (Victor, 1994, p.23). Finally, Ward places a particular weight on health, of oneself or one's spouse, as being a major reason for ageing (Ward, 1984, p.75).

All these seem to have drawn on the ground-breaking research done by Gray and Moberg, whose 1962 book relied greatly on their earlier separate postgraduate research in the early 1950s. They give, as others subsequently showed, four answers to the 'Why?' of old age: physiological, psychological, sociological and chronological (Gray and Moberg, 1962, pp.12–15).

In trying to discover why old age occurs, we cannot simply say 'It is because I've reached my *n*th birthday'. Society also has its unwritten rules; outside factors and internal feelings impact our lives, our health and life experiences play their part: why I am old is not ultimately for society alone to say, it is highly individualistic and personal. This is why the rest of this chapter will deal with what people themselves say about old age, being elderly, and who are older people.

What do people say?

In the writings of others

The *British Gas Report* is a key document in understanding present-day approaches to ageing. In their survey, they asked 16- to 24-year-olds what they called older people. Of those surveyed 34 per cent said 'elderly', 27 per cent 'older people', 7 per cent 'senior citizens' and 2 per cent 'retired'. But the retired and over 55's, when asked 'What would you prefer to be called?', said 'senior citizens' (36 per cent), 'retired' (36 per cent), 'older people' (4 per cent) and a minute 5 per cent 'elderly'. Seventy per cent of the 16–24 group felt people were 'old' by 60, with a mean age of 54.8 – the threshold for the survey (55) (Midwinter, 1991, p.2). Whereas, as Biggs points out, 'Few elders would categorise themselves as older than middle-aged' (Biggs, 1993).

A letter to *The Times* seems to agree with this:

> Sir, My *Chambers Twentieth Century Dictionary*, 1901 edition, reprinted 1930, defined middle-aged as 'from about 35 to 50'. Having fairly recently qualified for a pensioner's freedom pass, I'll support the current definition: 'between youth and old age. Yours faithfully, Peter Stroud (Stroud, 1999).

However old a person is, they seem either to be completely surprised by their old age, or to deny it. Stafford quotes J.B. Priestley at 79: 'It is as though walking down Shaftesbury Avenue as a fairly young man, I was suddenly kidnapped, rushed into a theatre and made to don grey hair, the wrinkles and the other attributes of old age, then wheeled on-stage. Behind the appearance of age I am the same person, with the same thoughts, as when I was younger' (Stafford, 1989, p.11). Jerrome tells of an 82-year-old, visiting 'old people' who were chronologically younger than her (Jerrome, 1989, p.755).

Bernard Baruch, financier and adviser to American Presidents, celebrated his eighty-fifth birthday with the observation, 'To me, old age is always fifteen years older than I am.' Asked if there were any signs of his slowing down physically he replied: 'As I grow older, I find myself less and less inclined to take the stairs two at a time' (Baruch, 1955, p.25). Even older, *National Geographic* tells of 93-year-old Hal Wright being reporter, writer, editor, ad salesman and deliverer of his own Californian newspaper. Asked about slowing down, he asked, 'What for? I wouldn't know what to do with my time' (Weiss, 1997, p.5).

To top these, and give an explanation, the following speaks for itself:

> Linda, a woman who lived to the age of 106, left us a magnificent testimony. On her 101st birthday, she confided to a friend: 'I'm now 101 years-old, but I'm strong, you know. Physically I have some disabilities, but spiritually there is nothing I can't do, I don't let physical impediments stand in the way, I pay no attention to them. I don't suffer old age, because I ignore it: it goes ahead on its own, but I pay no heed to it. The only way to live well in old age is to live it in God.' (Pontificium Concilium pro Laicis, 1999, p.13)

All of which leads to my own survey, in which I hope to give some more personal answers to the What? When? Who? and Why? of older people.

My 1998/9 survey

As the first chapter indicated, it became obvious very early on in my interviewing that simplistic, straightforward answers to any questions would not be forthcoming, and nowhere was this more apparent than in dealing with definitions of who was (or was not) an 'older person'. However, as I hope to show, some excellent indicators were given.

Compared with other questions, dealt with in later chapters, two interesting factors are worthy of immediate comment:

1. There was a remarkable reluctance to be specific in detailing what it means to be 'old', or when one knows one

has got there. Many a reply would begin, 'That depends on . . .' This led to all sorts of conclusions, as we shall see.

2. There was no difference at all between those of different denominations, or those with no church connection, or men and women: thus there can be no comparative table, though there were some differences between age groups. The questions were exactly the same for each and every one of the 200 or more who spoke with me.

Three complete answers

Let me give an overview by setting out three complete sets of answers to the five questions which relate to the specific issue of old age. Appendix 1 has these in detail, with the age chart used to give a simplistic guide only, which was on a separate card, being given to each interviewee. For easy reference, the questions (3 to 7) were as follows:

3. Your first reaction: What does the word 'elderly' mean?
4. When do people start being elderly? (The chart was divided into 5-year sections)
5. When do people start being old? (Chart)
6. To which age group do you belong? (Chart)
7. Do you think of yourself as being young/mid-life/elderly/old?

As these three examples will show, no-one was going to be strait-jacketed by my wording, nor provoked by my words: and virtually everyone gave me their exact age. I will only make one preliminary observation: note the ages of the people, as they describe what they consider themselves to be.

Winnie (non church attender, living in the town)

3. I don't mind the word elderly – I can't bear it if anyone calls me 'An old woman', but I don't mind 'Old lady'. I think of others as elderly but not me. I've got a sister who's two years younger and she looks old – but she is not well. Being elderly is to do with *health.*
4. When I was 32 my mother died at the age of 52 and I thought she was old then. But in this day and age you are not old till you have turned 80.

5. I was with a lady the other day who has turned 90 and she was *old.* If people start to wander in their mind then they are old. It all has to do with health, not age.
6. 88.
7. Not old. I am a bit elderly because I am slow in my movements and I am losing my sight. I have no aches and pains. My grandson said to me the other day, at the age of 10, 'You've always been old Nanny'.

Harold (a church attender, living in a village)

3. People with a wealth of experience, failing health, and more kindly – people who have mellowed over the years.
4. It depends on the individual. I have met quite a lot in their 50's who say 'I'll be glad when I've retired' and for them that is the start of their feeling old. People who have no hobbies in their 60's become old people: if you don't change then you are going downhill. Yet I know people in their 80's who are young at heart. If I had to put an age to it I would say 61 to 65.
5. There is a wide range – it depends on the individual. Some are sprightly in their 70's. People in their 80's must accept that they are elderly. You would start in your 70's but it depends on the individual.
6. 83.
7. I like to think I have a young outlook on life. In our church there are elderly people who believe we should stick to the old traditions. The vicar should concentrate on the young. I don't think in an elderly way – the young people are the congregations of tomorrow and I don't think the vicar is neglecting me.

Pam (a city church attender)

3. Me – now! – very much to my annoyance.
4. It is very difficult to say when someone becomes elderly because it is different for everybody. My friend Jean is six years older than I am (she is 79) but she is not elderly. But I am handicapped and so I feel elderly – it is not so much a physical age but how one's health is. I know a 92-year-old who walks up hills, goes to keep-fit, does the garden and is annoyed that the local Tory party does not use her for canvassing – she is not old. If I have to put an age then one is elderly after 65.

5. Old is a way you feel and whether you feel you can manage – it is any age after 65.
6. 72.
7. I am old because I can't get about: I know I look old because I walk badly.

I have given these answers verbatim and accept that all these give subjective definitions. They give some idea of what will follow: one can be 88 and 'a bit elderly', 83 and 'have a young outlook', or 72 and say 'I am old'. But to avoid the danger of commenting too soon on a minimal sample, here are the major answers to the questions about 'elderly' and 'old' as given by young people (up to 30), middle-aged (31–59), church leaders (ordained and lay), those 60 plus – who also said what they thought they themselves were. The numbers interviewed in each group are given in Appendix 4.

The young on 'elderly'

Although there were some, as would be expected, who placed the beginning of 'elderly' earlier than other groups, most chose somewhere between 66 and 75 as a chronological starting-point: which was older than their majority choice for 'old' (61–70). The young had few criteria for what made a person 'elderly'.

1. It depends on who the person is, summed up by my 15-year-old son, one of the first people I interviewed. 'Your first reaction to "elderly"?' 'You.' His grin told all, and he adjusted his answer to 'Nanna' (but his first answer showed his initial feeling). Grandparents featured in other replies: it was not the age but the role which mattered, even to those at the upper end of this age range.
2. Looks. 'Grey hair' said Nick (22), Matthew (16) and Simon (14). 'Hair going white' was a similar reply from Odie (24) while Ruth (14) chose the words 'wrinkled' and 'stooped'.
3. Health. This featured minimally, with only one person (Matt) speaking of 'old and frail'. However, it was implicit in no less than four references to a 'zimmer frame', and another to 'walking stick'. Thus it was the appearance of

frailty or failing health, rather than illness, which the young associated with 'elderly'.

4. Far and away the factor which counted most with the young was the attitude of older people, which made them 'elderly', or the attitude of the young towards older people, dubbing them with an older title. It is, again, a subjective approach which has emerged. To show these two viewpoints, here are comments from Steve (22) and Rebecca (14):

   Steve (in reply to, 'What does "Elderly" mean?'): 'Boring. You become elderly the minute you are restricted by what happened in the past and start to live in the past. There is no age to this, because I know a lot of old people who are brilliant, and people my age who act old – it's a state of mind.'

   Rebecca (to the same question): 'When they feel they are.' But then she added, to give the contrary view, 'My Dad thinks he's a kid. I think he's a boring man who tries to communicate with the youth. He's middle-aged – 39.'

These young people were affected by whether those they knew who were 'elderly' were good ('Experienced' – Trevor, 19) or not-so-good ('Strict people' – Simon, 19); 'Complacent, and always making complaints' (Anthony, 17). Most saw it as a balance. Rob (17) saw it as 'a matter of lifestyle, not age: you can be young and considerably elderly, or elderly with a youthful outlook'. Charlie in her mid–20s, has 'one Gran who is quite young at nearly 90, whilst the other who is only 70 has given up on life because she wants to die'. Tracy (19) and Steve (20), who go to the same church, showed how there can be diametrically opposing views about the same people. Steve's reaction to 'elderly' was 'boring and sceptical'. But Tracy talked of 'the elderly in the church – people who are more mature and pretty amazing: people to look up to'.

It begs the question: is a person elderly because of our attitude? From a youthful standpoint it would seem so. Whereas 'old' is a slightly different thing – for the young.

The young on 'old'

What is old to the young? Age counts most here. Fifteen-year-old Dave believes that 'the youngest you become old is between 41 and 45. The oldest is between 56 and 60.' Twenty-six-year-old Charlie admits that 'to the children I work with I'm old: old now means much older for me'. Odie (24) says it is '20 plus on my age – the generation above me'. To make most people feel old, Jez at 26 told me, 'I'm going to start worrying when I hit 30!' Odie's comment about the next generation is echoed in some young people seeing their parents as their idea of old. 'When you're a parent you're old' (Rebecca, 14). Old people are 'when they're older than me (46–50)' said Tracy (19), adding, 'My Dad's old – he's 49.' Very many fewer of the young were concerned with attitude here. Those who did spoke of 'when you become narrow-minded' (Anthony, 19), how 'people act' (Becky, 14) and old being 'in the mind' (Amy, 15).

As we get older ourselves, we can forget our own youthful views about those who were our seniors. To the teens and twenties, the late forties is a lifetime away. In looking at the relationship between the church and older people, we must hold in our minds that the younger end of church life has a huge bridge to cross to reach and understand their elders. Age does matter – but not as much as attitude. It is the relationship which counts here.

The middle-aged on the 'elderly' and 'old'

As I interviewed comparatively few in the 31 to 59 age group, I intend to deal with them more briefly. For the term 'elderly', attitude mattered not at all. Health, and its consequent burden on this group, was a factor. John (in his 50's), talked of elderly people 'being in a state of being decrepit', and their 'disability through ageing – as in my own family .... crippled with arthritis.' Marie (48) saw elderly as 'infirm', while Mike and Sue spoke of their elderly relatives as 'work'. How can you tell someone is elderly? A 45-year-old doctor gave his dictum: 'I have a rule of thumb. When you start giving your age at your next birthday, then you are old. For example, "I am 86 next birthday". I use elderly and old interchangeably.'

However, when it comes to the word 'old', attitude is everything: which may account for some placing 'old' before 'elderly' when giving a chronological answer. Ruth (44) said of the word 'old', 'It can't be defined by age – it is a mental attitude. I would say, if I had to put an age to it, over 70, but you can be old at 30.' As if to prove this, Kate, aged 30, answered the question as to what is 'old' by admitting, 'It depends: me in certain circumstances – I was old to a 14 to 16's group I was leading at Easter. There is no age where it is possible to say someone is old.' Chris, at 40, said that, as far as he was concerned, 'It depends on the individual. If you feel old, then you say you are "old", but if you feel like a young child, you won't say you are old.'

This middle group are less direct than the young people, probably because they are closer to being old themselves. They are wise enough to see that children and teenagers will view them as much older, if not specifically old, and they are coming to terms with their own ageing. Some put 'old' chronologically before 60 – their own age group. This makes the description of an 'older person' even less clear.

The leaders on 'elderly'

There are those who believe church leaders find it hard to agree. The young and middle-aged seemed fairly united, with three or four definitions for 'elderly'. The more interviews I had with ordained and lay leaders, the more reactions I acquired for what the word 'elderly' meant: a dozen will have to suffice here, such was the lack of unanimity. None put 'elderly' under 60, but age was not the dominant factor. When it was mentioned, it was as a question: one priest (himself under 40) asked, 'People can start being elderly under 40 – can't they?' A pastor suggested 'pensionable age', while a priest of 66 confessed, 'I would hate to be thought of as elderly or old'. This latter seemed to be a sad comment on getting old, as well as being unrealistic: what would his parishioners have said he was?

Some did not like the term 'elderly', preferring 'senior citizens', as they saw 'a person, not the age'. Janet, a lay leader, wanted the positive emphasized, seeing 'elderly' as 'fulfilment and wisdom'. A New Church pastor spoke of 'people mature in years – past retirement age. I also have the idea in the word "elderly" of people with experience, wisdom and life knowledge.' By contrast, a number stressed the negative connotations of 'elderly'. For one lay leader, the word meant 'care – you need to look after the elderly'. Frances, another lay leader, looked at 'when people become totally dependent on others physically.' A Salvation Army captain thought of 'the helpless ... people who are dependent on the system'.

There were leaders who spoke of those who were *not* elderly. A vicar put it like this: 'The secretary of my Fabric Committee is 80, and she climbed to the church roof recently with me. She is not particularly elderly.' In other words, the way that person was perceived coloured the vicar's view on the word 'elderly'. In similar vein, but with the opposite conclusion, the Bishop of Coventry saw 'elderly' as 'dependent and vulnerable, undervalued. Often frightened. I based this on my mother-in-law who I saw yesterday who has Alzheimer's disease.' This kindly and sad approach was not always present: one Minister said 'elderly' was 'someone past their sell-by date', while a lady lay leader pictured 'little old ladies with grey hair and glasses'.

Once again, attitude played a part in the whole question of ageing. 'It all has to do with an attitude of mind', said my very first interviewee, the Bishop of Warwick. 'Some people start to be elderly at 20. There are lots of young people in their 60's who don't start to be elderly, whilst some in their 20's or 40's do start to be elderly. It is not a matter of chronology, it is more an attitude.' Ian, a lay worker, said it was about 'attitude and perception about value compared with wrinkles and pension'. As the Precentor of Coventry Cathedral put it, 'You can be 13 going on 50', or, as a pastor commented, 'I have seen old 50-year-olds and young 70-year-olds'. Perhaps the most poignant comment of all came from Roman Catholic Bishop Pargiter: The elderly are 'most of our people who go to Mass'. Perhaps therein lies some of the reason for the more negative comments of others.

The leaders on 'old'

Not much can helpfully be added here, on top of the leaders' definition of 'elderly'. It is worthy of note that the highest numbers who gave a chronological age put it at 81 to 85, very senior indeed. Some were blunt, none more so than the Roman Catholic Archbishop of Birmingham: 'I'm 70. I'm old.' The Methodist Superintendent said you became old 'about the 56 mark, because that's when you are becoming a grandparent'. A vicar described 'old' as a 'process of slowing down'. A pastor emphasized poor health as being the almost exclusive mark of being old, while a Baptist minister spoke of the 'less able-bodied'. But mainly, attitude was again to the fore. A priest put it like this: 'So many have "youthfulness of spirit". You're as old as your heart: it has a lot to do with spiritual attitude.' To back this, a vicar told me of a man he knew 'who's 34 and spends his life trying to be old', while describing himself, at 53, as 'an old teenager'.

An Anglican vicar summed up the views of many of the approaches I have described in this way:

> 'Different people become old at different times. There are people in their 80's who have lively minds who I know: they are open, gracious and receptive. I know some people in their 40's who are so closed in their mind that they are old already. However, generally "old" is when people get beyond retirement age and become frailer, and life has a different rhythm and pattern.'

We may not find a better definition of 'old' even if it is too subjective to be an overall final definition. But, before we conclude this search for definitions, we must ask older people what they themselves think.

Older people define 'elderly'

Even the heading is emotive: should it be, 'Older people . . .'? We shall see. What a delight it was to ask the older generation these questions about age! Because they were speaking about themselves, they were that much more personal. Bert (81) typified this when asked, 'When does "elderly" start?' His verbatim reply was:

> 'When I was a child in Manchester, there was little grass around and the only pleasure was to play in your own street – never in the next street! If someone died in your street it

> was compulsory that all curtains were drawn the day of the funeral, and the children couldn't play: I couldn't understand why. What did old Ted die of? Pneumonia or TB. How old was he? – "An old man – 61".'

Most answers which mentioned age specifically were qualified with an added comment, such as, 'Someone at least 80 and who looks like it' (Tom, 65). One or two were bizarre: 'I assume you get elderly when you do what you want to do – 18 plus'. But an elderly age seems to have a different connotation for those now in it. Ted, 81 years old, put it like this:

> 'It's [elderly] a relative term. When I was in my teens a student teacher was old. But when I came back from the war, I realized she was only two years older and I fancied her!'

One or two, like Baruch (quoted earlier) were still of the opinion that 'people who are elderly are older than you all the time', while others would react to 'elderly' by 'Don't mention that word!' (Dennis, 76 plus); and Marjorie's (87) 'I try not to think – I won't admit to being old. I know I am, but I won't say I am. There are an awful lot of us.' People like Edna (75) came straight out with the bald answer to 'elderly' as, 'Me – someone getting feeble but who tries to be independent'. But good health in an elderly person would bring the opposite response: 'It's according to your health. Some who are a lot younger than me are proper invalids. I don't think of myself as old' (Phyllis, 86).

Once again, individual attitude came to the fore. 'Elderly' is 'growing old gracefully' (Matthew, 72). 'It depends on your outlook on life, and illnesses' (Irene, 67). A husband and wife, interviewed together, helped each other in defining 'elderly': 'I can think of people who are elderly in their fifties' (Betty, 65). Husband Tony (70) immediately chipped in: 'I can think of people who are elderly in their thirties: it's in the mind'. It was clear that neither had it in *their* mind. To take this to the other extreme, Doris (90), a resident in a home for the elderly, told me: 'Some are elderly before they are 60. We have a 100-year-old here who is not elderly.'

Two things interested me in the overall answers. Firstly, the word 'elderly' was not considered offensive by any, as some under-65's tend to assume. Secondly, it was often interchangeable with 'old', so the above answers interlink with the following ones.

Older people define 'old'

Compared with the last section, age was more important in defining 'old'. For some it was by way of contrast. 'Times are changing,' said Ken (69). 'When I was in Russia you were old at 30. My father was old at 60. It now depends on your mental ability. I would say 80 plus.' A different contrast came from Walter (80): 'When I was young it was about 60. Ladies used to wear black bonnets. Now it's 65 to 70.' Alternatively, it is 'when the doctor says, "It's your age" ' (Phyllis, 84). In similar vein, 'I didn't realize I was [old] till I was 80,' said Mary (90). 'I was talking to two people at a bus stop and when I moved away they said, "She's a nice old lady!" '

To these comments on 'old' as an age must be added the contrast some saw between body and mind. 'You get old in your body but not in your mind' (Wilf, 83). 'If you are really old,' said Phyllis (81), 'it is not just in your body but in your mind: people who are confused are old'. Life itself contributes. 'It depends who you are, how you live, and the circumstances and what kind of life you are living' (Evelyn, 89). Health may be a direct cause of someone being old, say the elderly. 'Most people are not old unless they can barely walk' (Bob, 75). 'When you're doddery' (yet another Phyllis (86) – a very popular name in the 1910s!). Matthew (71) believes old equates with 'having difficulty seeing', while Graham, in his 60's, spoke of 'a touch of the old jitters'.

So often this subtle injection of humour served to encourage the conclusion that old age, to the elderly, is more an attitude than anything else. 'I'm 83 and I don't feel old,' Bert told me, 'because if you start to feel old they may as well put you in a box.' 'My father was 84 when he died, and was not old. But my next door neighbours are in their 70's and are both old,' Vic (70) told me. Ted (81) said he knew 'a 95-year-old who has a liquid lunch and he doesn't seem old'. My favourite was 80-year-old Ruby's reply:

> 'On the bus everyone is old – but many of them are younger than me. I'm going to go out fighting. I'm still interested in collecting china. I've lived alone for 25 years. You've got to get up and be an optimist.'

No comment is needed to such an enthusiastic approach, except that it leads us to ask the final question: What are *you* if you are an 'older person'?

How older people see themselves

If ever I needed to prove the point that the expression 'older person' is incapable of a simplistic definition, the evidence came out here. In analysing the answers to the question, 'What do you think *you* are?' the variety of replies was astonishing. People who get lumped together as 'the over 65's', 'the elderly', 'the Third Age', 'old people', refuse to be so categorized and generalized. Here are some of the things I was told.

Firstly, some 'older people' are *young*. Mr B said 'I'm 72 – I'm young in outlook. I like to keep myself young.' Dorothy (74) is 'still young. I love pop music and videos. I like young film stars and do exercises with the television. I'm bitter because I can't go dancing anymore – I've had a leg amputated.' 'I feel young' (Mr. F, 70). 'If you have all your faculties,' said Daniel (79), 'I feel you are still young'. Next came the '*middle-aged*', as 84-year-old Phyllis described herself, or '*late middle-aged*' (Charles, 69), or even '*three quarter aged*' (May, 80). Some see themselves as '*bordering on elderly*' (Dennis, 76 plus). 'I'm "*getting elderly*", admitted Marjorie (88), while Pearl, at 68, made the grudging concession: 'For the benefit of the authorities I am *elderly*'.

When the term 'old' is used, it also has its variants. '*I don't feel old* at 90', Emma claimed, while Michael said 'I'm 84 and *don't feel terrible (sic) old* yet'. '*I don't think I'm old* now: how should someone of 74 feel?' enquired Doris. Joyce, in her 60's, reacted like this:

> 'The children ask, "Have you got a bus pass? Are you going to use a walking stick?" It's *not an age*. I'm as madcap now as I was twenty years ago – I'm a *recycled teenager*. Age is a *state of mind*.'

It is fair to say that the largest percentage did call themselves, '*old*'. Jack said, 'I never felt old till I was ill last year when I was 75'. Even at the younger end, there were those who agreed, as with 64-year-old Roy, whose 'mind is twenty years old, but in my body I'm old'. Health was often the reason for using this word: 'Since my stroke I'm *getting very old*,' Elizabeth (76) responded. 'I feel old' said Graham (70) 'because I have bad legs', while Lily (89) agreed: 'I'm old when I feel ill'. Events take their toll, too: 'I'm old,' Margaret (78) explained. 'I lost my husband and eldest son within four months and that ages you.' Of course you can be '*old, but not decrepit*!' (Edith, 78), or '*old in my attitudes*' (Ray, 69), and even '*ancient*' (Evan, 78)! The fighting spirit says, 'I accept I'm old but I don't feel old – and I don't want to!' (Ernest, 68). Phyllis, at 82, gave a poignant answer: 'I look at my hands and they look like my mother's. When that happened, I knew I was old.'

Even those who know they are old choose other words. Bob (75) is 'a *mature* person', while Alan (66) is a '*senior citizen*' (the only one to use that term). Phoebe, at 87 is '*aged*', but 'still *young at heart*. I'm the *matriarch* of the family – three sons, ten grandchildren, twelve great-grandchildren.' Even more confusingly, 74-year-old Peter is '*young-old*' (though unknowingly he used the 'correct' sociological term), perhaps identifying with Betty (65): 'Some days I feel ancient, some days I feel as if I'm *in my teens*'. One or two do not want to come within any definition: 'I've got all my marbles,' Flo (82) reacted – 'I'm just *a person*'. 'What are you?' I asked Marcia (66). 'Very *lonely*' was the sad reply. 'I'm a blooming *nuisance*!' Oliver enthused. 'It's us,' Katherine offered from a group of over 75's. 'It's when your get up and go is getting up and going.'

'What are *you*?' What a variety of answers. How dare one categorize such a diversity of people? Ted, at 82, summed up everyone's answers. 'What are you?' Answer: 'Just *me*!'

Summarizing charts

From all the answers which used specific ages, the following box plots and graph show comparable numerical information across different groups. The shaded boxes in Figures 2.1 and 2.2 show the middle half of each set of replies. The dotted lines stretch out to include nearly all the answers: any unusually high or low ages are shown by single horizontal lines. Figure 2.3 shows the average age given, plotted against the age of rejoinder, using 25, 45, and 65 for the three age groups.

Some observations

I do not believe it is possible to ask 'What is an older person?', because the word should be, '*Who*?' To define by 'young-old'

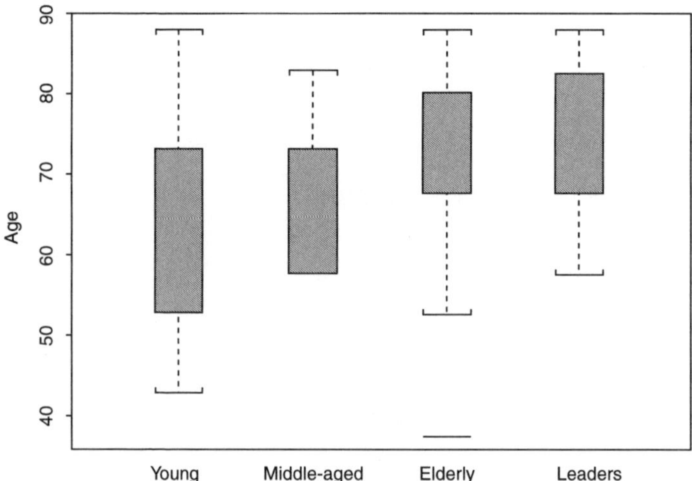

Figure 2.1 When do you become old?
The dotted lines indicate the age extent of all the answers given by each group. The boxes show the major age groupings given by the majority. One interesting feature is how the age of 'old' rises from 'young' to 'elderly'. Church leaders vary in age, but defined 'old' by age, the highest usage of all groups.

(55–64), 'mature-old' (65-74) and 'old-old' (75 plus) is simplistic in a most complex area.

Secondly, the age given by those who write about when 'old age' begins seems, by and large, to be too low for the start of the twenty-first century. If an age limit has to be given (and I question that), we need to listen to what ordinary people are saying in the 'older' groups, even though many of them are willing to suggest a starting point. So often our best definitions are in danger of being thrown into confusion. My own grandmother married when she was nineteen. Was that 'young' then – or now? She was married for 41 years: was she an 'old aged' widow at 60? Then, what shall we call the next 41 years, until she died just before her 102nd birthday?

Thirdly, so much depends on a variety of factors, such as

- Health, which itself needs to be seen as dividing into physical, mental and psychological.

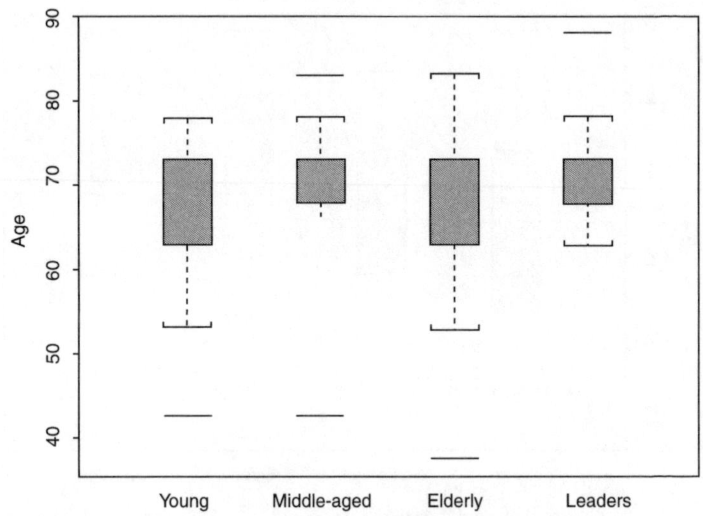

Figure 2.2 When do you become elderly?
Notes to Figure 2.1 also apply here. The single horizontal lines show where one or two people gave a reply which was a considerable way outside the norm. The word 'elderly' was given a much narrower age definition than 'old' in Figure 2.1, and is much more consistent across the groups.

- Personal experience in those who are younger, and circumstances in those who have lived longer, as each define 'old'.
- One's own age when making definitions of age.
- One's attitude as one looks at age. In days gone by, old age was much more accepted because of the comparatively few who reached it. Now, old age is not accepted by those who allegedly reach it, and those who even fight against the idea.

I have tried to highlight the enormous difficulties in defining an 'older person'. I have done this because it hugely affects how we deal with those we would put within this term. They may want to be so regarded – or they may not. It will certainly impact on the relationship between 'older people' and 'the church' (whose definition we will shortly seek).

Accepting all these caveats, one has to draw some sort of line, if only to be inclusive. In other words, if one does not set a lower

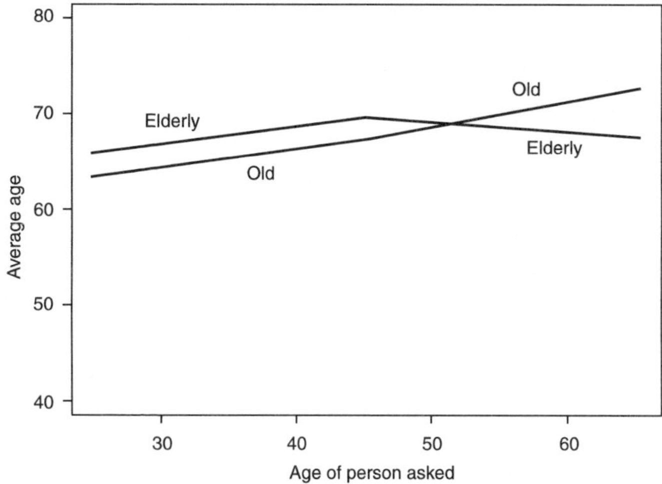

Figure 2.3 When do you become . . .?
This graph plots the average age given, plotted against the age of those answering. The significance lies in the way 'elderly' is understood by those aged before and after 45.

age for an 'older person', some may miss out on the benefits sought for them. My tentative age limit at the younger end of 'old' would read like this:

- People of 50 *may* be included, particularly if illness has prematurely aged someone.
- Those of 55 *could* be there, especially those who have taken early retirement and see that as a watershed.
- At 60, many *should* be considered as entering the phase of being 'older people'. The young will see them as such, and things like bus passes become available.
- For me, 65 *would* be the last lower age for 'older', with this being the upper limit for retirement.

I realise that this objective line-drawing at a point in the early to mid-60's flies in the face of the many subjective replies given by the interviewees. It could be argued that, ultimately, age is always subjective ('He's old at 30', 'She's a young 90-year-old'). It may be that one takes a specific age (The Beatles' 'Sixty-four') to make life easy. But governments and other major organizations invariably state an age and stick with it (a bus pass at 60, a pension at 60 or 65, a free television licence at 75, for example). As I have said, I will take a mid-60's age for 'older people' in this book, in order to be inclusive, and so none miss the benefits of and for those beyond that age. If no specific age is set, privileges as well as responsibilities can be missed. I accept that any age is arbitrary, and there will always be those who disagree either with the age stated or the stating of any age at all.

To conclude this chapter, here is one final set of answers, from an 'elderly' priest – Monsignor Tom Gavin of Coventry.

Q: Your first reaction to 'elderly'?
A: A vast picture of old people who carry their years in different ways.
Q: When does 'elderly' begin?
A: It depends on the mental attitude. The card with ages on is of no use to me at all.
Q: When does 'old' begin?
A: When people treat them like old people – for example, 'Sit down, here's a chair for you' – and you think 'Ruddy 'ell'!
Q. How old are you?
A: 76.
Q: What do you think you are?
A: I have still got plenty to offer – which is not always appreciated!

3

Ageism

Negative attitudes to ageing will come to the surface in this book, particularly in Chapters 6 and 7. Although every age group could cite unhelpful comments made against being a particular age, there tends to be such a constant negativism to ageing in later years that it has come to be defined as 'ageism'. For the relationship between older people and the church to be viewed thoroughly, some reference must be made to this, in order that it can be seen for what it is, and so avoided by those who are part of the church. This will be done by considering what ageism is, how it is practised by people at large, how older people themselves can exacerbate the problem, and how the church itself may be involved in ageist attitudes.

What is 'Ageism'?

Donald Reilly, a former deputy director for the National Council on the Aging (USA) was quoted, in an article in the *Baltimore Sun* of 25 September 1983, under the heading, 'Age Bias: It could happen to anyone', as saying: 'Agism is an odious social ill – which may be defined as a deep and profound prejudice against the elderly' (Apichella, 1989, p.27). Such a negative view can be further understood from Butler's definition in *The Encyclopaedia of Ageing* of 1987,

> Ageism is defined as a process of systematic stereotyping of, and discrimination against, people because they are old, just as racism and sexism accomplish this for skin colour and gender. (Johnson and Bytheway, 1993, p.200)

While there has been a great outcry against racism and sexism, ageism continues apace, with many less voices raised in protest. But, compared with the other two, every person has the potential to experience ageism (COHSE, 1991, p.8). Ironically, those who have ageist attitudes may well, ultimately, fall victim of their own prejudices unlike, say, white racists or male chauvinists (Frankin and Frankin, 1990; Report of the Social Policy Committee of the Board for Social Responsibility 1990, pp.55–6).

It is a problem both of terminology and attitude. To use terms like 'senile' is derogatory, but to call someone who is frail and old 'geriatric', when the word means a branch of medical science, is as wrong as calling a woman who has just had a hysterectomy 'an obstetric', or a sick child 'a paediatric' (Norman, 1987; Bond *et al.*, 1983, pp. 304–32). The caricature of older people which compounds an ageist view has been described in this way:

> The popularly held view of old age today is of very old people, usually women, living alone, socially isolated, managing on inadequate incomes, poorly housed, suffering ill-health, dependent on young carers, yet isolated from their families. Unhappy, withdrawn, but at the same time not taking an interest in making new friends, they have lost their energy, enthusiasm and drive, and are no longer concerned with education or personal development. Their deteriorating physical and mental health offers only the prospect of further decline and the ultimate sentence of old age – death. (Scrutton, 1990, pp.13–14)

How does this 'ageism' exhibit itself?

Ageism in the world

'I'm not ageist,' many would say. However, when that assertion is put to the test, there are those who may have to confess to their prejudices and negativism.

Growing old is a 'problem'

> We might start thinking that becoming old is the same as becoming a problem, that aging is a sad human fate that nobody can escape and should be avoided at all cost, that growing towards the end of the life cycle is a morbid reality that should only be acknowledged when the signs can no

> longer be denied. Then all our concerns for the elderly become like almsgiving with a guilty conscience, like friendly gestures to the prisoners of our war against aging. (Nouwen and Gaffney, 1976, p.17)

This is the first step in ageism. It is not to be unnecessarily rude, but to see growing old, and those who grow old, as a 'problem'. It may be for some a 'social problem' (MacIntyre, 1977, pp.41–3) where even those who formulate policies for health and social services use terms such as 'impending crisis', 'burden' and even 'disaster' when speaking of increasing numbers of those getting older (Coleman *et al.*, 1993, pp.1–2). As Burton-Jones points out, it is not the voices of older people speaking out in this way in Western societies. It is the culture of the young, including those researchers who generally have not reached old age themselves, who make old age seem to be a problem (Burton-Jones, 1997, pp.1-2). A recent Government report admits that people in general see old age, not only as a problem, but one which will 'increase in intensity' over the years, becoming 'increasingly insoluble'. Thus the needs and aspirations of older people themselves are not recognized (Sutherland, 1999, 1.11).

'Old age' is viewed negatively

Paul Tournier, himself a champion of older people, recalls Professor K. von Dürkheim asking some Japanese what was considered to be the supreme good in their country. 'Our old people', he was told. 'Alas,' Tournier comments, 'our Western outlook is quite the opposite' (Tournier, 1972, p.37). His pessimism was echoed by Rabbi Sidney Brichto at a seminar on Spirituality and Old Age, who spoke of a 'conspiracy against the old in which all of us, including the old, participate', where old age, instead of being a blessing, is now 'an inescapable disease which people try to avoid' (in Regan and Smith, 1997, p.24). Simone de Beauvoir, in her pessimistic book *The Coming of Age*, ends by saying, 'The vast majority of mankind looks upon the coming of old age with sorrow and rebellion. It fills them with more aversion than death itself' (de Beauvoir, 1972b, p.550).

Not that this is a new phenomenon. The Egyptian philosopher, Ptahhotep (*c.* 2500 BC) was of the opinion that 'Old age is the worst of misfortunes that can afflict anyone.' But, from then until now, 'We have lost an awareness of old age as a time of life valuable in itself' (Sutherland, 1999, 1.1). Old age is viewed as a state of decline and loss, rather than being welcomed for its gains and achievements (Howe, 1993, pp.3–11 – observation from Australia). The American, Martin Heinecken, agrees, speaking of our culture seeing only 'wrinkles, white hair, halting gait, cracked voice, trembling hands and all', and calling people 'old crone' or 'old codger' (Heinecken, 1981, p.83). Occasionally older people reply in kind, as the old music-hall song proudly spoke of 'My old dutch'.

Viewing old age negatively can be seen at every turn. Fashion magazines insist that 'you can't turn back time – but it is possible to slow its progress ... to minimize obvious signs of ageing'. The article, in a Marks and Spencer magazine, is headed 'Anti-Ageing' (Pearce, 1998, p.83). When society thinks of 'the aged ... we think immediately of dreary nursing homes filled with helpless, senile caricatures of human beings' (Clements, 1979, p.3). Thus the ending of life's course is 'in great crisis' (Phillipson, 1998, p.137). Whatever term is used to describe old age, it soon becomes a negative, as 'Le Troisième Age' has in France (Laslett, 1989, p.96).

The old are a burden

One of the major reasons for older people being viewed negatively is the perceived burden they place on society, both financially and in terms of human resources, with the need to care for many of them.

> In our own country at the moment all that we seem able to see is the ever growing number of failing elderly people who weigh upon the individuals who support them. Ageing is seen as a burden on society at large because resources have to be found to give older people incomes, provide for their ever-failing health, to maintain institutions for those who cannot be supported otherwise. (Laslett, 1989, p.1)

Organisations like Help the Aged make periodic pleas for a more humane approach, speaking of the segregating of elderly people into nursing or residential homes as 'ageist' (Frean,

1999) while the elderly face 'the steady decline of facilities' (Phillipson, 1998, p.7, p.16). This 'burden' on society is largely because of increasing numbers of those who reach old age (Talmon, 1968, pp. 186–96). However, the vast majority actually live in their own homes, as I will show later. Though this is 'the demographic triumph of the twentieth century' (Phillipson, 1998, p.105), the problem is that so many more reach 65 as a percentage of society as a whole (Clarke, 1996, p.40). This has led to frequent references in the media about 'unsustainable pensions' as the active population shrinks relative to those who are retired.

The old are marginalized and ill-treated

As has already been noted, ageism does not end with words or opinions, but leads to positive unkindness to older people. In reviewing the literature, it is remarkable how universal is concern about this. The Australian, Deborah Patterson, writing of the problems of the elderly in 1999, quotes the Copenhagen Declaration on Social Development (1995), that 'in all countries older persons may be particularly vulnerable to social exclusion, poverty and marginalisation'. She also refers to an article by Nikki van der Gaag in the *New Internationalist,* 1995, which says, 'What most of us fear about ageing – not death, but neglect; not the added years, but lack of love and lack of respect' (Patterson, 1999, p.1).

Simone de Beauvoir, writing in France, speaks of society being 'not only guilty but downright criminal' as far as old people are concerned, treating them as 'outcasts' (de Beauvoir, 1972a, pp.1–2). The Congress of the United States in 1976 stated that 'the economic, social and psychological factors associated with aging operate to exclude millions of older people from the full life and the place in society to which their years of service and experience entitle them' (Hunt, 1988, pp.5–6). Donald Heinz puts the American view most graphically:

> Unwelcome reminders of our repressed destiny, we clean them [the aging] from the attics of our consciousness and set them by the curb to be collected. Or we store them in warehouses at the edge of the town, until it is discovered they

> have died. We have come to expect from them an early social death, in case their biological deaths should tarry. (Heinz, 1994, pp.3–19)

The Vatican shares this concern, speaking recently of the problem of the 'marginalization' of older people (Pontificium Consilium pro Laicis, 1999, p.16). The Pope has said that Western society shows 'contempt' for the elderly, making them feel worthless (Gledhill, 1999b, p.5). In Northern Ireland, a survey of the elderly, living alone, found that 25 per cent felt they would not be missed if they were out of sight for a day, while 44 per cent did not meet people on a daily basis (Lampen, 1989, p.14). The 1999 Royal Commission on Long Term Care in the UK spoke of older people suffering 'social exclusion', putting them in residential or nursing homes where they are 'not only out of sight but also out of mind' (Sutherland, 1999, 1.6). Older people now have 'a crisis of invisibility' (Phillipson, 1998, p.124).

This worldwide awareness of the isolation of the old may be encouraging, but action of a positive nature must happen, or ageism can easily progress from this form of negative cruelty to positive unkindness: poverty, humiliation and misery (Bytheway, 1995, p.1). Older people become irrelevant (Grainger, 1993, p.26). 'As a general rule, society shuts its eyes to all abuses, scandals and tragedies [of old people], so long as these do not upset its balance' (de Beauvoir, 1972a, p.216). How can such an advanced society act in such a manner?

The old are discarded in favour of the young

In a society which glorifies the cult of Youth, anyone who is regarded as too old is discarded on the scrap heap as being past it. The concern is not just that this does happen, but that it happens earlier and earlier. 'We discard people too early' was the comment of CBS correspondent Mike Wallace (80), speaking of Walter Cronkite returning to broadcasting at 82 (Brodie, 1998, p.16). The complaint was that Cronkite had been replaced too soon. For some, 60 is too old. The Archbishop of Canterbury recalled MP Austin Mitchell realizing he was too old at that age to be considered for the New Labour Cabinet (Carey, 1998).

Ageism can come even earlier. Rob Warner says that, in many fields of work, 'If you're over forty-five, you're past it. Ageism reaches far beyond the workplace. It can be highly traumatic to experience ageism at fifty, but the treatment of those over seventy is often deplorable' (Warner, 1999, p.9). In 1906, Professor William Osler spoke of 'the comparative uselessness of people over forty, and the entire dispensability of people over sixty' (Laslett, 1989, p.97). All this, because 'we live in an age which venerates youth' (Hunt, 1988, p.3), and denigrates old age: described by Heschel as 'the cult of eternal youth', which he saw as 'idolatry' (White House Conference on Aging, 1961, in Gray and Moberg, 1962, p.145).

The very success of older people may cause this problem. Elizabeth Harbottle says that the younger generation can even be excused if they are resentful of 'YEEPIES' (young elderly energetic people into everything), going to the gym, retiring to the country, with plenty of disposable income, holidaying abroad, and not keen to babysit (Harbottle, 1998, p.7)! The alternative picture of old age as ugly, idle and degenerating is preferred (Featherstone and Hepworth, 1993, p.306).

Those who 'have not reached maturity' view the elderly as 'unalert, physically inert, narrow-minded, ineffective, sexually finished old people in poor health without proper medical care and without enough money to live on', according to pollster Louis Harris (Harris, 1974, p.8.) The views of the old are, therefore, worthless. As comedian Bill Cosby has said:

> In addition to never mentioning something that happened more than three weeks ago, there is one other thing you must never say: 'When I was your age'. You were never their age. You were older in the womb. (Cosby, 1987, p.133)

The director of Better Government for Older People, an initiative run by the Cabinet Office of the UK Government, criticized his own Government, saying how wrong it is to focus so specifically and single-mindedly on tackling the problems of children, while neglecting the role of older people (Shreeve, 1999). Rick Parfitt, of the pop group Status Quo, was asked if he approved of Prime Minister Blair's 'obsession with young Britain'. He replied that it was a 'big mistake ... in Britain we're wrong not to revere our elders' (Montefiore, 1997). He was in good company. Long ago in Rome, Cicero lamented that families were not what they used to be, especially in the way they cared for their elders (Victor, 1994, p.169).

This cult of youth, seen as versus age, produces a further aspect of ageism in the world at large.

The bad outweighs the good

> People today live longer and enjoy better health than in the past. They are also able to cultivate interests made possible by higher levels of education. No longer is old age synonymous with dependence on others or a diminished quality of life. But all this seems not enough to dislodge a negative image of old age or encourage a positive acceptance of a period of life in which many of our contemporaries see nothing but an unavoidable and burdensome decline. (Pontificium Consilium pro Laicis, 1999, p.13)

However much good there now is in growing older, the negatives still dominate. The talents and experience of older people are ignored (Laslett, 1989, p.5). Realistically, it is sometimes the fault of the old themselves. At a Seminar, 'The Grey Generation', one contributor commented, 'Where I live, in a town which is seventy per cent elderly or retired, they are the most impatient people I've come across; they have no patience, time to relate or courtesy' (Pascall, 1999). As Robin Gill puts it, 'Caring for cuddly animals is easy.... Caring for irascible people may be extremely difficult' (Gill, 1992, p.4).

Because of our culture of youth, many find these comments true, and 'contacts with the elderly are psychologically troublesome', with the old being 'a painful reminder of one's probable future' (Longino and Kitson, 1981, p.171). Very few want to be old (Kastenbaum, 1979, p.77); but we are all ageing daily (Harris, 1987, p.2). Even Age Concern entitled a booklet, no doubt tongue in cheek, 'How to avoid becoming an old codger' (Age Concern, 1993a). Ultimately, the bad, which outweighs the good aspects of growing older, is that death is waiting. Despite the glories of Autumn, Winter will arrive. Death is near (Lyon, 1985). Lord Hugh Cecil described old age as 'the outpatients' department of Purgatory' (Oppenheimer, 1999). The very meaning of ageing has been defined by the American gerontologist Lansing as 'a process of unfavourable progressive change, usually correlated with the passage of time, becoming apparent after maturity, and terminating invariably in the death of the individual' (in de Beauvoir, 1972a, p.11). The old then become 'unwelcome reminders of our own mortal course' (Heinz, 1994), and retirement 'a sort of slow preparation for death' (Creber, 1994, p.4). In fact, old age is the only way of avoiding death:

> Vieillir, c'est la préhension la plus immédiate que nous ayons de la pérennité. Quelqu'un a dit: Vieillir est le seul moyen que l'homme ait inventé pour ne pas mourir. [Getting old is the closest understanding we have to eternity. Someone has said 'Getting old is the only means man has invented for not dying'.] (Tritschler, 1991, pp.7–8)

This is ageism in a world which does not venerate older people. It leads to older people themselves believing it is true.

Ageism in older people

With such negativity in society at large, it is no wonder that older people are themselves affected by ageism. The problem is often felt and occasionally exacerbated by those growing old.

We do not want to grow old

One of the questions asked of everyone in my research was, 'What are *you*?' (Appendix 1, question 7). Here are some typical replies, with the age and sex (M Male, F Female) of the person answering: 'I don't think I'm elderly – though I know I am' (M, 73); 'Bordering on elderly' (M, 76+); 'I accept I'm old, but I don't feel old – and I don't want to!' (M, 68); 'Middle aged – I suppose' (F, 56+); 'Middle-aged. I don't want to be elderly 'til I am 81' (M, 56+); 'I feel about 70. I'm more middle-aged at 89' (F); 'I don't think of myself as old' (F, 86).

Therein is the problem. People do not want to admit to ageing, and 'many fear growing old' (Bell, 1980, p.4). Most people do not look forward to the 'last lap in the race of life' (Burton-Jones, 1997, p.8). The converse is true: 'We want to stay young forever' (Dulin, 1988, p.104). Camille Paglia, interviewed about getting older, 'retorted shrilly, "I am not happy about ageing at all. I don't agree with all this manic celebratory mode, the 'It's-fantastic-you-come-into-your-own' of women like Cher. Come off it. I agree with Oscar Wilde that youth is wasted on the young. I'm fifty-two now and I just can't stay up all night like I did"' (Mills, 1999). Simone de Beauvoir, some years earlier, said she had never come across one woman, either in life or in books, who looked on her own old age cheerfully (1972a, p.297). Hence further answers included these: 'I'm still young – I love pop music and videos. I like young film stars and do exercises – with the television' (F, 74); 'I'm young in my mind' (M, 71); 'I'm young in outlook. I like to keep myself young' (M, 72); 'I don't feel old. I'm very active' (F, 76+); 'I'm aged, but I'm still young at heart, young inside' (F, 87); 'I'm getting on middle-aged, though I feel young' (F lay leader, 46+); 'Not old, I will probably never think I'm old' (F, 61); 'Very active elderly' (M, 71+); 'Young at heart' (M, 66); 'An old teenager' (M Vicar, 53).

Mary Thomas wrote an article entitled 'The Curse of Older Age' (a highly emotive title), in which she said:

> If you were to call a thirty-five year old man or woman middle-aged, you would be considered rude. Call a person over sixty or seventy elderly, what do you mean? I am seventy-four but not elderly. I am merely older than someone younger than me. (Thomas, 1999, pp.10–11)

The implication in all these comments is clear: people want to stay young. To get old is not good. Is this not ageism? Turgenev said that the worst of all vices was being over 55 (Turgenev, 1862). How does someone come to terms with being old, while feeling young? It has been called 'one of the existential dilemmas of ageing in our culture' (Jerrome, 1989, p.775).

Old age brings its problems

Older people see their lives as being increasingly limited in what can be done. So they want to be 'elderly not old' (F, 81). But the limitations are there: 'Not old. I'm a bit elderly because I'm slow in my movements and am losing my sight. My grandson said to me the other day at the age of ten, "You've always been old, Nanny!"' (F, 88). As Henri Nouwen has said,

'As you grow older it is very important that you face the reality that your life has limits' (Nouwen, 1995, pp.1–8).

> From both a humanistic as well as a biographically orientated gerontology, there is concern over the absence of meaning in the lives of older people, and the sense of doubt and uncertainty which is seen to pervade their daily routines and relationships. (Moody, 1992, pp.294–5)

From this follows an answer which says, 'I'm old – but not decrepit! I try to keep on as well as I can' (F, 78). The Roman Catholic priest mentioned at the end of the last chapter, who was aged 76, told me, 'I've still got plenty to offer'. An 81-year-old man told me he was 'middle-aged: you are old when your memory lets you down'. The 'meaning' Moody speaks of makes a 64-year-old man tell me, 'My mind is twenty years old, but in my body I'm old'. Often the regret is caused by inactivity, or loss of status, or lack of income through retirement (Townsend, 1986; Phillipson, 1993, pp.15–44). Or there is a sense of deterioration, causing one person to reply, 'Since my stroke I'm getting very old' (F, 76), while another said, 'I feel old because I have bad legs' (M, 70). 'If I could get on a bus – I have bad balance – then I wouldn't feel so old' (F, 90). Corrie ten Boom, after her stroke, faced 'the greatest trial in her life' (Rosewell, 1987, p.110).

It has been called 'heroism' to preside over the disintegration of one's body and mind (Morrison, 1998, p.11). 'Because of my illness, I'm old' (M, 76). Even this can be ageist, equating old age with being ill. Similarly, older people see themselves often as a burden (Tinker, 1989, p.25). They may feel restricted, especially in the countryside (*Faith in the Countryside*, 1990, p.90). Some may feel trapped in a nursing home, with the feeling that they might as well be dead (Treetops, 1992, p.3). One lady (66), living on her own, told me she was 'very lonely'. Evan Marsh speaks of being 'bored, uncertain, unhappy', and asks, 'Is this how we have to end our lives?' (in Johnson and Slater, 1993, p.21). We fear becoming 'debilitated, helpless and dependent' (Cosby, 1987, pp.15–16).

Such are the thoughts of many older people. They do not view old age with happiness. The ageism of society has caused them to adopt a negative approach themselves. Does the church help them, in such circumstances?

Ageism in the church

Later chapters allude to a certain negativity towards older people within churches. But do these amount to ageism as such? Two church writers in the 1990s in Britain would answer, 'Yes'.

> Ageism means blatantly discriminatory attitudes towards older people. Sadly it is as common in our churches as it is in the rest of Society .... Even Christian ministers can be heard complaining about the older members of their congregations and stressing the need for more resources for youth work. (Creber, 1994, p.5)

The significance of this observation is that the writer is himself a Church of England vicar in the Midlands of England, doing research into older people. The second comment is from Rhena Taylor, Director of Outlook, a Christian organization working specifically with older people.

> The Western world has been for many years in the grip of ageism, described as 'a deep and profound prejudice against the elderly'. The church has shared in this prejudice. Yes, there is a care line, possibly a lunch club, a friendship club and a weekly meeting for the over 60s in the church, but no one can pretend that church programmes involving older people are high on the list of church priorities, and provision for their spiritual care is often non-existent. (Taylor, 1996b, pp.13–14)

Echoes of these views were reflected in an occasional comment by ministers during my research. One country parish vicar said about her attitude to older people: 'I feel frustrated by them. I am less tolerant with them than with the younger ones.' A city minister said, 'I admit I'm ageist.' Quite a number of the replies detailed later show that no provision or activities are available for the elderly in some churches.

Older people are ignored by the church

The North American Congress on the Church and the Age Wave predicted that ageism in the church would diminish, while church programmes and staffing would reflect age-related concerns, with ministry focusing on 50 to 70-year-olds

(Yessick, 1995, p.7; Garner, 1996, pp.77–84). Rhena Taylor is not impressed: 'The danger of debates, reports and seminars is that they do not directly touch the person in the pew and I'm not sure how long it takes before they do' (Taylor, 1998).

In some major reports, older people are scarcely mentioned. In the 400-page report, *Faith in the City* (Archbishop of Canterbury's Commission on Urban Priority Areas, 1985), pensioners are mentioned once (p.19) and the elderly in two paragraphs (12.3 and 4, p.273). A strong letter was written by the then Director of Age Concern to the then Archbishop of Canterbury, regretting the Report's lack of focus on older people in Urban Priority Areas. 'Our concern ... reflects our wider concern that the established Church of the nation and its clergy seem to have lost much direct contact with older people.' The church's position was rigorously defended, meetings arranged, and the Church of England later produced its Report, *Ageing*, in 1990 (Report of the Social Policy Committee of the Board for Social Responsibility, 1990). Yet the Church of England still only has a breakdown of members before and after the age of 16 (Tongue, 1998). The secular world fares no better. *The Good Retirement Guide,* 492 pages, has no reference to 'church', even in 'What to do when someone dies' (p.453). There are 130 pages on finance, chapters on leisure, health, work – even caring for parents: but nothing on the spiritual life of older people (Brown, 1998).

The Archbishop of Canterbury has acknowledged that churches and society are not good at encouraging the gifts of those in their 'third age' (Carey, 1998). Writing for the United Reformed Church, Nigel Appleton says that the old most commonly are mentioned in intercessions for the 'old, frail and sick', little acknowledgement being given for their positive gifts. 'The church has adopted an attitude of benign neglect towards the needs of the majority of older people' (Appleton, 1998, 2.06). There is a lack of services to meet their needs and a dismissal of their contribution – a 'pervasive ageism' (Regan and Smith, 1997, p.27).

Older people are on the outside

The Report *Ageing* (see above, pp.117–18) spoke of older people's concerns about the future of an ageing church, which can lead to those very people being neglected in order to bring in a younger congregation. When it comes, therefore, to considering those outside the church, older people are generally overlooked in outreach (McFadyen, 1997, p.11; Taylor, 1997). This would equate with my own experience. At a 1999 meeting to prepare outreach with a church in the Midlands of England, church leaders spoke of those they would like to contact, including youth, twenties to thirties, thirties to fifties, 'street kids', young mums: but no one mentioned the over-fifties.

Yet my fieldwork shows that many older people have a love for God, but from outside the church. They are like Santuzza in Mascagni's *Cavalleria Rusticana.* In this 1890 one-act opera, Santuzza has had an affair in her Sicilian village, and she feels unworthy to attend the Easter morning Mass. She stands outside and, in a deeply moving aria, adds her voice to the Easter hymn. The elderly may not have wronged, but can be made to feel on the outside – and join in from there.

Here again is the youth *versus* old problem, in the same way they appear to compete for public funds (Daniels, 1988, p.4). 'For the most part, the church has adopted a youth culture. . . . In the church, as in the world, older people have become second-class citizens rather than senior citizens' (Beasley-Murray, 1995, p.180–1). In the United States, 'Many of our churches are not prepared for an aging community and congregation. Most churches that I know have a youth minister and a youth program ... but very few churches offer any kind of an exciting program for the elderly' (Yoder, 1996, pp.417–37). Gray and Moberg spoke of 'the neglect of the aged' and an over-emphasis on young people by churches in a society where youth is king (Gray and Moberg, 1962, pp.19–36). A Free Church minister said to me, during my research, 'I like older people, but we can have too many.' A young minister admitted, 'I find relating to older people very difficult because of the age gap.' Writers continue to warn of modern, youthful worship alienating older people, especially where major changes have been made (as with older Roman Catholics who worshipped before Vatican II) (Fahey and Lewis, 1984, pp.145–53).

Older people in residential homes

Regan and Smith did a survey of older people's residential homes and found that clergy and senior church members placed a 'regrettably low priority on providing services for homes in their area' (Regan and Smith, 1997, pp.33–4). Further, many residents had been persuaded, or had persuaded themselves, that they could or should no longer go out to worship (p.41).

A particular need here concerns those with dementia – some of whom live with their families. Major research into this has been done by a Scottish church minister, Hugo Petzsch. Before referring to his writing, a generally agreed view is that 'many victims of Alzheimer's Disease die emotionally and spiritually alone' (Cohen and Eisdorfer, 1986, p.260). In life, too, 'spiritual needs are often overlooked ... especially for the cognitively impaired .... Clergy might feel that persons with dementia are not responsive, and therefore not appropriate to visit.' Marty Richards and Rabbi Sam Seicol, who wrote those words, speak of residents with dementia being included or excluded without consideration of current needs or previous religious preferences or patterns when worship services and religious programmes are offered in a home (Richards and Seicol, 1991, pp.27–40). As almost all dementia sufferers are older people, ageism is again to the fore.

Petzsch (1984) researched the relationship between dementia sufferers and the church in depth, and justice cannot be done fully to his research in an overall book of this nature. His research led him to say that there is a 'fairly bleak picture of the Christian ministry to the severely demented' (p.15), and that 'the predicament of dementing people is an area of neglect' (p.18). The ageist approach is described by Petzsch in the following terms (p.19):

> Another aspect of the churches' practice open to scrutiny in this area is the general provision of services for the severely demented. While it is recognised that many churches would find it practically impossible to accommodate the demented in their services it is worth pondering the reasons. A sobering contrast can be drawn between the churches' response to the demented and their response to young children. While both

> groups have in common a tendency at worst to be incontinent, smelly, noisy and difficult to control, a considerable amount of energy is expended on providing special services for the young and on integrating these to some degree into the congregation's main diet of worship on Sundays. It is not difficult to imagine the initial response of most congregations to a dementing adult or elderly person who was brought to a normal Sunday service. The implications of this parallel might lead one to think that the churches are implicitly endorsing a very materialistic view of man. That is, that he is only of worth when he holds the ability or potential to contribute actively to society. While this is the case with children, who are seen as the hope for the future, it is patently not the case with the severely demented who, whatever they may have contributed during their life before illness, are now regarded as being incapable of contributing to society.

With the elderly dementia sufferers, is the church ageist? Are they, like other older people, part of the 'psychological phenomenon' where the aged are 'often seen and yet not seen' (Clements, 1979, pp.8–9)? I will look at what can be done in my concluding chapters.

Final thoughts on ageism

In society, among older people themselves, and especially in the church, ageism must be seen for what it is, challenged and removed. 'Every man desires to live long, but no man would be old,' wrote Jonathan Swift (quoted in Hunt, 1988, p.1). Ageism must be opposed for that most selfish of reasons – for ourselves. 'Failing a nuclear holocaust, almost all of us will have the good fortune to live to be old, and many of us will be very old. It is in our own interest to combat ageism' (Norman, 1987, p.23). 'Interdependence between generations is vital' (Victor, 1994, p.249).

The final word on the subject is with Tom Kirkwood, the then Professor of Biological Gerontology at Manchester University. Interviewed in *The Times,* he said that 'we are terrified of ageing much more than we acknowledge', and went on:

> I speak to older people a lot and they feel less valued than other members of society. We should be shouting that this is not what society is about. Ageism needs to be challenged, because it is a dismissal of old people. (Ahuja, 1999, p.12)

How can a new relationship be established between older people and the church, to help banish ageism? As this book progresses, I hope to suggest ways which could help.

4

What is 'Church'?

As there was a need to define 'older people', so there is a need to answer the important question, 'What is "church"?' To understand the relationship between the two, it is vital to see what is meant today by the term 'church', and whether there is any agreement between those who lead churches, those who attend them and those who do not.

It is necessary to emphasize at the outset that, as in defining 'older people', there is not going to be a simplistic, one sentence answer in this chapter. However, as with chapter 2, an answer will be sought from those who have studied this subject, and from the detailed answers given to the first part of Appendix 1, questions 1 and 2. These, as with the questions in Chapter 2, were answered by all the participants – leaders, young, middle-aged and older people – this latter group divided into church and non church attenders.

What *is* 'church'? This chapter will show a great diversity of answers to this question: hence the need for the first point, by way of introduction.

A variety of definitions

In the Questionnaire, interviewees were given two bites at the cherry. I felt this to be appropriate because these were the very first questions they were asked, and it helped to put them at ease:

Question 1: What is the first thing you think of when you hear the word – 'church'?

Question 2: Now you've said that, what does the word 'church' mean to you?

This enabled both an immediate reaction and a more reflective observation. In analysing the answers, it appeared wisest to combine the answers into one to get an overall picture. Very few people gave one single definition and the variety of views, even from one interviewee, is exemplified in these two answers, the first from a Free Church minister, the second from a New Church leader:

Minister: Answer 1: 'A building.'
Answer 2: 'Home. Family. Lighthouse. Mooring place. Open doors.'

Leader: Answer 1: 'Worship.'
Answer 2: 'People. Friends. Learning. Fun. Community. God – I left him rather late!'

In other circles, this would be called hedging one's bets, and is not a new phenomenon. Spinka refers to a sermon by John Hus, preached on October 19, 1405:

> Hus defines the terms used for the church: the word sometimes refers to the edifice, sometimes to the congregation of the faithful; at other times it refers to particular churches such as the Roman Church or the Prague Church. 'In the third mode the church is the totality of the predestinate, called the mystical body of Christ, the bride of Christ and the kingdom of heaven'. (Spinka, 1966, pp.60–1)

Spinka goes on to contrast these definitions with those given by a contemporary of Hus, Stephen Pàlec, who gives six definitions of the church in his treatise *De aequivocatione nominis ecclesia* of 1412:

> In the first place, he applies the word 'church' somewhat inaptly to the church building, because God is worshipped therein. In the second place, the church is 'the congregation of the wicked and iniquitous men, as heretics and schismatics', although this usage has no merit. In the third place, the church stands for the general Council gathered to consider matters of faith or other ecclesiastical concern. ... The fourth significance of the word refers to the prelates and other officials heading to the church ....
>
> In the fifth sense the word 'church' signifies the universal and total congregation of all the predestinate or believing .... the sixth significance of the term 'church' refers to the community of all those who are baptised and believe ... the Apostles' Creed. (Spinka, 1966)

Despite Spinka's comment about the inappropriateness of defining 'church' as 'building', we shall see shortly that a number do define it thus, but the variety he draws from Hus and Pàlec is typical of many who cannot give a single definition. They stand in stark contrast to Philipp of Hesse, in his *Confession of Faith* of 1550, whose single definition of 'church' is almost aggressive in style:

> We all hold to and believe one Christian church. . . . For there can be no other church than that of the old fathers and martyrs, who for Christ's sake suffered and were opposed to the Arians and heretics. And no one can or will show me another Christian church. (Quoted in Littell, 1964, p.34)

One is left wondering if one would become a martyr for disagreeing. However, most would not give such a blunt, single answer in their definition of 'church', as we shall see.

Having glanced at two approaches, it may help to look at a couple of dictionary and encyclopaedic definitions, before launching into the several choices offered by scholars and interviewees. The first is from the *Oxford Dictionary of the Christian Church*:

> Terminology. The English 'church' . . . comes ultimately from the Greek *Kuriakon* '[thing] belonging to the Lord', which was applied originally to a church building. The Latin *ecclesia* . . . although used of the building, comes from the secular Greek [and] meant an assembly, primarily of citizens in a self-governing city. . . . In the Septuagint *ekklesia* was used of the 'assembly' or 'congregation' of the Israelites and especially of those 'within the covenant' as opposed to 'the stranger in your midst' (Deut. 23.3). (Cross, 1974)

This definition makes Spinka's observation even less plausible. Further help is found in *The Encyclopaedia of Religion*, which refers back to the Hebrew, as well as the Greek:

> The gathering of the people for the worship of God was designated in Hebrew by the word *qahal*, which the Greek Septuagint translates eighty-one times as *ekklesia* (sic) . . . The 'spirit of Christ' causes the new Israel to take form as the body of Christ. For 'body of Christ' we might well say 'church' or 'churches'. *Ekklesia,* which had been used to

> translate *qahal* and which in the Greek world meant the convoked assembly of citizens, occurs sixty-one times in the writings of Paul; in Acts the word is used twenty-three times for the local community.

By way of further explanation, the *Encyclopaedia* makes the observations that this 'church' is 'a community in a particular place', that 'this community is the church of God', but part of all other churches, and finally that 'these realities are heavenly ... the realities are eschatological' (Congar, 1987).

We now turn to the views of over 200 interviewees, and observations from writers. What is 'church'? As I come to look at the specific comments, the following charts (Figures 4.1. and 4.2) show the initial reactions of all those questioned, whatever their status. At the end of the chapter, I give the overall charts (Figures 4.3. and 4.4) to both the questions set out at the beginning of the chapter. Figure 4.1 shows the overall position, with Figure 4.2 giving a breakdown of the 32% 'People' section by numbers.

There now follows a detailed account of the different responses to the questions regarding what 'church' is, following the percentage breakdown in Figure 4.1. I have tried in each case, where appropriate, to show how leaders, younger and mid-aged church members, older church members and non attenders differed. However, in many cases below, it will be seen that there was a degree of unanimity, as I will also seek to show.

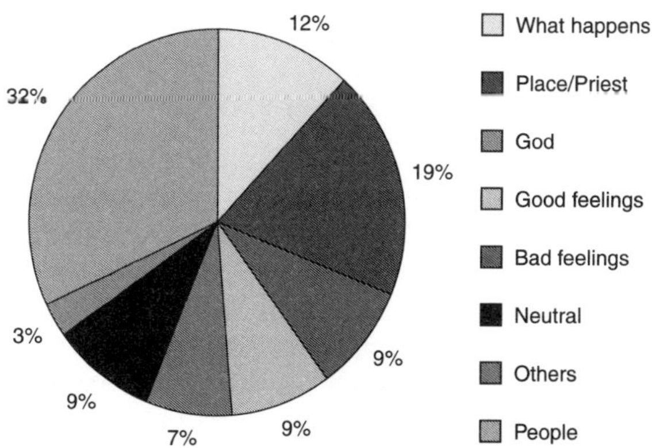

Figure 4.1 Initial reactions to 'What is "church"?'

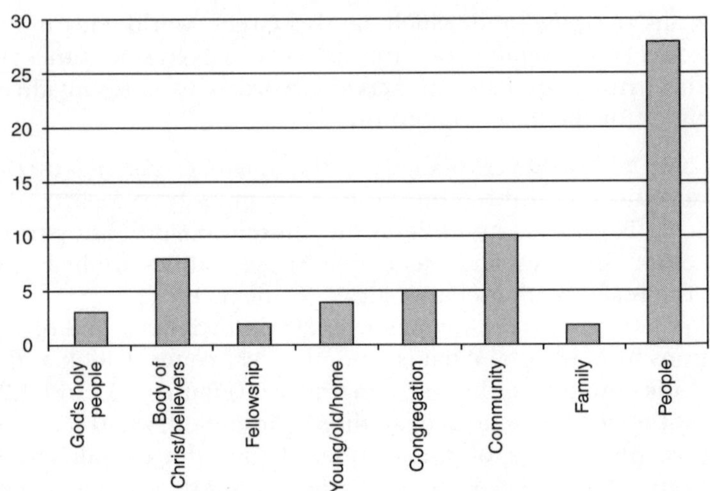

Figure 4.2 Breakdown in detail answering 'People' (32%) in Figure 4.1. by numbers

I will now give an answer to the question 'What is church?' beginning with its being described as the building itself, or its minister.

Church is – a building and a priest

'What is "church"?' Of all those asked 19 per cent defined 'church' as the building or its minister.

> 'What is a church?' – Our honest sexton tells,
> ''Tis a tall building, with a tower and bells'.
>
> (Crabb, 1810)

'The building – the physical building – a very honourable place in this village.' So said John, a man over 76 who did not attend church, but who regarded the local parish church as epitomizing what church meant to him. Like Lord Eldon, he was not a pillar of the church, he was a buttress: he supported it from the outside. Of the 19 per cent (above), over half (12 per cent compared with 7 per cent who defined church as its minister) of all those interviewed said they equated the word church with a *specific* building, quite often naming a particular edifice ('St John's,' 'St Boniface'). Of these, half were elderly, dividing equally between churchgoers and non attenders.

Among the leaders, an Anglican vicar, asked for his initial reaction to the word "church", replied, 'Holy Cross Church – a picture of the building was the first thing I saw when you said the word "church".' It was interesting that this sort of reply was not confined to those mentioning older buildings. A New Church leader answered the same question thus: 'A vibrant, lively building where people can come and experience life and get involved. A place for plenty of activities for the community.' 'The building has a lot of feeling for me,' said Pam (72), 'The history of the building is important.' Some would include the building in their overview of the word 'church', as 82-year-old church attender Frank said:

> 'It depends on the church. At the church my children go to in Cambridge the church is first class and very concerned in outreach. But sadly some churches alarm me because they are chiefly concerned with maintaining the building, and the people outside matter very little. Some people on TV, when they portray the church, I say "Praise the Lord". With others I think that if that is all God means, "I'm sorry for you" '.

Frank seems to equate 'church' with the building, the people, its relationship with those on the outside and its portrayal. As the heading for this section implies, 'church' may not just be the building, but also the minister of it.

> Our picture of the church usually begins with a romantic rural setting in which a beautiful medieval church, built on the highest piece of ground in the area is surrounded by a quaint mixture of attractive old housing .... From the church emerges a clergyman (usually in our mental picture, an elderly one). Often more liked than understood, he is – after the building – what people mean by 'the church'. (Warren, 1995a, p.7)

Two non attending older people saw 'church' as being specifically the priest (ex-Catholic) or the vicar (ex-Anglican). Wilson sees this as a unique feature of the Christian faith, saying that, 'The designation "church" defines an autonomous corporate institution hierarchically organised and served by a professional priesthood. Churches that conform to all these specifications are found only in Christianity' (Wilson, 1968, pp.428–37). Troeltsch would see the priesthood as one reason for the church's survival. 'So long as all participated in faith in the priesthood, the sacraments and the unity of religious knowledge it [the church] was indissoluble' (Troeltsch, 1931, p.96). Historically (though less so since Vatican II), the Roman Catholic Church in particular relied on the priest to be the key figure in making church be church:

> The pre-Vatican Church stressed the virtues of loyalty, the certainty of answers, strict discipline and unquestioning obedience (Greeley, 1972). In this model the priest was viewed as a 'man apart' and the 'sacred' ministry of the priest was asserted over the priesthood of all believers (Moore, 1975). In the pre-Vatican theology with its fidelity to tradition (*Pro Mundi Vita*, 1973), God was seen as remote, unchanging and perfect (Neal, 1970). (Hornsby-Smith, 1987, p.32)

Though things have changed, as Hornsby-Smith implies, many older Catholics would still hold to this pre-Vatican II model, especially those who do not attend and, therefore, know less of the changes. Nor will this be limited to long-standing denominations. When a newer church starts up, its leader may be the focal point for what 'church' is, as Weber showed:

> A religious community arises in connection with a prophetic movement as a result of routinization (*Veralltäglichung*), i.e. as a result of the process whereby either the prophet himself or his disciples secure the permanence of his preaching and the congregation's distribution of grace, hence insuring the economic existence of the enterprise and those who man it. (Weber, 1965, pp.60–1)

It certainly seems to be the experience of a number of 'house churches' that their success or failure depends on the main leader; his or her decline may well lead to the dissolution of that particular church. The same sometimes occurs in a Free Church, unless there is a strong central organization to help maintain continuity.

Perhaps it is a problem of terminology. When people say, 'I'm going to church', they mean setting off to a building. When a person says they are 'Going into the church', they mean becoming an ordained minister. There is no popular word which means that the church is anything else (Warren, 1995a, p.34). Thus to equate the church with the message, a Free Church leader said church was 'a place where the Gospel is preached'. On a lighter note, one young person told me that 'church' equals 'pews'! Only two people equated 'church' with a specific denomination (a Roman Catholic bishop, and one of his older non attenders).

The last word on the church being a building and a minister lies with 80-year-old Ruby, who goes to an Anglican church:

> 'My faith is very weak. I go to church every Sunday. I love everything about church. I enjoy the church as if I were going to the theatre. The vicar has to grab me in the first two minutes of his sermon or my mind wanders.'

We now make something of a quantum leap. Church is sometimes seen as the building, or the leader, but more often it is those who attend.

Church is – people

By far the highest number of answers given in the definition of 'church' (32 per cent) associated the word with the people who go. However, there was still a great variety of expressions.

People

The specific word 'people' was used by 14 per cent of *all* interviewees, the highest percentage for any definition. This means those respondents who literally equated 'church' with the specific word 'people', rather than its denotations and connotations. Two church leaders put it like this: 'People – and those who *should* be there'; 'People, not the building'.

They were in good company. The theologian Hans Küng says:

> *We* are the church, and we *are* the church. And if we are the church, then the church is a fellowship of those who seek, journey and lose their way, of the helpless, the anguished and the suffering, of sinners and pilgrims. (Küng, 1968, p.33)

'The church', asserts Briscoe, 'is not somewhere you go to, it is something you are' (Briscoe, 1999). It is highly significant that, with one notable exception, very few elderly chose this definition, while only six church leaders did *not* (and those six who did not use the specific word 'people' chose another word which was similar). It was only mentioned by three of the 60 non attenders among the elderly, and by only four elderly attenders out of 52 – not counting the aforementioned exception. These were elderly attenders of New Churches, *all* of whom said 'church' is 'people'. By far the majority of New Church leadership, full-time and lay, agreed. This was so, even though these New Churches had, in some instances, fine buildings where they worshipped.

From this general term of 'people', we now look at how it was construed in more specific terms.

Family and Community

Only one elderly person used the word 'family' to define 'church'. Remarkably, of the eleven who did, eight were young people. Fifteen-year-old Amy was typical, saying church is 'a family of people who believe in God and worship him'. Both leaders and older people need to see how younger people feel about them. Perhaps it has something to do with their feeling of equality in a family, particularly in partaking of the Sacraments (Troeltsch, 1931, p.72).

The other word which commanded a lot of attention was 'community': a fifth of those who used a 'people' word chose this to describe 'church'. This fits with Küng's views that the church is 'a new community'. Given his own treatment, it is hardly surprising that he states, 'The new group of disciples may be seen as the eschatological community of salvation' (Küng, 1968, p.81). The Roman Catholic Archbishop of Birmingham described the church, when interviewed, as 'the community of Jesus Christ in which the sacraments are given and people are taught the Gospel'. A black church leader extended this to embrace outsiders, saying church is 'a focal point for the whole community – not just the church community, meeting spiritual and physical needs'. He sees it as 'ministering to young people, children and senior citizens, engaging in social programmes, being the primary deliverer of spiritual programmes'. It should, he concluded, give 'fellowship, and an environment for love, compassion, healing and reconciliation'. In this way, Troeltsch (1931, p.62) sees the church community as 'the religious Communism of Love', while Robin Gill devotes a whole chapter in his book *Moral Communities* to 'Churches as Moral Communities' (Gill, 1992, Chap. 4).

It is significant to note that the word was hardly mentioned by older people (four, all Anglican attenders); could it be that they do not find the church is a community, or a family, for them? The perception of leaders may not be theirs.

Body

Several definitions (8 per cent in all) were used to describe 'church' as a 'body', meaning a group of people linked like a physical body, but spiritually.

- *A 'body of people'.* Harold (83), who goes to a village Anglican church, told me that church means 'the better aspects of life: a body of people who all think in the same sort of way. Church is important,' he went on, 'it is a way of life. If more people adopted Christian ideas, it would cut down the horrible side of life.' This is an interesting comment, from an Anglican, as Free Churches would normally see themselves more in this way: for example, this 'voluntary association' is an essential mark of the Anabaptists (Littell, 1964, pp.82–113) and, indeed, *all* Free Churches (Troeltsch, 1931, p.656) though a decline in numbers may lead to *all* churches fitting Harold's definition (Troeltsch, 1931, p.381).
- *A 'body of believers'.* The leader of the Baptists for the Warwickshire area described the church as 'the gathered community of believers, identified by a commitment to Christ, having received Jesus as Saviour and Lord. The church then has a family and there is an extended community of people in the family life, but who are not part of the gathered family of believers.' This exclusivity and yet inclusiveness will be seen again, but this 'body' definition is a limiting one.
- *'God's Holy People'.* This has a similar ring to it as the previous one, and was used primarily by Roman Catholic leaders, as a variant of another term they used, 'God's

> pilgrim people'. Again, there is a sense of an exclusive organization – a mark of the Baptists, Independents and Congregationalists, according to Weber (1965, p.65).

The church is viewed as the people of God and, by implication then, as a pilgrim church .... The church is a pilgrim not simply for the practical reason that in the modern age it no longer calls the tune and is everywhere finding itself in a diaspora situation; rather, to be a pilgrim in the world belongs intrinsically to the church's excentric position. It is ek-klesia, 'called out' of the world and sent back into the world. (Bosch, 1991, pp.373–4)

The danger of this definition, however true it be, is the way it separates the church from the world. Bosch may be right in theory, but in practice the church may, acting on such a description, retreat from the world. As Michael Winter says,

> The parish as we know it is now an obstacle to the kind of mission which the church must exercise .... The construction and maintenance of ... costly buildings keeps the Catholics in a psychological ghetto of inward-looking activity, while the authentic problems of mankind are largely ignored. (Winter, 1973, p.6)

The terms 'body of believers' and 'God's holy people' to define 'church' are almost certainly correct theologically, but may give the appearance of being so exclusive as to justify the view of Weber (1930, p.145) that this turns a church into a sect. It is not the purpose of this chapter to argue the pros and cons of the terms 'church' and 'sect' but the matter is debated between Troeltsch (1931, p.993) and Littell (1964, p.iii), while Beckford distinguishes between church and sect in an article in *Current Sociology* (Beckford, 1973, p.95). The point to be made here is that, once again, the elderly did not use the term 'God's holy people' at all, whereas leaders did. Again, the significance of this is important: leaders are using some terms which are not perceived by their older members and non attenders.

- *'Body of Christ'.* Two church attending older people identified the church with the 'Body of Christ', as did four leaders. In his book about older churchgoers, Apichella says that 'the church today needs to recapture the vision of the body of Christ as an extended family, and not just a building' (Apichella, 1989, p.138). The definition is helpful as it can be viewed as inclusive of *all* churches into one society (Mission Theological Advisory Group, 1996, p.33). It gives the idea of oneness, one Body, the '*whole* people of God' (Küng, 1968, p.125). It also brings Jesus Christ into a definition, whereas many of the other 'people' descriptions of church can make the church appear to be a social or familial gathering and little else, as if anything to do with God is an optional extra, as the following may demonstrate.

Fellowship and Friends

Küng described the church as 'the fellowship of aspirants to the Kingdom of God' (1968, pp.95–6). Seven older church attenders agreed with him, echoing the words of Kate, a New Church middle-aged member (the only younger or middle-aged interviewee to use these terms): church is 'a group of people on Sunday mornings in a building – but people going round helping each other. The bit before and after the meeting itself is what really matters.'

As already hinted, the implication could be the side-lining of God: the service in the middle matters less than the personal contacts either side. But it is socially beneficial to have this fellowship, especially for the lonely and bereaved. Betty (79) sees church as 'a community of friends'. Dorothy, an elderly village churchgoer, looks at church as 'a place where you go to meet with friends and other people, to be near God and get spiritual guidance and learning'. Bearing in mind how unfriendly churches seemed to be for some of us earlier in our lives, these concepts do matter:

> As networks rather than institutions are the means through which people increasingly relate to one another, it is vital that the church itself discovers how to become a network of loving relationships. (Warren, 1995a, p.125)

Young and old

These terms were used very infrequently (four people in all, including two leaders), but show that 'people' can occasionally mean a specific age group. It was sometimes used in sad terms, as when an older Free Church attender said this:

> 'I am concerned about our church – it is very elderly and we don't know how to encourage the young people. They come in, see us all being old and turn and go. There is no one in their age group to look after them. Our congregation is aged 55 to 85. When the old go there will be no congregation.' (John)

On the one hand, John points to the essence of Christianity being that it welcomes, so none need 'turn and go', be they young or old, men or women (Weber, 1965, p.105). The church should be, for old and young, a place of care (Gill, 1992, p.81). On the other hand, the existence of a church which caters for older people gives it the opportunity to be 'a community which takes up the burdens of unemployment, handicap, loneliness and sickness of its members' (Turner, 1983, p.3, quoted by Hornsby-Smith, 1989, p.93). It is a dilemma: but can the church just be 'young' or 'old'?

Gathering and Congregation

These terms were used almost exclusively by older people (six out of seven), attenders and non attenders alike. Nan, an elderly non attender, still sees church as 'a congregation where you say your prayers'. This sits comfortably with Article XIX, 'Of the Church', in the 1662 *Book of Common Prayer*:

> The visible Church of Christ is a congregation of faithful men, in which the pure Word of God is preached, and the Sacraments be duly administered according to Christ's ordinance in all those things that of necessity are requisite to the same.

Hus saw the church as 'the congregation of the faithful to be saved' (Spinka, 1966, p.394), while Küng says that '"Congregation", "Community", "Church" are not mutually exclusive terms, but should be seen as interconnected' (1968. p.84).

Social structure

Only one (a Roman Catholic young person) used this term to describe 'church'. He is backed by writers on the subject. David Bosch tells us that 'we now recognise that the church is both a theological and a sociological entity, an inseparable union of the divine and the dusty' (1991, p.389). Troeltsch sees the church as a 'Sociological phenomenon' (1931, p.36), a 'social whole' (p.203) and a 'social system' (p.78). Hornsby-Smith says the church, 'like any other social institution, is in a dialectical relation with the society in which it exists' (Hornsby-Smith, 1991, p.141). However, a great more needs to be said to explain 'church': 'social structure' is dangerously limiting on its own. Even though it be true, it is not the whole truth.

Home

It was two Free Church clergy (one a senior leader) who saw 'church' as 'home'. Perhaps they spend a lot of time there! Alas, the only older person to use the term, did so retrospectively. Margaret, a 76-year-old non attender, said this:

> 'Where I came from it was like going home. But it's not like that in Coventry: I have never had the feeling that I'm part of it. The people who go are all out-of-towners. There is not the same community spirit.'

The word 'home' is able to incorporate most of the different terms used under the heading 'people'. Church is seen by many as those with whom they meet, rather than a building where they meet. But, for others, church means the things which happen, as we will now consider.

Church is – what happens

Every eighth person in the entire sample, when asked what church meant to them, answered with something which occurs in the course of a service in a church building. 'Church' becomes an event, something one *does.*

The Mass/Communion. 'In contemporary ecclesiology the church is increasingly perceived as sacramental sign and instrument .... The new terminology is, perhaps understandably, used more extensively in Catholicism than in Protestantism' (Bosch, 1991, p.374). To substantiate Bosch's observation, all but one who said that 'church' is the sacrament of Mass were, indeed, Roman Catholics, of whom Angela (77) was typical. 'What is church?' Answer 1: 'The Mass.' Answer 2: 'The priest means a lot to me.'

Services/worship. Four mentioned the word 'services' to describe church (all Anglican attenders, two of them older); but the word 'worship' was more frequent (fourteen people in all), and used by four elderly non attenders. Majorie, an 88-year-old, said that church is 'worship – I miss it because I cannot go because I cannot sit long enough with my arthritis'. As we shall see later, the church needs to hear such a *cri de coeur,* and find ways to take simple worship services to such as Marjorie.

Hymns/singing.

> ... As some to church repair
> Not for the Doctrine, but the music there
> (Pope, 1711)

Despite the new and exciting music in the newer churches, it was Anglicans and Roman Catholics who specifically related 'church' to 'hymns' and 'singing' (eight in all, including three older attenders). One might see this as a limited answer, but that is how some do see church: good music is important.

Bible/prayer. These were mentioned by five people (two young attenders, three older – all non attenders), the one equating prayer with church being significant in two illuminating comments. Mary, an older Roman Catholic, said church was 'going in and speaking to God – thanking him for health and strength'. Pam, an elderly Anglican, said church is 'somewhere to pray and visit and be at peace'. The significance lies in the fact that neither is a churchgoer in that they do not attend services. But the church building is their refuge for private prayer; clergy need to keep the building open, and have people available to meet such needs.

Sermons. For those who preach, it is sobering that only one elderly attender mentioned the sermon. So much for Luther's view that, 'wherever the Word is preached, there is the Church' (Troeltsch, 1931, pp.479–80).

Outreach. Bosch (1991, p.375) reminds his readers of the oft-quoted Archbishop Temple, that the church is the only society in the world which exists for the sake of those who are not members of it. An Anglican vicar told me that the church is 'a missionary agency: a group of people chosen to shine God's light in the world'. But only three others went along with this definition of 'church', none of them older. As we continue to answer the question, 'What is "church"?', one matter to consider is: where does God fit into the definition? This next section seeks an answer.

Church is – God/life

When I came to analyse my findings from the 200 plus questionnaires, I only then realized how infrequently God got a mention. Only 7 per cent equate church specifically with God, or Jesus (though one or two did use the term 'Body of Christ', as we have seen). Of the several who said 'church' is 'God', four out of fourteen were elderly non attenders. Two of the four who said 'church' is 'Jesus' were in the same category (as 87-year-old Marjorie said: 'church is "The Lord Jesus" '). Answers such as 'the Kingdom of God', 'the love of God', and 'the Cross' were each mentioned no more than twice. God may be in danger of getting left out of his own church.

However, a small number (4 per cent) saw church as their basis for life itself. Among Roman Catholics, Betty and Tony, elderly attenders, said 'Our children would tell you it's our life. We never have a minute to spare because all we do is to do with the church.' In similar vein, Maureen told me, 'It's part of my life – I couldn't live without it.' Turning to elderly Free Church members, Roy claims, 'My church is my life: it's my reason for living.' When asked about what church meant to her, Ruby spoke in these terms: 'God saved me almost from the gutter – my marriage had broken up. I would have done away with myself, but God changed my life.'

These answers reveal a deep optimism in some people. They lead to the last definition I discovered, where 'church' is a matter of the emotions.

Church is – feelings

When one says the word 'church' to some people, it evokes feelings more than anything else. There were some surprises here, too.

The negatives. Even though 60 elderly non attenders were interviewed among the 200 plus, an overall total of less than 5 per cent had bad feelings when speaking of what church meant to them. Of this 5 per cent, half were those elderly who classed themselves an Anglicans, but no longer attended, and a quarter were young people (attenders).

The strongest comment came from an Anglican vicar. With a great deal of laughter, when asked what 'church' was, he replied: 'It is important – and the thing that causes me most pain in my life.' More sadly, non attending elderly Pam said church was 'factions, hassle, feeling pushed out'. Bob (75) said church was "too highfalutin"'. For Roy (65), church is 'boring: it's something you've got to go through. I was an altar boy and played pranks, but I found church very boring.'

For one, church was 'work', for another, 'tradition'. Walter (80) saw the church as 'another means of gaining power over the people', but 'people are beginning to see through it'. Matthew (72) finds church is 'a complete waste of time, a bunch of hypocrites: all churches should be turned into old people's homes'. These are strong words from a non-practicing Roman Catholic. An elderly husband and wife were bitter about their local Anglican church:

> 'The people who go – they don't seem to help others compared to those who don't go, because those who go only work for the church. We've never got help for the village from the church people.'

In like manner, Alan, a 70-year-old former Free Church member, spoke of the church as:

> 'A group of people who are self-serving and who have very successfully looked after their own interests to the disadvantage of the surrounding population for 2000 years: a very successful small business.'

Elderly Anglican non attenders mentioned lack of help, money, self-interest and factions. But overall the negative feelings were few and far between.

The positives. Compared with the 5 per cent who spoke of 'bad feelings', 7 per cent found the church to be the source of good feelings. It was country folk who felt this way, as Phoebe

(87) said: 'A loving environment: there is the feeling that people have worshipped there. I feel it in my church, as if arms are enclosing you.' Several non attending Anglicans in villages still found that church meant quiet and peace, typified by Tom, for whom church is 'peace and quiet inside – and a very nice view from the churchyard'! Bert (81), attends a village Free Church, and says it is 'peace on earth. Our church had a notice,' he said, 'which read, "This is a very noisy world: come in and have a rest in peace".' Others spoke of the help and comfort, feelings evoked by the word 'church'.

For one, 'church' is 'security', for others, 'faith'. Ernest (67) said church is 'my faith and my priests and my soul'. Rather winsomely, 88-year-old Winnie said this:

> 'Good things. I wish I were better. I don't go to church, but I am a believer. I wish I had a faith which I followed, but I don't. You can't help believe in Jesus Christ.'

For Ena (83), church is happy feelings:

> 'What happy memories from being a child, when my mother took me and I grew up as a member of the church. There is nothing like a church: it is peaceful and you can go in and there is an aura about it.'

Ena's thoughts are summed up by Phyllis (82): 'I wouldn't be without it'.

The neutral feelings. Eight per cent had what one might call a neutral approach as to how they felt about church, mainly comprising elderly non attenders. For one or two it was 'hatched, matched and despatched' (a phrase used specifically by Ted (82)). Likewise Dennis (76), for whom church is 'weddings and funerals and christenings – family life growing up'. For Wilf (83), church is simply 'somebody to bury me', while Ray (69) sees church as 'the Christian religion'. Daniel (79) said church reminded him of 'boyhood – I was made to go'. For some attenders, church means 'going', or they have 'always been'.

Four (two middle-aged attenders, two older non attenders) felt the church is just an 'institution', echoing Hornsby-Smith's view of the Roman Catholic church in the 1950s as a 'bureaucratically administered religious organisation'. He cites Butler (1981) as showing that 'the Second Vatican Council endeavoured to reform the Church so that it would be more responsive to the needs of people living in the contemporary world' (Hornsby Smith, 1991, p.191). Beckford employs the term 'bureaucratization' in describing the Church of England's synodical government (Beckford, 1985, pp.125–38). There are those who agree with him.

Inevitably, there are those for whom the church means nothing at all, at least today. Josephine (74) said church meant 'not much. Years ago it meant I went every Sunday.' Pearl (68) said, 'I'm indifferent'. But these were few (three older non attenders and, remarkably, one clergy): most had an opinion of some sort, putting a question mark over the thought that 'for the majority of people in this country our churches are irrelevant' (Warren, 1995b, p.2).

As promised, the following charts give the overall views, and can be compared with those shown earlier. Figures 4.1 and 4.2 gave initial reactions. Figures 4.3 and 4.4 combine initial reactions with the secondary questions (by adding them together) regarding a more considered reaction. Figure 4.3 gives the summary, while Figure 4.4 gives a breakdown of the 49 per cent 'People' section by numbers.

To summarize

The amazing fact is that the word 'church' evoked over 70 different reactions and definitions. Although most defined it as the people or the building, minority views spanned a great

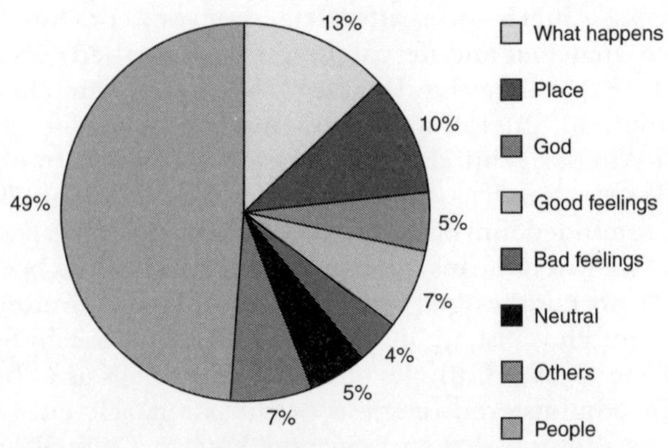

Figure 4.3 Overall views on 'What is "Church"?'

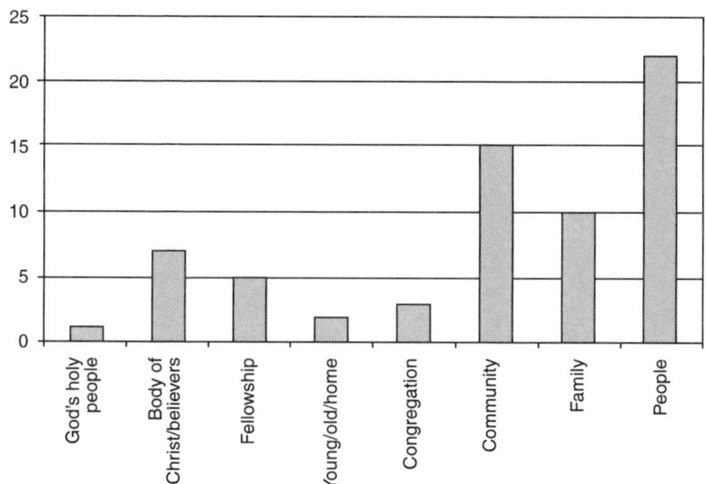

Figure 4.4 A detailed breakdown of the 49% answering 'people' in chart 4.3 by numbers

breadth of ideas. 'Church' has dozens and dozens of meanings. One cannot assume it is only one thing.

We have seen some diversity of definitions given between those who lead, those who attend, and those who do not. For example, many more who attend, compared with those who do not attend, see the church as the 'people'. Perhaps that is inevitable. It was the younger attenders who saw the church as their 'family', and who also used the word 'community' – something hardly mentioned by older people. It may only be a matter of generational terminology: older church members used the word 'friends' more often. There may be some significance also in 12 per cent speaking of what happens (the Mass, hymns, prayer being three examples). It was interesting to note that God was mentioned infrequently.

The conclusion must be similar to that of Chapter 2: it is as hard to define 'church' as it is to explain the words 'older people'. As a point of reference, the word 'church' will have to include building and minister, the people who go, what happens and the feelings all these evoke.

It may be that the next chapter will cause even more confusion, because the church is not static: the last decades have brought about great changes in the church – as we shall now see.

5

The Changing Church

When conducting a series of qualitative interviews, one is never completely sure when one set of questions will almost universally spark imaginations, producing enthusiastic answers. Although questions on the meaning of 'church' were appreciated, it was the further questions on changes in the church which generated a greater interest amongst respondents. This chapter seeks to give the results of those responses.

An overview

The history of the church in the last 40 or 50 years has been one of considerable change: worldwide, inter-church, within individual denominations and with the emergence of the New Churches. Worldwide, the church has seen the explosion of Christianity across Africa and South America, and in single countries like South Korea. The Second Vatican Council has brought remarkable changes to the Roman Catholic Church, while the Alternative Services Book reformed worship for the Church of England. Inter-church and, indeed, inter-faith consultations are now part of a permanent agenda. From small-scale House Churches, the New Churches are a growing factor on the British church scene.

Little wonder, then, that very few saw 'no change' when answering questions 8 to 12 at the beginning of Appendix 1 (which relate specifically to changes in the church over the last few decades). Of those who did, or gave no answer, all but four did not attend Church. Significantly, some church leaders see little or no progress. A Captain told me that 'Worship in the Salvation Army is pretty much the same'. The Baptist lay leader of an elderly village congregation said, 'There has not been a great deal of change here, not as in many churches. Most of our congregation are elderly and have been for years.' A New

Church leader, more surprisingly, spoke of little change in graphic terms: 'Having to take stock of where the church is: it has its head up its backside and we have to work out how we get it out'! The secretary for the area United Reformed Church admitted, 'There have been no great changes in the URCs'.

These answers are not typical of the majority, who spoke in one way or another of change. My purpose here is to detail the *perceived* changes, those specifically referred to by those interviewed in the Coventry and Warwickshire area. Further reference should be made to *Building Missionary Congregations* (Warren, 1995b), and Hornsby-Smith's detailed accounts of the major changes in the Roman Catholic Church (Hornsby-Smith, 1989 and 1991). His 1989 *The Changing Parish* contains detailed tables analysing the situation pre- and post- Vatican II (pp.17, 31 and 121, for example). His own research for *Roman Catholic Beliefs in England* (1991) shows that among dormant Catholics 'there was not even any knowledge that the Roman Catholic Church had changed in recent decades' (p.30) whereas, ten years on, I would have to say there is now a greater awareness of change among lapsed Catholics.

However, in reviewing this literature, and from personal observations from visiting most denominations over the last 40 years, the following is a summary of the major changes, although individual views from those interviewed will follow.

The Church of England had only one official set of services for nearly 300 years: the 1662 *Book of Common Prayer.* There was an abortive attempt to change this in 1928, but Parliament did not endorse the amendments, and the unofficial Prayer Book was little used. Its changes were limited, in any event. But at the beginning of the 1980s, the Church authorized the *Alternative Services Book* (ASB) with a very revised liturgy, and even a rewritten Lord's Prayer. This came after a form of Family Service, produced by the Church Pastoral Aid Society in the 1960s, had opened the door to change. From both of these have followed various further variants and usages. More revisions are in production. As a result of all these, older members of congregations have, in part (my research shows), gravitated to churches with older styles of services, or to more traditional services in their own churches.

It is, as has already been suggested, in the Roman Catholic Church that even bigger changes have come about, described later in this chapter by some as nothing short of a revolution. Formerly the Mass was in Latin, entirely priest-led, the priest celebrating with his back to the congregation. The Council of the church met in the early 1960s, culminating with what is now called 'Vatican II'. This Council encouraged churches to celebrate the Mass in the vernacular, for the priest to face the people and involve the congregation, making the services more relaxed; for the laity to play a much greater part both in the services and the community as Eucharistic Ministers; for the Bible to be studied, again in the vernacular (the *Jerusalem Bible* being one example), and read similarly in the Church.

The Free Churches have seen varying changes. Some, as indicated above, have remained substantially the same. Others have introduced new orders of service, and new hymn books. Like other churches, a great deal of new music has come in, influenced by the charismatic movement, the Taizé Community in France, the Iona Community in Scotland, Spring Harvest Celebrations, holidays like New Wine, and singer/writers such as Graham Kendrick.

The New Churches are, as their name suggests, very new. They arose from out of the House Church movement in the 1970s, and are still evolving. They have great appeal to the young, with comparatively few older members. Though their changes continue, the earlier comment from one leader shows some teething problems in the movement.

Finally, almost every denomination is experiencing a shrinkage in the numbers of worshippers, as some will comment on in this chapter. The overall effect is that England may not now be considered a 'Christian country', which puts the church into a new sociological position.

In this chapter, I am seeking to show what my interviewees themselves perceive as changes, and especially how these have impacted upon older people. As with the answers to 'What is "Church"?' in the last chapter, I have grouped changes under several major headings. Figure 5.1 will give a guide for what now follows.

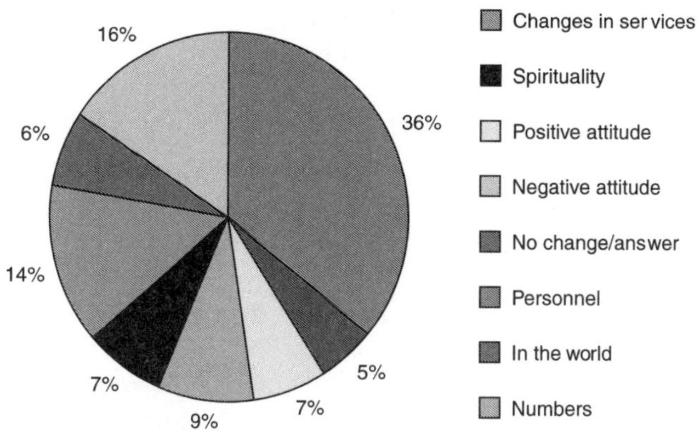

Figure 5.1 Overall changes in church life

Changes in services

Of all those asked about changes in the church, 36 per cent (a very considerable percentage) referred to what happens in the services, with major references to new liturgies, styles of worship and music.

Liturgies

> 'The Mass used to be when the priest took his beretta and turned his back on the people and spoke in Latin. The laity were tolerated, and were physically not part of what went on: the roodscreen in Cathedrals showed this. Then – the church was the clergy. Now – *we* are the church, which is much healthier. There is less attention to status in the church of the clergy. Things have opened up. There is a better understanding of the message of Christ – which is for *all* of us. This is seen in the liturgical services.' (Frank (65))

Frank clearly loves modern-day Roman Catholicism! Maureen, 78 years old, speaks of services being 'open and much better'. Bishop Pargiter told me that 'Vatican II was the key event. The changing of liturgy happened between 1965 and 1970.' For the Anglicans, too, there have been similar changes: 'ASB and all that,' a vicar said. 'We are no longer a church of the *Book of*

Common Prayer. The Church of England has grown in non-prayer book numbers – family services, seeker services.' Although a few have objected (as will be seen later), it is clear that most clergy and people have a feeling of new-found freedom.

Latin to English

Perhaps because this is uniquely a Roman Catholic matter, almost everyone in that denomination mentioned this. 'The change of language into the vernacular is the main change – being able to understand,' said one elderly churchgoer. Most of those who disapproved of this do not now go. 'They should have kept the Latin,' Angela (77) said. 'I was brought up with it, and I liked it. Times change and the church changes.' Another said that the change 'should never have been allowed or accepted'. Evan (78), who does attend, said the change from Latin to English 'created a lot of discontent amongst a lot of the older generation', though he himself was glad that Mass is 'more simple now'. If the church is to regain its older lapsed members, some concessions may be needed, it would seem.

Most were glad of this language change, led by the Archbishop of Birmingham: 'Most people would rather have the Mass in English'. One priest, ordained just post-Vatican II, spoke of the 'great excitement' then, while another said that 'The use of English is fantastic – it is so much easier'.

Worship

All denominations have experienced some changes in worship over the last 40 years, as the elderly have had to adjust to newer styles and practices. The Roman Catholics have introduced a Saturday evening vigil mass (a move many like, said one priest). The less formal style now is valued by some. Phoebe, at 87, spoke warmly of this: 'There is less regimentation: there is loosening up. When I was a child we didn't say a word.' There was a positive approach from 82-year-old Joyce (an Anglican attender):

> 'It is much more informal. It is very much more friendly than it was. The informality is good. I don't like the changes

> because I love the words of the set services – the modern words grate a little. I miss the choir. But I realize the need for more modern language. But it is more relaxed now and that is good.'

Harold (83), goes to a village Anglican church. He is even more enthusiastic:

> 'There is a much freer attitude towards the church. We do things now we never used to do: you can applaud, have a light-hearted attitude and there is a group with instruments – I think that is all right. As a child and a teenager I *had* to do it because my parents made me. I regarded clergy as awesome figures: there was not a lot of smiling and welcoming. If you didn't attend church you were thought of as wicked. We have got away from that – children are more amenable to our approach.'

Some spoke of better worship, and with approval of more modern styles. One even said sermons were better! Others were not so happy. 'It's all too modern,' said one, 'But it is the old ones who go.' 'I don't like modern services at all' (Ruby, 81). 'I didn't really like the "Peace" [when the congregation shares peace in a physical gesture, usually a handshake but sometimes a hug] and found it very embarrassing. By all means 'Peace be with you' and everything – but it never strikes me as necessary.'

Music

As Shakespeare said of dreaming, 'Aye, there's the rub' (Shakespeare, 1599). New music, and the abandonment of older hymns and tunes, was a major source of comment and occasional controversy. Despite its frequent use in the media, only two spoke of 'happy clappy', one in terms of 'Happy clappy *dancing*'. Ruby (again) doesn't like 'happy clappy services – you can do that in school halls'.

There is a big division here, which is clearly a generational problem. Some older people really struggle with the newer songs, but none seem completely unaccepting; what they want is a balance. Here are four comments:

> Phyllis (81, ex-Anglican): 'Modern churching is to bring as many as they can with little orchestras and jazzing it up: it should be a quieter time, not too flippant.'

> Dorothy (69, Anglican attender): 'We have a lot of modern hymns – some are good and some are diabolical because they are too repetitive. I like the good old Ancient and Modern hymns.'

> Pearl (68, ex-Anglican): 'I am always nervous when I catch sight on TV of Songs of Praise when they have modern bands. I literally take a step back. I want 'Praise my soul the King of Heaven' and such hymns. We have to move on – what appeals to young people today is not necessarily for the older. I puzzle why.'

> Terry (65, New Church attender): 'There is more emphasis on modern choruses, we don't sing many old hymns. I'm not happy with some of the music, but I go along with it. It's not my cup of tea. I don't like the Americanisms as they sing: there is no need to call God Gaaaard!'

It is significant that three of these four are mostly 'young-old', and the church will have to accommodate them for some decades – or lose them. It is also noteworthy that Terry goes to a New Church: what will this new denomination do for older people?

Youth

To exacerbate the dilemma, here is what a young married couple, who attend a Methodist church, had to say:

> 'We are unhappy with our moving into the twenty-first century with the huge proportion of the elderly in our church. We have no young people. It is good to cater for all, but we are not catering for young people at all, or for young families. It is chicken and egg – are we only catering for the older people and therefore not catering for the young because we don't have them, or don't we have them because we're catering for the older people?'

Gary, 80 years old, went along with this:

> 'The younger element don't indulge in the church now. I wonder if it's the way they conduct the services now – as if it were years back, and not looking forward: we need more jazzy singers, as long as there is a "church" feel. It needs to be like "Sister Act".'

But Hilda (83) told me, 'It's a young church. I feel I don't belong because I'm fading out' (she goes to a New Church). As the Bishop of Coventry says: 'There is a greater awareness of the generational differences which are wider than ever and therefore the young people's culture is not just a bit different but radically different: therefore styles of worship are harder to unify.'

'Things ain't what they used to be' (Persons, 1941)

'Good', say the young. 'Alas, yes' say some older people (though not all). Marjorie (87) put it like this:

> 'I went as a little one to Sunday School. I don't like people standing up and saying "Praise the Lord". There have been changes in hymns and the Lord's Prayer. It's not like it used to be. I don't like the jumping and dancing during hymns. I'm pleased to see children go.'

'The main change,' said Dorothy (69), 'is the loss in the richness of the services and the words – ours is a lovely language. I don't like modern hymns: the music is pathetic for the words. You say a few words and then there's a big gap. I don't like the new Bible or the Lord's Prayer being changed – they are so beautiful. I resent these changes very much. I like the Psalms in the 1662 Prayer Book and the wording.' As this elderly lady goes to the Cathedral, which is more formal than many churches, how do older ones cope in other situations? 'There has been a change from it being a "proper service" to a service which is not so proper,' was how 82-year-old Olive summed it all up.

Services have changed in so many ways. No wonder so many chose to speak about this as the change they saw within the church in the last few decades. For some it is a new liturgy, for the Roman Catholics a new language. There have been changes in music and styles of worship, even changes in those attending.

Behind all these thoughts are the spoken or unspoken changes in life itself. It could be argued that no century has seen as many changes as the twentieth. Those born in the first half of this last century have seen their whole way of living alter irreversibly: from the corner shop paying 'on the nail' on a Friday to the Supermarket's credit card; from an extended family to fragmented nuclear ones; from front doors opening onto a neighbourhood street to 'behind closed doors'. Many I spoke to looked back with great nostalgia. What remained permanent? The church? This was their final point of stability. Now it has moved on, too. Changes in the church are to be seen as part of the overall happenings in society.

By way of summary, Figure 5.2 gives a bar-chart summary of what has been said so far.

Not only have services changed, but another big alteration has been in those who lead, as we now consider.

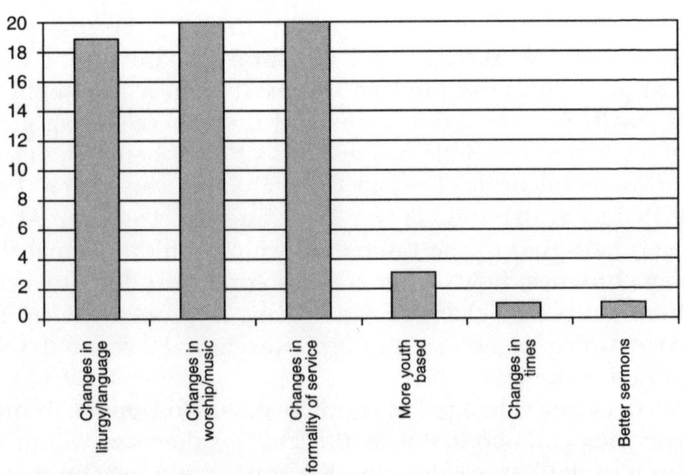

Figure 5.2 Detailed breakdown of 36 per cent in Figure 5.1, commenting upon changes in church services (numbers)

Changes in personnel

The ordained ministry

Inevitably, when conducting an extensive survey, one sets out with some preconceptions as to the answers one might receive. When asking about changes in the church, I anticipated major comments about the ministry of women, especially from Anglicans. Yet of the 200 plus I saw from every denomination, only four mentioned this, with three of these being positive (two of them, lady vicars!). Only one non attender was unhappy. So much for what I expected!

However, there were several who spoke of the changes in the ordained leadership, especially the fall in numbers. 'When I was younger,' said one, 'there were three or four priests living in the Parish House, with two or three daily Masses. There is now one priest and one daily Mass – if at all.' Almost every denomination has seen a similar decline, with priests, clergy and ministers covering several parishes and churches, especially in country areas. Hornsby-Smith (1989, p.1) gives several reasons why 'the Catholic parish has been transformed', including 'major social changes ... dramatic shifts of self-understanding, theological orientations and ideological legitimations'. I would have to add – a huge decline in those entering the priesthood. I shall refer to this again shortly, when dealing with overall decline.

Hornsby-Smith, in his later book (1991, pp.208–9) cites Burns and Stalker (1966) to show that the Roman Catholic Church has moved from the 'mechanistic' to the 'organic' in its organizational change, this being 'suitable for the changing social and religious conditions in the modern world'. He also refers to Kühn (1970), who shows that the 'old authorities are quietly being discarded and new ones legitimated'. My research would suggest that, even more influential than the changes in organization, has been the impact of so many fewer priests to do the work.

More than that, quite a number of those interviewed spoke of the character of their ordained leaders. However much the organization may change, and however many or few may be in ordained ministry, the reaction of the church attender or non churchgoer is to the man or woman at the helm, and how they conduct themselves, even more than how they conduct the services. Sociologists and theological writers may have their explanations for changes in the church, but when I asked 66-year-old Maria what made the difference, she simply said, 'The church changed when a priest let me down'.

What leaders do matters. Matthew (72) does not go to church. He says they are 'a bunch of hypocrites. A vicar will run off with someone else's wife. Priests in the Roman Catholic Church are misbehaving.' 'In my day,' Phyllis (81) told me, 'you looked up to your ministers'. This is how Charles, a 69-year-old former Anglican summed it up:

> 'The church has changed a heck of a lot. Our vicar was a smashing chap. He was very good to us kids – an inspiration. Our current vicar is not great – he is not impressive. The church is personality: it depends on the vicar. I don't like them if they are too staid, and if the church is too stiff.'

In similar vein, Elizabeth (76) said:

> 'I was brought up in church. Everything I did had to do with church. I never went when we came here to Coventry before the war because we were not catered for. Everything I did I did in church. You don't see the vicar now. No-one came to our house to see about the funeral when my mother died. I was very upset because my mother was a real believer.'

These negative views came from several people, but there were those who viewed the clergy more positively. Pam (72) was glad that 'the clergy are not "up there" any more. In my father's day,' she recalled, 'he would never criticize the clergy for anything.' Kay, over 76, attends a Free Church, and has found that 'you can talk to the minister – he is more approachable'. Joyce, in her 60's, goes to a New Church. 'It is more personal,' she said. 'The leader is approachable. You can go to him, talk, laugh, because he is one of us. He is not the head of the church and us just out there. The church is together.'

Even at the top, the old snobbery is going. Bishop Barrington-Ward, recent Bishop of Coventry, and with an Eton and Cambridge background, rejoiced to tell me that 'our Archbishop of Canterbury left school before the sixth form. The Archbishop of York also is not from the old Eton and

Cambridge conventional background. It is more possible to be not upper class and be a leader in the Church.'

Thus, some see positive moves by ordained leaders. What help is perceived for those who feel either disadvantaged or abused by the church?

Use of the laity

Of those asked about changes, 5 per cent mentioned with approval the increased participation by the laity in the running of churches. As clergy numbers have fallen, so the laity have been given their opportunity. One older lady spoke this way:

> 'The Cathedral I go to is more formal than most churches, but is a lot less formal than most Cathedrals. We have less clergy – only three now – and therefore there is more and more lay involvement. The lay people have always been involved, including the Cathedral Council which is like an ordinary church's PCC. To get things done, the laity have to do it. I am pleased the laity are more involved.'

An Anglican lay leader saw the main change in the church as being 'the development of lay leadership and ministry compared with everything being clerically led'. For the Roman Catholics, this has been revolutionary. A country priest described it to me:

> 'We used to have a hierarchical '50s church. People prayed, paid and obeyed. Before 1965 the priest did everything in the church and the parish. People went to church, the Mass was in Latin; the people did not matter particularly – they were an audience who went to watch the Mass by the priest on their behalf.
>
> Now, in England, since 1965, there is active participation in the Mass. Readings are in English. There is lay ministry – Readers, Eucharistic Ministers – people have hit the Sanctuary by storm. It is useful to have the native language because there is now active participation. A lot of people found it very hard. They are happy now – they wouldn't go back, at least, very few would. There is collaborative ministry. All those baptized, every contribution is valid.'

Frank, an elderly Roman Catholic attender, echoed this with approval:

> 'We have come an enormous distance. This is a very open parish [in the city] and it is the people not the priest who are the parish. In 1962 the laity were there to do as we were told. We have come from the priest telling us what to do, but now the *people* decide.'

Free Churches have enjoyed such liberty for many years, but lay people in every denomination seem to be more and more active, a situation welcomed by the vast majority – though the decline in clergy numbers is a big concern, as we shall now see.

Changes in numbers and status

Decline. Some 12 per cent of all those who answered the questionnaire in Appendix 1 spoke of the decline in numbers and clergy as the major change in the church over recent years, most of them older people who spoke with sadness.

Leaders referred to churches closing and clergy disappearing. The Methodists are struggling very badly. A country minister told me, 'The main change in this area has been that thirteen to fourteen churches are now down to seven in thirty years. Of these, one only has one afternoon service per month, and another one evening service per month.' Another Methodist minister in a town spoke of 'a declining denomination. Methodist figures daftly suggest that the church will be extinct by 2006. It is not a powerful force.'

Meanwhile, as Roger (an older Anglican attender) pointed out, there has been 'vast desertion from the Church of England'. John, aged over 75, does not go to church. His words may appear somewhat cynical, but they ring many bells:

> 'I started in a village church in Yorkshire: it was a village community and we went to church on Sunday mornings – I was propelled by my mother to the nearest Church of England. It was a centre for Sunday mornings and it was impressed upon one. Now – unless you are a deeply religious family, or into nearly old or plain lonely – these are the only people who turn up. In our village the Evensong has fourteen in a church holding a hundred, mostly widowed ladies who

> are seeking a prop and company and therefore it does a good job for them. There must be many more who don't get together like that.'

Another Anglican non attender, aged 81, said, 'The church has deteriorated due to generations of people not caring – from the '60s onwards.' People did once go, as Graham (70) did: 'I went to Sunday School, and went to church when I was in the Navy. I went because I wanted to – it meant a lot to me.' In a later chapter we will consider if help can be offered in situations like this.

The Roman Catholics have not fared any better. 'There has been a lot of falling off and not going to church compared with when I was younger' said 84-year-old Michael, an attender; 'Rain or shine you had to go. Now they don't take any notice.' A member of the Roman Catholic hierarchy spoke like this:

> 'There is a lack of priestly vocations, and a decline in the numbers of nuns and sisters. In our diocese there used to be two or three priests in every parish. Now they are all one-horse missions, or amalgamations. We have had about forty priests from the Anglican Church in the Diocese who defected over women priests and that has kept some of our parishes going. There are very few candidates even to the Irish priesthood because of the sexual problems in the Catholic Church there. Very few are entering the priesthood here. In the whole Diocese which goes from the North of Staffordshire down to Henley-on-Thames there were *no* people coming into the ministry in 1998.
>
> There has been a huge departure of people from the church. It used to be a mortal sin not to attend mass. The church still teaches this, but the people don't believe it.'

The Baptists in the countryside tell me that 'the age of the fellowship has got older and we are not getting young people in – they have drifted away'. Another Free Church member in a village says, 'I don't think people want to go now', while Edna (76) bemoans the fact that 'there are not the families in church now'. As Marjorie (88), who goes to a Free Church in the town, remarked, as she agreed about the loss of young people: 'At fifteen to sixteen the church has no attraction: we have to change in some way.'

One wonders if these comments, which are typical of many, are being heeded by the church. As Dr Peter Brierley, a major researcher into church statistics, said to me, 'The church is one generation away from extinction' (Brierley, 1999b). Is there any hope?

Growth. However, there seems to be another side to be seen. Some churches are growing: New Churches and some evangelical Anglican churches, but, as an Anglican vicar told me, 'The separation between churches collapsing and churches growing is one of the big changes.' Another said that 'there is a rising in morale in the Coventry Diocese'.

This is the dichotomy: many fewer attend, but there is a much better spirit among those who do. Roman Catholic Bishop Pargiter said:

> 'Overall, though there are fewer going to church, those who go are much more active. They go on lay theological courses, lay scripture courses, there are lay catechists and the laity participate in parish councils, which is very positive.'

In his inimitable way, Monsignor Tom Gavin agreed:

> 'There are more people helping, more getting their oar in. When I see the numbers and the working together, they tell me about someone who I have not known who wants a visit. People turn up in ruddy 'undreds (sic) to pray for the dead – there's a great family feel.'

One wonders why such enthusiasm does not result in greater numbers attending. This will have to be considered later.

Loss of status. This tricky balance has had its impact nationally. A young New Church member explained it thus:

> 'People have become disillusioned. The church has lost its place in Society as a moral, stable place. People now choose to go mainly because they have become Christians as opposed to "religious" people [i.e. church-going as a "habit" or a "duty" has changed to become a voluntary matter of belief]. There has been a demise in the organized church – Methodist, Anglicans, Baptists.'

'The Church of England is not now part of the local community as it was thirty to forty years ago,' said one city vicar, and added,

'I wish so many hadn't left. I wish secularization hadn't happened.' But it has. As Pearl (68) who does not now attend an Anglican church said, 'The church is no longer part of our structure any more, compared with everything being based around home and church in my early days. There was a togetherness and everything was interdependent.' The Anglican Cathedral Precentor believes that 'we are no longer able to assume even the nominal loyalty of the Nation'.

Betty (78), a Roman Catholic attender, spoke of the 'lack of obedience in the Catholic Church'. Walter (80) agreed: 'The church has lost a lot of its power: the Catholic Church still has power and even they are losing their congregations.'

Ecumenism and Outreach. Is there any attempt to draw closer to each other and to the world to restore the situation? An astute observation was made by a teenage Roman Catholic from a country church in these terms:

> 'We are trying to get closer to the Church of England and the Protestants – to become more united, eventually to be one in the same church. This is the only way for the church to survive because of dwindling numbers.'

Bishop Simon's greatest regret was 'the failure of the Anglican/Methodist conversations'. A Roman Catholic lay leader spoke of a change in her own attitude, 'an acceptance, an openness, prejudices breaking down between churches'. Even if the oneness the teenager spoke of does not come about, surely there are those who hoped for a greater sense of togetherness.

In relation to the great world outside the church, a minority spoke of signs of hope here, as the church seeks to adapt and reach out again. But very few mentioned this. It is more a question than an answer, and best summed up by one Anglican vicar:

> 'In my teens there were a lot of assumptions about the clergy and the church: there was a strong tradition of children having some contact with the church. Now the vast majority of people in the country do not have the first clue about God, the church or prayer – only a vague race memory. They have no idea about Jesus – thoughts are mixed up with new age, spacemen and Buddhism. The church has a very different

job to do now. You can't assume anything. People have heard the word "crucified" and have no idea it has anything to do with the Cross: we are back to the first principles.'

The general picture given by the answers in this section is one of steady decline (with a few exceptions) both in numbers attending church and in the church's standing in society. How has the church reacted spiritually?

Changes in spirituality

How have all these changes affected the very core of the church – its spirituality? Again, here is a curate's egg.

Good changes. 'The good side is the recovery of the Body of Christ and the discovery of the Holy Spirit and the emphasis on the Spirit giving vitality and freedom' (Bishop Simon). But has this reached the grass roots among the elderly? Win (80), an Anglican, said that 'they don't preach in the Spirit: the Holy Spirit is not there and therefore there is no power'. Perhaps here is the heart of the matter, as a Roman Catholic priest told me: 'Only the Holy Spirit can renew.'

The church needs this, as do its individual members. The change then is personal. Barbara (69), an Anglican, when asked about changes, told me:

> 'The dramatic change for me came when I did Alpha four years ago – I never realized what I had missed because I always had a feeling about people who "saw the light" – I thought they were over the top. My sister reckoned it was because we had always been there and that's why we didn't feel anything. I found out that I'd got as much to discover as the outsiders – now I realize how close you can be to God and the Holy Spirit – there is a living faith for me now. The change has not been in the church but in *me*: the church helped me to make this change.'

Whatever 'it' is, Barbara has found 'it'. Does the church need this discovery, too? David, an Anglican in his 60s, felt it does:

> 'It is best where the church is more focused on Jesus, and less on trappings and organizations. Where there is lack of change, especially at the top levels and on the institutional

> side, the church becomes more fossilized and not responding to what is going on, even within itself.'

Some see spirituality improving. Ann said that she did not 'remember meeting Jesus in church as a teenager', but, 'I can do now in the [Anglican] church I go to'. Peter spoke of the Roman Catholic Church in similar terms:

> 'We've traditionally been "the church that likes to say 'No' ". That is still the official stance, but loyal Catholics now accept people and humanity much more than the headlines say. Christ's teaching says "Yes", and that sets standards. We now let Christ come through more.'

Bad changes. Very few spoke of a decline in spirituality. One did not like the 'lack of respect and talking – they forget they are in the House of God'. Another said the church faced the danger of 'worldliness'; a third that 'things were more sacred' when she was a child. Roman Catholics miss the 'mystery' and the 'mystical', and some spoke of the 'lack of reverence'.

Vic, 70, was 'brought up High Church. If you were taking Communion you were never expected to talk on the way back, which they do now.' Even a New Church leader felt 'we are now too liberal in our behaviour and it has swung too far. There is not enough reverence and awe: people see God more as "mate" than "Father".'

Two things did stand out as changes for the worse spiritually. The first was the decline in pastoral care by ministers. One elderly Anglican said this:

> 'The clergy are not pastors any more, and we are sheep who look up and are not fed. There is no visiting of the elderly. The clergy have lost touch with the people – they never visit. I have been in hospital many times, my husband was on a kidney machine for six years and no clergy ever visited. I feel very bitter towards them.'

This was a typical response for a number of older people, who felt uncared-for. Some clergy can appear positively rude. Freda (in her late 70's), recalled her last vicar, who 'made some very big changes including music and styles of worship. When we asked him about it he said, "Well, if you don't like it you know what you can do" '!

There does need to be a reassessment in some church quarters as to how individual people are treated pastorally, especially older people. Many clergy seem to the elderly more like managers than shepherds. In their defence, there are certainly fewer clergy than heretofore. Also, there may be a certain diffidence in visiting those in mixed marriages, especially for Church of England and Roman Catholic clergy.

The second matter is the lack of spirituality in the country. Ernest (68) put it like this: 'People are more affluent and affluence excludes God: they feel they don't need God and sometimes they feel they *are* God.' Bert, at 81, goes with this: 'The modern people only have one thought: they are hell-bent on pleasure, and Sunday is the only day they can get it. They do their gardening too.' (*pace* – so gardening is no pleasure . . .).

Phyllis (81) believes that, in this spiritual desert, 'people are beginning to search for something to hang on to: material things count for nothing. You need inner peace.' Two bishops look for an answer. Bishop Pargiter looks back and says, 'Somewhere along the line we have missed out on the instruction in the faith.' Bishop Colin of Coventry looks forward: 'In the next ten years we need to return to our spiritual roots.' Both want the church to come up with a spiritual answer for the Nation's needs.

This whole question of spirituality is a further difficult area. On the one hand, there were those who regretted a lack of reverence, a sense of too much familiarity with God. God has become too 'folksy', too 'matey'. There is little silence for personal prayer and worship. But others value Jesus being brought closer, a 'friends and brothers' Christology appeals to this group. It is another 'no-win' situation.

Changes in attitudes

A few people mentioned attitude changes, and other problems, but not in any great number. Positive and negative answers were about equal.

Negatives. These were wonderfully varied and inconsistent with each other, as will appear:

'A big identity crisis in the Baptist Church: who are we and where are we going?' (a minister).

'A loss of sense of Mission' (a Methodist minister).

'The Roman Catholic Church 'has tried to keep up with the changes in society, but has lost its way in the process' (an elderly attender).

'People are sitting on their little seats – doing funerals – with no invitation to get people in. The church has not changed with the times' (an elderly Anglican attender).

Referring to unity: 'There has been a lot of deconstruction, but little construction' (a United Reformed Church minister).

'The faith is not taught properly. People don't believe the basics' (an elderly Roman Catholic attender).

'In the previous generation, older people were shown respect' (an elderly Free Church attender).

'Church is too pompous' (a non attending elderly Anglican).

'The church has lost its commercial grip' (a non attending Free Church older man).

'I don't like the pews being taken out' (a non attending Anglican lady).

'I don't like change' (previously quoted Ruby, 80).

One has to reach the conclusion about not being able to please all the people all of the time: most denominations got in there somewhere, and church leaders have to accept that any changes, or none, will cause some unhappiness somewhere to someone.

Positives. A comment by a number was how the church is now more tolerant, and less rigid. The lack of divisions was picked up, and put well by a Roman Catholic town priest:

'There has been a big healing process. What changes people is repentance, and the healing of wounds of divisions. There has grown to be a courtesy before Christ for others.'

To show that some churches, and ministers, in the view of some respondents do get it right, here are two final comments:

> 'Back to my childhood and teens I lived in fear of what we were taught about sin and the dire consequences. Now more manifest is the love of Almighty God compared with negative punishment.'
>
> 'Church is far more friendly. The atmosphere has changed. Church is more welcoming.'

There is going to be an inevitable tension between the needs of generations: to pull in the young by producing a style for those who are not yet in church, which consequently does not appeal to those older ones who are there. Getting this balance right may depend on attitude more than anything.

To summarize

As with the question 'What is "Church"?', there were more than 70 separate views on what changes the church has seen. Almost everyone asked spoke of one change or another. The Figures earlier in this chapter show in pie chart and bar chart form how the answers divided. As I have said, a remarkable 36 per cent spoke specifically of changes within the services themselves, especially those in the Episcopal denominations. Indeed, almost every Roman Catholic mentioned the change of language from the Latin. A considerable number (14 per cent) spoke of changes in personnel: but only 2 per cent in total referred to women in ministry. Twelve per cent spoke of decline in numbers, with only one person speaking of growth. Overall, the diversity of answers was the greatest feature: the percentages are almost all too small in the 70 plus different answers, other than those above. Nor is there a particular bias in one or another denomination (other than the Latin, mentioned above).

It is noteworthy that all the problems and changes find considerable uniformity in comments made across the denominations. No one denomination stands out as being exceptionally 'good'. The question must be, how do the churches feel about these reactions, especially from older people? How does the church feel about the older people themselves? We shall next seek an answer to these questions.

6

What does the Church say?

This chapter seeks to find what the Church thinks of older people, and where they are to be included, or excluded. It concentrates upon the responses of church leaders, clergy and lay church members, details of whom are set out in Appendix 4. All those interviewed were allowed to define 'old' as they pleased (as described in Chapter 2) but, if they questioned an age limit, 65 was specified. Chapter 8 will give older people their opportunity to respond by asking their feelings about the Church. Reference should be made here to Appendix 1, Questionnaire 2: 1 to 4 and Questionnaire 4: 1 plus Appendix 2 (Theological Colleges), though these will be mentioned specifically in the chapter.

Problems in forming an opinion

For anyone to form a considered attitude to anything, they need to be aware of and think through certain facts. The more research I conducted, the less certain it seemed that the church had the necessary statistics to enable a realistic opinion to be formed about older people.

Knowing the size of the problem

All leaders (hierarchy, headquarters, ordained clergy and leaders, plus lay leaders) in each denomination were asked the following two questions as the first special questions for them alone (Appendix 1, Questionnaire 2):

1. What percentage do you estimate are elderly attenders (65+) in your own church/denomination?
2. How will this percentage change in the next twenty years: more/same/less?

An easy pair of questions, one would think: look up the tables of statistics for the area and the specific church, and make a reasonable guess as to how these would change. If only it were so. Virtually no-one in any church or denomination seemed to have any idea of how many older people belonged to either, though most were willing to hazard a guess. In one village church, the vicar told me she had 15 per cent of her congregation who were 'elderly'. Her husband, a lay leader, when replying to the same question gave the percentage as 30. She said this would rise in the next twenty years: he said it would remain the same.

In an area where the percentage of the population (adults and children) not attending church in 1997 was 88 per cent (Brierley and Wraight, 1997, p.1), compared with a national figure of 89 per cent, how many older people did church leaders see within the 12 per cent of churchgoers? In considering the answers which follow, it is salutary to realize that statistics are readily available. *Prospects for the Nineties* (Brierley, 1991) gives breakdowns of denominations, age distribution, church-going in the regions of England, with a comparison between 1979 and 1989. The national percentage of those attending in 1989 (1979 in brackets) who are 65 and over is:

Anglicans	22%	(19%)
Baptists	19%	(18%)
Roman Catholics	16%	(13%)
Methodists	30%	(25%)
Pentecostals	13%	(14%)
United Reformed Church	30%	(26%)

In his later work, Brierley does not give such details (Brierley, 1999a), but it is easy to obtain the 1991 facts and figures. Similarly, the *Social Focus on Older People* (Matheson and Summerfield, 1999, p.40) has a breakdown of religion by age from 1996 figures, showing the percentages of those over 65 who claim allegiance to a denomination: for example, 40 per cent Church of England and 9 per cent Roman Catholic. The Baptist Union surveyed its churches in 1997, giving just over 40,000 out of a total membership of 96,600 as being 50 plus, in replies from 1,352 churches (Jackson, 1998, p.5).

With such help available, what did the denominations have to say about their figures? A spokesperson for the headquarters of the Church of England, in August 1998, informed me that they have no national statistics by age, apart from a breakdown between adults and children, thus having no way of knowing the percentage of its elderly worshippers. In my geographical area of research, I was told that 'Churches are not so good at recording statistics. We have to rely on the National Census' (Holtum, 1999). This gives a head-count for Sunday attendance at church, with no age breakdown. Three Reports on Urban Priority Areas (UPAs) have been made by the Church of England since 1985, with little reference to older people (Archbishop of Canterbury's Commission on UPAs, 1985; Archbishop of Canterbury's Advisory Group on UPAs, 1990; Bishops' Advisory Group on UPAs, 1995). Although the 1985 Report, *Faith in the City,* gives 'Older People living alone' as one of six indicators of a UPA (p.10), it hardly refers to older people, apart from an input from Age Concern. The subsequent Reports fail to mention older people specifically, compared with many references to (*inter alia*) ethnic minorities, single parents and the unemployed. The Reports do show that the Church of England is serious about the needs of society, but there is a need not to lose sight of older people amidst other concerns. The reference to Age Concern shows their acknowledgement of older people (Nissel, 1982), which is not overtly reflected in any of the three Church of England Reports.

Other denominations fare no better. Hornsby-Smith's tables from the Catholic Education Council's Summary of Parish Statistics are divided only into Mass Attendance, child baptisms, receptions, first communions, Confirmations, Marriages and Deaths (Hornsby-Smith, 1989, pp.2–3). The Secretary to the Archbishop of Birmingham told me that the Roman Catholic Province has no statistics relating to its elderly. The only statistics they keep are related to Baptisms: under one year old, one to seven, and over seven years – that is all (Garrard, 1999). The United Reformed Church has no statistics which officially break down ages. They only have details of children and young people, and adults (Marshall, 1999). Similarly, the Methodists have no age breakdown for older people, and could not help with any statistics in this regard (Cardell, 1999, pp.41–3).

Statistics from church leaders

If the headquarters of each denomination were not able to help (apart from the Baptists), would their leaders be able to shed a clearer light?

How does the Church of England in an area see the situation? What is the percentage of older people (for this question they were specified as being over 65) in the Coventry Diocese? 'There are a disproportionately large number who are over 65. I estimate it to be 5 or 10 per cent higher than the sociological ageing problem': the Bishop of Warwick; '40 per cent' (the last Bishop of Coventry); '60 per cent' (the present Bishop); '65 per cent' (the Archdeacon of Coventry). When interviewing individual vicars and leaders, it seemed that their own church's figures affected their view on a guess for the Diocese as a whole. Here is a selection of Anglican answers:

> 'In my church and the Diocese, about 50 per cent.'
>
> 'In my church 45 per cent: the Diocese 60 per cent.'
>
> 'In my church 10 per cent (most of our congregation is under 25): 50 per cent in the Diocese.'
>
> '70 per cent in my church: 40 per cent in the Diocese.'
>
> 'In my church 15 per cent: in the Diocese 33 per cent.'
>
> 'In our church plant, 5 per cent: in the main church 15–20 per cent. In the Diocese 40–50 per cent.'

There is no great consistency there! What about the Roman Catholics? 'I have no idea how many are 65 plus' (the Assistant Bishop); 'I can't say' (the main priest at Birmingham Cathedral); '50 per cent plus' (the Archbishop). What of the priests, their churches and the Diocese? The following are some of their guesses.

> '50 to 60 per cent are over 65 in my church. In the denomination: 60 to 65 per cent. The daily Mass has 80 per cent older people.'
>
> '50 per cent in one church: 20 per cent in the other, because there are many young family houses. In the Diocese – goodness only knows.'

'I have no idea, because I care for them all equally: 30 per cent is possible.'

'70 per cent here.'

'In my church, 80 per cent. In the denomination 60 to 70 per cent. We have not got the young people.'

'My church, 20 per cent. The denomination, 30 per cent.'

Again, these variations make analysis difficult. But in the Free Churches, the percentages of older people are very high. The Methodists' Superintendent puts their figure at 50 per cent over 65'. The United Reformed Church puts it at 75 per cent, with 80 to 85 per cent in the Nuneaton and Bedworth areas. The Baptist Area General Superintendent sees their attendance as being 60 per cent over 65's. And their churches?

A Salvation Army Captain has '80 per cent here, 50 to 60 per cent in the denomination'.

A U.R.C. Minister: '60 per cent here, 70 per cent in the denomination'.

A Baptist: '40 per cent in my church and the denomination' (and in conformity with the national statistics).

Another Baptist: 'Out of 35 people in our church, 66 per cent are elderly. In the denomination, 60 per cent.'

A Baptist lay leader: '90 per cent here. In the denomination, almost the reverse in the towns: 20 per cent plus.'

New Church leaders: '10 to 12 per cent'; 'six out of about 100. It's probably the same generally.' 'We have one person out of 150 members who is over 65, and out of 225 attenders we have here on a Sunday.'

Black Church leaders: '30 per cent here. The denomination, 40 to 50 per cent.' '14 per cent in my church: 40 per cent in the denomination.'

Twenty years on

If much of the above is guesswork, and very inconsistent, then a look into possible future trends has no hope of being anything other than speculation. There is little to be said here. In analysing the many replies from leaders across the board, virtually everyone predicts a rise in the percentage of older people attending church. It is all said sadly, and reflects on the attitude towards older people: no more, please, unless we can't help it. The whole problem of a rise in the percentages of older people is that it leads to a psychological negativism towards any work to reach more of them, or even to concentrate on the needs of those who do attend. For example, here is a comment from a spokesman for the Anglican Cathedral:

> 'The Cathedral is heading for a crisis because the core was there at the Consecration [in the 1960s] and we wonder what will happen to the young people who go off to college and leave. If we cannot attract and hold the young and middle-aged then we are in a real crisis. The Cathedral offers a middle-aged spirituality: it can offer a slower, quieter faith and people can grow slowly. We don't have to justify our existence as other churches do.'

There is no hint here of working to reach the old, though they are appreciated (as a later answer will show). In similar vein, the former Bishop of Coventry said this:

> 'I hope we will gain the initiative for young people. If we don't, we are doomed to shrink terribly. On the other hand, more of the population will be elderly and therefore the ratio in the church will not get less. I think a lot of the elderly, they are such a tonic, and they can attract young people. You can have many a church gathering where the majority are grey-haired: a lot are in their late forties and fifties and over that, and we need to redress this because it is disproportionate. We need an attitude to welcome and want the young.'

The dilemma is obvious: if there are few young, the church must go for them. However, the corollary is dangerously subtle: there will be no sense of urgency to help those who are older, inside or outside the church. The imbalance can work against the majority. The concern is not for the older ones: enough is enough. All energy must strain for the next generations. As a lay leader in the Roman Catholic church put it to me:

> 'I worry about the Catholic Church: people either go from a very early age, or not at all. In my street alone only six out of thirty-two Catholic families go to church. There are no threats any more!'

Ageing in the church is a deep problem across all denominations (apart from the New Churches, who wish they had many more older people, but acknowledge that their styles of worship are hard for those 65 plus). One minister told me, bleakly, 'It is possible there will be no church here in twenty years.'

Reports to help leaders

Two denominations have, in recent years, produced Reports to help their churches. *Respecting the Gift of Years* (Appleton, 1998) is supposed to encourage individual United Reformed Churches to take action in helping older people. But when I told local ministers of the URC about this, and asked if they knew that their national church had written it, a typical response was, 'Did they?'

Similarly, the Church of England produced a major Report, *Ageing*, in 1990 (Report of the Social Policy Committee of the Board for Social Responsibility, 1990), with a workbook *Happy Birthday Anyway* (Board for Social Responsibility, 1990). David Skidmore, Secretary to the Board for Social Responsibility, admits that no substantive work has been done since then, but *Happy Birthday Anyway* 'succeeded in its aim of encouraging a great deal of discussion at local level' (Skidmore, 1998). The excellent Report and Workbook did not need further work: the problem is to get them to grass roots level and read there. The majority of clergy told me, 'I have never heard of the 1990 Report', when I asked them about it. Others responded by saying:

> 'I did read *Ageing* and I have it still. It was encouraging because we need to be reminded again and again of the needs of older people.'

> 'I have seen the Report *Ageing* but I have not read it.'

> 'I have never seen *Ageing*, even though it was produced while I was at theological college.'

'I have not seen *Ageing* or its workbook' (this from a major leader).

'I was on General Synod when *Ageing* was brought to the church' (the Archdeacon). 'It did not result in any Diocesan initiative, but had the indirect effect of putting older people on the agenda.'

'I regret that very little was done with *Ageing*: there was too much on at the time. It was passed to the Board of Social Responsibility Officer but there was just one thing too many. It was never tackled sufficiently.' What a sad response from Coventry's former Bishop.

Thus in two denominations help is at hand, but seems not to be used. It is difficult for ministers in the church to form considered opinions if the writings of their own leaders are not known.

Theological training

If the ordained ministry is to start out on the right foot in its approach to a particular group, some responsibility must lie with their trainers. I spoke with leaders in four theological colleges, and afterwards understood where part of the problem lay regarding older people. There is very limited teaching about them. I will refer to the colleges by their denomination only: as none is in my research area, I felt free to choose ones within striking distance of it. The questions used in this part of my research are in Appendix 2.

The United Reformed Church College I visited spends a considerable time studying Pastoral Care. There are special sessions on work with children and young people – but nothing relating to older people. When asked if any training is given specifically for work with the over 65's, the answer was a blunt one: 'Absolutely not'. The one concession is that once only an expert gives one two-hour lecture about older people. Students have to pick up ideas for activities with older people when on placement with particular churches: there is no teaching on this, or advice on speaking to older people. The students have to reflect on work with the elderly and the housebound, after their placements. One of the nine reflections is about pastoral care, part of which is about the elderly. All this happens (or does not happen) in a College in which he told me that '80 per cent of the URC is elderly – the church is an elderly institution'.

The Church of England College was similar. Though there is a pastoral course, and two optional courses on children and young people, specific training on working with older people is limited to a two-hour optional session in the final year to look at old age, ageing and disability. A third of the College would attend such a lecture. 'Do you give advice about the housebound and those in residential homes?' Answer: 'There is a little bit in pastoral visiting – one hour – and a passing glance at elderly homes and housebound.' This is in a two- or three-year course. An attempt is made by the College to steer about half the students to the elderly and housebound on placements in churches, but, 'Alas, incumbents want them to do children's work'. Like the URC, 'It depends on the good practice of the parishes they are involved with'. The College will 'touch on the uses of active retired people. Also the role of the elderly in understanding the nature and character of a congregation'. Some work is done on bereavement. The most telling comment was this: 'We do look at the need for sensitivity in services; that is, that there is a balance for young and old. I have a session on "all-age" worship, on being child-friendly, but not on being old-age friendly!'

The Methodists' College told me, 'We could do more'. Their College does an extensive Pastoral Care course, and there are no less than sixteen hours of compulsory lectures on the Child Protection Act. But the course on the elderly is (yet again) voluntary: only half do it. The course on the housebound is also voluntary. 'What practical ideas are taught concerning attracting the elderly to church?' Answer: 'None, so people hear it.' An expert speaks to leavers every two years about the elderly: if it is your year, you hit – or miss. No ideas are suggested for activities for the elderly, though in the homiletics and communications course there is some teaching on preaching to young people and the elderly. There is an intensive two-day course on bereavement.

The Roman Catholic Seminary fared best: perhaps it has something to do with the training lasting six years. Students do work in schools, but also in the hospital, with a lecture from a geriatrician. On their placements with churches, they visit the elderly, and 'work amongst the elderly features in pastoral lectures'. The students do learn how to visit the elderly, especially by taking Holy Communion to the housebound. An encouraging response came when I mentioned speaking to older people: 'We could do more in the preaching area, and I will think this through for the homiletics classes' (this from the Seminary Head). I was left with the feeling that, although they said that more could be done, an effort was being made to help prospective priests learn how to work with older people.

The picture generally is not encouraging. If clergy-to-be are shown in most colleges that learning about older people is optional – voluntary – and that the churches they visit on placements want them to work with the young, what message is being transmitted? Herein lies at least some of the problem as to the approach of clergy to older people.

Buildings

An unspoken problem, but one which often speaks louder than words, is the church building itself. As a practical answer to the question 'What does the Church say?', the welcome – or lack of it – may say everything.

Some churches are extremely difficult to get into for older people – especially those who are handicapped. One older lady said to me that she was embarrassed to take her husband to church in his wheelchair. It was impossible to get up the steps at the front, so she had to push him round to a side door – which was almost always locked. Such a fuss was made at opening it that they felt they were being a nuisance. Once inside, there was nowhere except the aisle for his chair.

Others cannot understand a service not having at least some old, familiar hymns. They struggle to see the overhead projector, especially if they cannot stand. It is rare to have large-print words as an alternative. Similarly, notices are written in small, fine print. To reach the Communion rail means climbing more steps – or being singled out by the clergy processing down the church to one older person who could not make it to the front. If there is no public address system, there are those who fail to speak loudly enough.

Older church buildings in particular cause these problems. Some churches I have visited have made real efforts: ramps, a good P.A. system, a 'loop' system for the audibly impaired, sensible lighting, and a thought-through service. But many more are asking the question: Is our attitude to older people hampered by the plant we have – and what should we do about it? I will seek positive answers in Chapter 10.

The Black Churches

> 'A great problem is what is happening to the elderly who are first generation immigrants from the Commonwealth, especially from the Indian sub-continent and the West Indies. So many of the latter are going back to their homelands. We need to see this as a matter for urgent sociological investigation.' (Edwards, 1999)

This comment made to me by the General Director of the Evangelical Alliance, Joel Edwards, himself of West Indian descent, needs to be heard urgently. How are the churches who attract these immigrants to view them? I have pondered this deeply, and come to the conclusion that Edwards is right – we need urgent sociological investigation. Every piece of research has its own limits, and I fear that this present study cannot do proper justice to such a big subject. I trust others will take up this particular cause enthusiastically, and that Joel Edwards will forgive my ducking the issue. However, the views of some black ministers have been sought and will be included in the following sections and chapters.

Church leaders' feelings about older people

The Hierarchy

The Archbishop of Canterbury was interviewed by *Reader's Digest* prior to taking up his office. He was asked, 'If the Church of England were a person, how would you describe it at present?' His answer, though somewhat droll, is a key as to how leaders in the church view the old:

> I see it as an elderly lady, who mutters away to herself in a corner, ignored most of the time. When you are in trouble, you go to this granny and get a sort of eternal tap on the head and everything is alright again. (Carey, 1991)

The significance is not in the slight sarcasm, but in the implied approval of this 'elderly lady'. Almost everyone in leadership in the church, despite their ignorance of numbers and their poor facilities, appears to like older people. Typical of those many leaders with a very positive attitude is the Bishop of Warwick. Asked, 'How do you feel about the elderly in your church?' he replied:

> 'Wonderful! The elderly make a valuable and important contribution to the church. They need the church to make their journey of faith, and we need their input as we need any age group within the church.'

This unqualified approval was echoed by the URC District Secretary, saying how older people 'take active parts' compared with the younger members who have families or work away and who, as a result, 'are not so actively involved'. Similarly, the Roman Catholic Assistant Bishop commented:

> 'We have a lot who go to Mass everyday. The old and sick are praying all the time: there is a great amount of holiness in the elderly in parishes. Many are working hard and, when they cannot, they pray. Their faith is enormously deep. I am not so sure about the depth of faith in the young people – there is great outside pressure on them.'

Such enthusiasm is, however, quite often qualified, especially when comparing older people with those who are younger. This can be in numbers, or attitude. 'There are not too many older people – it is just there are not enough younger ones' is how the Bishop of Coventry put it. The Precentor of Coventry Cathedral agreed, adding a further difficulty:

> 'I have no problem about people being elderly. We couldn't do without them – we have huge numbers of volunteers and almost all of them are elderly. The problem is that they are getting much older and we are not sure what to do when they are too old.'

The Archdeacon of Coventry went further:

> 'I am sad: not because they are there, but, if so high a percentage are older, then the number under that are fewer, and the Christian faith is for every age. The danger is that so

many old folk do not seem the sort of people who are the "storm troops" of the church and are therefore not necessarily engaging in evangelism. They are not doing nothing, but they are more there for what they can get out of it than what they can put into it – and Christianity has demands. None of us live as we should as Christians, and none of us are as committed as we might be.'

Two final thoughts from those in hierarchical positions are apposite. When asked what he felt about the elderly in the church, the retired former Bishop of Coventry said, 'It depends on their attitude. We want older people to grow and move' to attract the young, and themselves 'to stay young and fresh'. Likewise, the Area Baptist Superintendent spoke of older people having 'potential', which 'should carry the major parts of the church mission'. So although there is universal approval of older people from those who hold senior leadership positions, they have their 'if onlys': if only there were more young; if only the older people were able to do more; if only they were livelier.

Clergy and lay leaders

Ordained and lay leaders who are more at the 'coalface' are, by and large, equally enthusiastic about older people. They were also asked how they felt about older people in their churches. A typical reply came from a country Anglican vicar:

> 'Brilliant. It is really crucial that the elderly are there and enabled to be part of the living community for the benefit of young people who can learn from their wisdom, love and all they have learned over sixty years of being Christians.'

A city vicar expressed similar sentiments when he said:

> 'Marvellous. They are our greatest supporters. The older people are concerned about the church going on after they die. They are more and more interested in the young people. The old people love the young people doing things and therefore we can do simplified things in worship because the young people are involved and the old people love it. It is their grandchildren. Some react, "it was better in the old

> days", but a new lot of old people have now come in. They are so supportive. They pray for us even when they are housebound.'

Such high praise! The Roman Catholics would support this approach. One priest spoke of older people as 'wonderful'. He said his church has 'prayer friends': older church members who take young Confirmees as friends, to encourage, instruct and pray for them, and spoke of how these older folk are valued. Even when the rest of the church is not so good, another priest speaks well of his older ones:

> 'I think they're marvellous. I think of a hovercraft – which is no good resting on the ground – it has to float and be empowered. The church is like that: we have been so static we have lost our spiritual empowerment. There is no life. The elderly retain a grace of renewal, and the younger ones have to discover this.'

A priest in a country parish spoke of older church members as 'committed and supportive'. Another country priest enthused at their 'very important contribution to the parish', and their encouragement of the young. A lay worker said they are 'lovely! Without them nothing would get done.' A Methodist minister out in the country went even further:

> 'They are great! Without the elderly, churches would close. The retired bring time and energy: they are wonderfully loyal. The elderly as a group are the most generous in giving: which is interesting because they have limited income.'

These wholly positive feelings are tinged with a regret among New Church leaders, in their predominantly young churches: if only there were more older ones! One expressed the sentiments of others:

> 'I feel very positive about them. There are too few. Elderly people have so much to contribute by wisdom and experience. Maybe they cannot do so much: there's a value in being there, listening to others, sharing with them and praying. If church is about family and community and we have no elderly then we miss a whole dimension. I would love to see more.'

Some qualified opinions

It is at this grass roots level where certain negative feelings are admitted. A Methodist minister told me that she had 40 per cent older people in her congregation: 'Some are wonderful, some are a pain in the neck – like the other 60 per cent!' Without going as far as saying that, there were certain concerns expressed by church leaders about older people.

Compared with the New Churches, almost everyone else has an imbalance the other way. To put it bluntly, there are proportionately too many at the older end. A Church of England vicar who has 70 per cent of his congregation over 65, explained his dilemma:

> 'They are a dear people, but I can't build a church out of them. There are not too many. They are part of the church at the centre: but you can't build an organization with them.'

A Black Church pastor also struggled with an imbalance:

> 'I love as many of the old people to be there as possible – if there are enough young people as well. If the church is only elderly, it is not growing: you need a good mix. I have been to elderly churches which are like ten green bottles hanging on the wall, and when you go back there are less.'

Coupled with the perceived problem of there being too many older people is the suggestion that they cannot move the church forward. Another Black Church pastor spoke of his feelings in this way:

> 'Good, because they are more faithful traditionally. They are the main givers. But the older folk are very traditional and slow to embrace change. This tends to lead to conflict about what is good and bad. They think in black and white terms (*sic*): they can't see what is culturally transient compared with the fundamental truth. We need to be living epistles today.'

One senses his frustration at being held back by some of his best people, who also hold most of the purse-strings. In another Free Church, where 80 per cent are over 65, the minister said that he was glad the older people came, 'but we need to look to the future'. He admitted that 'the old people have done their best, but now they are older and incapable of doing things. I like old people but we have too many.'

Numbers, lack of drive and an unwillingness to change: these are the main preoccupations of ministers in relation to their older congregations. For some, there is a third element.

> 'I try to be positive. I admit I am "ageist" – I accept that. I find relating to older people very difficult because of the age gap. I struggle to communicate. I struggle with their tradition that "We've always done it this way".'

There speaks a young Free Church minister about a congregation which is 40 per cent over 65. The problem, he says, lies within himself as much as with the older group: he says that he has to learn how to lead, taking bold and maybe unpopular decisions, whilst bringing the older members along with him. He agreed that this is both frustrating and well-nigh impossible for him at his age and with a congregation which has been there much longer than he has. A Church of England vicar, in an old village church, put it even more strongly:

> 'The old – I feel frustrated by them: those who wish for "a golden age" which never was. Others are in favour and keen. When they complain, I don't like it. I don't like it when I can't help them understand. They think the Family Service is "irreverent", "entertainment". I dislike their refusal to see things differently. I am less tolerant with them than with the younger ones. They still want the psalms chanted.'

One is left wondering if such an impasse gives that church a very happy future, at least in the immediate run. The above comment certainly contrasts with the vicar who said that his older people were 'brilliant' (the first comment under the 'Clergy and lay leaders' sub-heading above): he has a very similar setting, yet a totally different approach.

Suffice to say that these qualified comments were in the minority. With an overall positive feel, how does that impact on how the church leadership helps older people?

Specific activities and help

Do leaders who express their enthusiasm for older people in such generally glowing words, turn these words into action? What special activities and provisions have they?

Hierarchical hopes

Those who lead the denominations and branches of the church are very much aware of the needs of older people. The Evangelical Alliance, representing many thousands of churches, has detailed their perception of these needs in their unpublished paper, *Life Beyond Sixty*. In a chapter 'Problems of Older People', these are set out as physical, mental, financial, emotional, psychological, cultural and religious: interestingly, in that order (Lambert, 1997, Chap. 4). To help older people cope with such a multiplicity of difficulties, each denominational head I spoke with said that his or her section of the church had the facilities.

Among the Roman Catholic leaders, more than one mentioned the Society of St Vincent de Paul, an organization whose members visit the sick, needy and elderly. Eucharistic Ministers take the Holy Communion each week to the housebound. This happens, according to a senior figure, 'in every parish'. Another told me that the parish priest would visit 'once a month: priests are very good at visiting the sick and housebound'. The Church of England hierarchy were equally enthusiastic about their clergy. One said that 'most clergy spend time with the "critical" and the elderly – good quality time. This includes taking Communion to the elderly.' A second leader gave more detail of help given:

> Providing a worshipping community in every community in the Diocese, in towns and villages. 'Most people have a place of worship within walking distance – which is very important for those who find it hard to get about.'
>
> 'We provide patterns of worship with which the elderly are familiar and happy.'
>
> He spoke of 'support and pastoral care in each congregation including home visits and home communions.'
>
> 'There is social support in both the rural and urban communities for the elderly.'
>
> 'There are opportunities for the elderly to contribute their gifts and energies, and the chance to carry on learning.'

His enthusiasm contrasts with some of the comments in the previous chapter. We shall see if the older people themselves agree in Chapter 8, and if his clergy agree in the next section of this chapter. But here is the standard being set: is it being attained? One other leader mentioned the help the Mothers' Union gives.

How do the heads of Free Churches feel about their catering for older people? The Methodists speak of Sisterhoods, Ladies' Associations and Men's Fellowships. The URC has Friendship Clubs, lunch clubs, meals for the elderly and Ladies' Fellowships. The Baptists have lunch clubs and friendship hours. Only in this latter denomination was there any hint that all might not be well. 'The organization does nothing special for old people' I was told. In correspondence with the Baptist headquarters nationally, it was encouraging to hear that 'many of our churches offer practical help for older people in various ways'. However, the writer continued, 'I think we are aware that, with much emphasis usually given to youth, this is a neglected area that deserves greater and more thoughtful attention.' He was hopeful of progress (Sparkes, 1998). The Baptist Union agreed at their 1997 Assembly to address the 'needs of the elderly' (Coffey, 1998).

The question arises: is the optimism of those in senior leadership fulfilled on the ground?

Grass roots realities

The Bad News. Of all the churches seen or referred to by interviewees, no more than half catered specifically for the elderly.

The hopes of Roman Catholic leaders are sometimes not fulfilled in the local churches. 'We have nothing really for the older people. The church does not have anything for older people,' said one priest. 'Senior Citizens meet monthly and have outings and parties. In the denomination we rely mainly on what the parishes do rather than the denomination providing anything. The elderly are part of other groups,' was another's reaction. There seemed to be very little on offer specifically for older people. 'Have you anything special for older people?' I asked a third:

> 'No. Nor for any other sector, because I am too busy managing the plant. There is no age-targeting in our ministry. Laymen should do this – but there is no money so the clergy have to do the work.'

'No,' said another: though, 'The ladies' group are mainly older women. The men don't seem to want a group, but they join the ladies as and when they can.' A lay leader also said, 'No: there is nothing at my church, nor at the neighbouring parish.' Another lay leader agreed, and mentioned a learning centre – which was 50 miles away. Not one lay leader said 'Yes'.

The positives of the Church of England hierarchy were also met by some negatives. 'Does your church have special activities and provisions made for the elderly?' 'No' was the one-word reply from the leader of a key church in the Diocese. 'We have no facilities' said a second. 'We do nothing particularly' replied a third. Yet another had only 'No' as the answer. 'We have a youth worker, but no elderly worker. We do nothing really for the older people' was a further reply. They were not the only negatives.

In the Free Churches, 'only the Sunday services, and the ladies' circle on Thursdays (only about seven go to that)' said one, as if the Sunday services were a special provision for older people. A Methodist minister said that, 'apart from the women's fellowship (men do come!), nothing. There is nothing in the denomination. There is a network of women's work to which the older go, but it is not specifically older.' 'There is nothing specifically for older people' said a Baptist lay leader about his church. In a similar way, one church leader simply answered, 'No'.

The Good News. The above does seems very negative. A considerable number of churches do not seem to fulfil the hopes of their senior leaders, and very little is done specifically for older people. However, a minority of churches have very different approaches of a very positive nature.

One Roman Catholic church is pleased with its easy access for wheelchairs, 'which is why we have our healing services there'. A second has a Tuesday Society for the over 55's, with concerts, talks, whist, trips to shows in other cities, and holidays abroad. Their lay people take Communion and the parish news sheet to 50 or more housebound members each week. A great deal of visiting is done by priests and deacons, and the young people 'quite often go and sing' for the elderly. Lifts are arranged for those unable to get to church under their own steam, and pilgrimages arranged. The Society of St Vincent de Paul visits, and gives practical help, and there is an annual dinner for over 100. All this is in one parish, where the priest spoke of 'a great community spirit because we are God's Holy People'. This proved to be in the minority in the Roman Catholic churches I researched. Only one other spoke of specific meetings for the over 50's, making three in all.

Specific Church of England churches also have good plans and activities for older people. One has a community centre in its hall, including a day centre, open every day for its multi-faith neighbourhood elderly. Another has services in the sheltered housing and the nursing home in the parish. A third runs a lunch club every Monday, Wednesday and Friday: 'The elderly organize it, run it and come – most of those who come are not church people,' the vicar said. He conducts a special Communion for older people each week on a Friday morning. In one town parish, 80 people receive a home Communion each month, while ten old people's homes are also visited. One clergy person said she was thinking things through carefully, having a monthly Songs of Praise with the older hymns, and 'many elderly come'. A country parish has both a Ladies' Fellowship and a Men's Fellowship where the average age at each is 70. Another has 'tea parties'. But another could only manage a once-a-month club, and agreed that this may be too infrequent.

In all these cases I have tried to extract any positives available. The majority of Church of England churches did not cater specifically for older people, other than as general members of congregations.

One reason why older people are provided for (when they are) is simply by reason of a group ageing. 'Groups have evolved to be elderly,' a Methodist minister explained. His church does a great deal:

> 'The Sisterhood has an average of 70. The Ladies Association start in their 60's. The over 60's club has 80 members (all of whom are over 70): this is semi-religious and is a social gathering. All of these meet weekly. The Men's Fellowship is for older men in the evening – their average age is 60. The Retired Men's Morning plays canasta and snooker – the eldest of 96 beats everyone at snooker. Every three months we have a Housebound Service when we bus in people who are housebound for a service and tea.'

On top of this, the Methodists seem to be the leaders in care for the elderly among the churches: 'Methodist Homes' have sheltered accommodation, nursing homes and dementia and domiciliary care. From these homes, and from private homes, another Methodist church brings older people to church in the church minibus, the Minister taking regular Communion to those who are housebound. 'I recognize them as important,' she told me. A number of Methodist churches run lunch clubs and coffee clubs for older people on a weekly basis. A United Reformed Church has a social twice monthly, described by its Minister as 'an arty-crafty, keep-fit, line-dancing event'. His church has a weekly lunch club, a Ladies' Circle and 'a call-in-for-coffee on Tuesday mornings: which came from observing the loneliness of people'. They have tea dances once a month. The Minister's observation on all this activity is germane: 'All bar the lunch club have started in the last eight years because I grew up with older relatives and appreciated them'. Some Baptist churches have lunch clubs. One boasts 'the best thing in the village': a fortnightly meeting for the over 55's.

Some New Churches try to serve their few elderly attenders, one running a very successful weekly meeting for older people. The New Testament Church of God, predominantly Black, is particularly impressive. Its 'Tuesday Club' meets (incongruously) three days a week, funded by the local authority. It is for high-dependency older people (for example, stroke sufferers). The church provides a hot meal, laundry, hair care, baths and showers, and a social element including worship, keep fit and reminiscing. 'The whole day is very holistic,' the Minister said. Such facilities seemed unique.

The view from the pew

'What do you feel about the elderly in the church?' This question was asked of church attenders who were *not* older people, nor leaders. The majority of answers were carefully balanced, admiring those they knew who were older, but concerned about some problems.

Those few who expressed only negatives were unhappy about the inability of older people to move with the times. 'The elderly don't want to change' said Natalie (16). Adèle (17) agreed: 'They want the rules, not to bend the rules, not to change, not to develop for the youth.' 'They are very set in their ways,' was 48-year-old Marie's comment. Rob (17) even included his parents' generation in this problem, while Steve (20) disliked the criticism he received from an older couple who moaned at him every week for the way he worked the sound and lights in the church. But even in this negative group, there was an interesting contrast. A married couple, each aged 25, members of a Methodist church, were asked how they felt about older people. The wife said that they 'really frustrate me. They hark back to the way things were. They talk about the past and can be very annoying.' Her husband, in reply to the same question, said, 'They're great!'

A considerable number had nothing but praise. 'They are very nice people: I like their company and their love' (Laura, 20). 'The journeys in faith they have done are very important for those who listen – they have wisdom from their experience' (Odie, 24). 'The church wouldn't seem like church without them' (Rebecca, 14). 'They are very supportive to us young people. They care about us as a youth group and as individuals' (Anthony, 17). Matthew, 16, spoke of 'one lady who is about 70 to 75 who keeps me going. She has a smile on her face, and she is always thanking and encouraging, even when she has problems of her own.' 'A lot of the old people pray for the young people and are interested in what they are doing and have a lot to do with them', Tracey (19) told me.

These enthusiastic comments were repeated by several others in their youth or middle-age. Modified praise came from the majority. Ruth (44) was typical:

> 'We are all part of God's family: the elderly are very necessary because they have a lot of wisdom. Sometimes they are inflexible and unwilling to go forward as the young people do. They are people with a lot of time which could be harnessed if they were willing and if they were true believers. They have a lot of experience.'

There were quite a few caveats. David (15): 'Some are good and nice, all-round friendly and talk with me. Others tell you off for the smallest thing you do.' 'They are fine, but some don't approve of us younger ones' (Becky, 14). Paul, 23, spoke of his Roman Catholic church's older people: 'I'm quite appreciative of them. They are devoted, and this encourages me. But the negative is there is such a large proportion of elderly.' Simon (19) from a New Church, said that 'some are great, some of the elderly are not so great.' But, 'There are too few going to church.' The numbers game seems a no-win problem!

Several qualified answers were particularly refreshing, because the younger people answering were prepared to accept some blame for poor relationships, or for their own perceived failure. 'I'm envious of them,' said Martin (33), 'because I fear seeing empty churches when they pass over: my generation will fail them.' 'I don't speak to the elderly,' Michael (18) admitted. 'That's a fault on my part and theirs. I chat to some of them and they have interesting things to say and they are interested in me.' John, in his early 50's, feels guilty, as he sits behind the older ones in church, because he realizes they need the help he could give: 'Probably their sink is leaking, the central heating is not working and, being a DIY addict, I could help them – but I don't.' Pam (23) admitted that 'the church as a whole does not make the effort to include them. "They don't matter because the young people are the church of the future": I don't agree, because the older people are wise.'

At least these answers give hope for negotiation and compromise. From almost all those who were younger church-goers there was a sense of valuing the older people, a desire to include them and a willingness to reach out.

Final thoughts

This has been a chapter of paradox. On the one hand, there is enthusiasm for older people; on the other, the realization that the needs of older people 'may easily be overlooked' (Hughes, 1999, pp.6–7).

> If it is fair to say that some Christian churches have rather neglected their older members, and this is a criticism which comes mainly from the churches themselves, then they should consider how they might change their policies and practice to rectify this matter. They should ask themselves whether they do enough to acknowledge the contribution of older people ... to the life of this religious community. They should ask themselves whether they are doing enough for

> those older people who are at risk of losing touch with the religious community which matters to them. Finally they should ask themselves how, in fulfilling their responsibilities for nourishing the spiritual life of their members, by providing the kind of pastoral care which is their special sphere of competence, they might take account of what is distinctive in the position and circumstances of older people. (Howse, 1999, p.103)

These comments from Hughes and Howse would be at one with my research. The picture given is one of contradictions. On the one hand, there is often a majority of older people in churches. On the other, few seem to be doing very much to help them. As with Chapter 4, the tensions between attracting younger, newer congregations and caring for older members have not been resolved. Hierarchical hopes are not being met, and this would appear to be equally true right across the denominations. There are notable exceptions, but these seem to be spasmodic at best. What needs to be done?

These matters will be considered shortly. But, first, a return to basics: as the next chapter will explain.

7

Older People – and God

Any research must, at some stage, go back to the roots from which it derives. Thus, a study of quantum mechanics will almost certainly contain major references to Erwin Schrödinger's wave equation, as Sir Isaac Newton will provide the starting point for a study of the laws of motion, and the whole area of relativity. How could a right-angled triangle be studied without Pythagoras' geometrical theorem? In a religious treatise on the Muslim faith, the Koran and the teachings of its founding father, Mohammed, will be often quoted; so too the Old Testament and the Talmud for the Jewish religion; Marx, Engels and Lenin will be leading figures in any research on communism – and so forth.

In considering the church and older people, it is essential at this juncture to go to the source of the church's thinking, the guidelines, as it were, which shape its views. I refer to the Scriptures, Old and New Testaments, the Bible. This collection of books and writings is the primary basis for the church's actions, and gives the benchmark for the church's behaviour.

As soon as the pages of the Bible are opened, it is apparent that growing old, ageing and dying are the normal pattern of life. By the third chapter of the Genesis, after the first human beings have disobeyed God, he tells them, 'Dust you are, and to dust you will return' (Gen. 3.19); words which find an echo in many a funeral service, 'Earth to earth, ashes to ashes, dust to dust' (The Order for the Burial of the Dead, *Book of Common Prayer*, 1662). W. R. Bowrie, writing on Genesis 3.19, observes, 'From the fear of death [man] cannot escape .... He will be compelled to face the fact which he has always tried to deny – that he is man and not God' (Bowrie, 1952, pp.512–13). This book of Genesis also gives the age beyond which people are almost certain not to live. After listing a number of men and women who lived to vast ages, culminating in Methuselah reaching 969 (Gen. 5.27), God sets the upper limit at 'a hundred and twenty years' (Gen. 6.3). Inevitably there are many, like S. R. Driver, who see Methuselah and others of his ilk as 'not to be understood as . . . real persons', merely giving a general picture of life long ago (Driver, 1904, p.75). Whether that be the case or not, by the time the beautiful poetry of the Psalms was written (c.1000 BC), a realistic life expectancy is, in seventeenth-century language, 'threescore years and ten; and if by reason of strength they be fourscore years, yet is their strength labour and sorrow' (Psalm 90.10 AV). 'The length of our days is seventy years – or eighty, if we have the strength' is the more prosaic NIV translation.

Despite a lengthy argument in favour of 135 as the top age possible today, Teresa Hunt in her book *Growing Older, Living Longer* fails to convince that 120 has been, or is likely to be, passed, and her own arguments when citing the oldest known human beings suggest that the Genesis limit is to be preferred (Hunt, 1988, pp.9–11). The norm of Psalm 90 is also Hunt's discovery, though Genesis and Psalms find no reference in her book, which is surprising. Even though she argues in favour of life getting longer, she, like everyone else, must agree with the writer who tells us that there is a 'time to be born and a time to die' (Eccles. 3.2). Ageing happens universally: as the greatest psalmist of all, King David, put it, 'I was young, and now I am old' (Psalm 37.25). Not only that, but it all seems to happen so quickly, and a person's life is like a mere passing moment when one stands back and views history in its entirety. Perhaps it was never better expressed than in the paraphrase of Psalm 90.4–5, penned by Isaac Watts in his hymn 'O God, our help in ages past':

A thousand ages in Thy sight
Are like an evening gone,
Short as the watch that ends the night
Before the rising sun.

Time like an ever-rolling stream,
Bears all its sons away;
They fly forgotten, as a dream
Dies at the opening day.

The fact of ageing and death is not in dispute. But what in the Bible has helped the church to formulate its views, and on what should it base its current thinking and attitudes? To that I now turn.

The downside of ageing – and its answers

It is possible to look at ageing in the Bible with pessimism. This is the tenor of the style of 'the Teacher', writing to a younger reader in the book of Ecclesiastes:

> Remember your Creator in the days of your youth, before the days of trouble come and the years approach when you will say 'I find no pleasure in them' – before the sun and the light and the moon and the stars grow dark, and the clouds return after the rain; when the keepers of the house tremble, and the strong men stoop, when the grinders cease because they are few, and those looking through the windows grow dim; when the doors to the street are closed and the sound of grinding fades; when men rise up at the sound of birds, but all their songs grow faint; when men are afraid of heights and of dangers in the streets; when the almond tree blossoms and the grasshopper drags himself along and desire no longer is stirred. Then man goes to his eternal home and mourners go about the streets. Remember him – before the silver cord is severed, or the golden bowl is broken; before the pitcher is shattered at the spring, or the wheel broken at the well, and the dust returns to the ground it came from, and the spirit returns to God who gave it. 'Meaningless! Meaningless!' says the Teacher. 'Everything is meaningless!' (Eccles. 12.1–8)

Such total negativity, with its clear references to failing sight, lack of teeth, deafness and general debility, leads to one expositor putting it thus:

> Old age is depicted as a time of fading light and is compared with winter, when storm clouds darken the horizon. Even after the rain has ceased, clouds again gather and obscure the luminaries in the skies. Luster (sic) and joy, warmth and sunshine, have gone. (Atkins, 1952, p.84)

The passage later finds an echo in the words of Jaques' famous lines in Shakespeare's *As you like it* (Shakespeare, 1598). Although every one of the 'seven ages' of a person's life has a negative and often barbed comment, the worst description of life is saved for old age, where

> Last scene of all,
> That ends this strange eventful history,
> Is second childishness and mere oblivion;
> Sans teeth, sans eyes, sans taste, sans every thing.

Happily, this sense of hopelessness is exceptional in the Scriptures. Although there are other references to the pains and problems of becoming older, these are invariably counter-balanced with an antidote. In Psalm 103, David speaks of approaching death, saying that God 'knows how we are formed, he remembers that we are dust' (v. 14). He goes on in the following verse, 'Man lasts no longer than grass, no longer than a wild flower he lives, one gust of wind, and he is gone, never to be seen there again' (JB). Matthew Henry, in his classic Commentary, says of this verse,

> How short is man's life, and uncertain! The flower of the garden is commonly more choice, and will last longer, for being sheltered by the garden-wall, and the gardener's care; but the flower of the field, to which life is here compared, is not only withering in itself, but exposed to the cold blasts, and liable to be cropt (sic) and trod on by the beasts of the field. Such is man. (Henry, 1960, p.430)

If that were the end of Psalm 103, the parallel with 'the Teacher' of Ecclesiastes would be obvious. However, David continues (in verses 17 and 18), 'But from everlasting to everlasting the Lord's love is with those who fear him, and his righteousness with their children's children – with those who keep his covenant and remember to obey his precepts.' As Henry continues, 'Such is man. God considers this, and pities him . . . God's mercy is better than life, for it will outlive it.'

There is hope. Death is not the end, and despair is not in his thinking. David's most famous writing emphasizes this, as he deals with the problem of facing death, either his own or through a bereavement. Addressing God, he says, 'Even though I walk through the valley of the shadow of death, I will fear no evil, for you are with me' (Psalm 23.4). The Old Testament is at pains to emphasize this help God gives, whatever the changing circumstances brought about by ageing, with its hurts and difficulties. As the elderly find weariness increases, they are encouraged by the Scriptures to turn to a changeless God.

Isaiah points out that even younger people sometimes struggle, but God has the solution:

> Do you not know? Have you not heard? The Lord is the everlasting God, the Creator of the ends of the earth. He will not grow tired or weary, and his understanding no-one can fathom. He gives strength to the weary and increases the power of the weak. Even youths grow tired and weary, and young men stumble and fall; but those who hope in the Lord will renew their strength. They will soar on wings like eagles; they will run and not grow weary, they will walk and not be faint. (Isaiah 40.28–31)

For older people, this constancy of God is to be the answer to their ageing. As Lowther Clarke underlines, 'This omnipotent God cares for every member of his people' (Lowther Clarke, 1952, p.538). The very last book of the Old Testament has God saying, 'I the Lord do not change' (Malachi 3.6). No wonder older people are glad of the hymn 'Abide with me', and the lines

> Change and decay in all around I see,
> O Thou who changest not
> Abide with me.
> (Lyte)

The New Testament picks up this theme of realism and hope. It does not hide the fact that growing older has its problems and burdens, but seeks to show that even the downside of ageing is, at worst, survivable, and at best, can be filled with real hope. An ageing Paul, weary from his travelling and the opposition he has encountered, writes of the difficulties in his own life, but follows each one with an answer:

> But we have this treasure in jars of clay to show that this all-surpassing power is from God and not from us. We are hard pressed on every side, but not crushed; perplexed, but not in despair; persecuted, but not abandoned; struck down, but not destroyed. We always carry around in our body the death of Jesus, so that the life of Jesus may also be revealed in our body. Therefore we do not lose heart. Though outwardly we are wasting away; yet inwardly we are being renewed day by day. For our light and momentary troubles are achieving for us an eternal glory that far outweighs them all. (2 Cor. 4.7–10, 16–17)

His optimism outweighs the potential pessimism which could have been expressed through his several hardships. 'It is in comparison with glory that the affliction appears light' (Barrett, 1973, p.147). Jesus himself also recognizes the way life tends to weigh people down, but provides in himself the relational answer, beautifully worded in the almost poetic language of the Authorized Version:

> Come unto me, all ye that labour and are heavy laden, and I will give you rest. Take my yoke upon you, and learn of me; for I am meek and lowly in heart: and ye shall find rest unto your souls. For my yoke is easy, and my burden is light (Matt. 11.28–30, AV).

The NIV 'weary and burdened' for 'labour and are heavy laden' gives a slightly different wording, but adds little. The concept is there: Jesus Christ will share the load with those who, through frailty or age, are struggling with life. There is an answer, according to the Scriptures, to the problems of getting older. His invitation is full of compassion: as Bishop Ryle comments on these verses, 'It is the only place in Scripture where the "heart" of Christ is actually named. It is a saying never to be forgotten' (Ryle, 1856, p.119).

The upside of ageing

As I have indicated, there is realism in the Bible about getting older. Far from being negative, however, this realism is almost invariably coupled with optimism, and encourages a positive attitude for both those who are older and those who have dealings with them.

Indeed, God seems to reserve some of his most positive help for those who are ageing. The Old Testament has several encouragements to promote this premise. God speaks through Isaiah: 'Even to your old age and grey hairs I am he, I am he who will sustain you. I have made you and I will carry you; I will sustain you and I will rescue you' (Isaiah 46.4). God is not treating older people as forgotten: even when they feel helpless and hopeless he will be there with his presence and his strength in their weakness and need. More than that, the Psalms encourage older people to believe in themselves as increasingly valuable as they age:

> The righteous will flourish like a palm tree, they will grow like a cedar of Lebanon; planted in the house of the Lord, they will flourish in the courts of our God. They will still bear fruit in old age, they will stay fresh and green, proclaiming, 'The Lord is upright; he is my Rock, and there is no wickedness in him.' (Psalm 92.12–15)

The indication is that life is no downward trend with God. Despite ageing bodies, the inner person is to become increasingly beautiful and useful, with 'fruit in old age' (Psalm 92.14). The great nineteenth-century Baptist preacher, C. H. Spurgeon, says of these verses:

> On the summit of the mountain, unsheltered from the blast, the cedar waves its mighty branches in perpetual verdure. So the truly godly man under all adversities retains the joy of his soul, and continues to make progress in the divine life. (Spurgeon, 1976, p.178)

Was this the inspiration for Robert Browning's lines in his poem 'Rabbi ben Ezra'?

> Grow old along with me!
> The best is yet to be,
> The last of life, for which the first was made:
> Our times are in His hand
> Who saith, 'A whole I planned,
> Youth shows but half; trust God: see all nor be afraid!'
> (Browning, *Rabbi ben Ezra*, v. 1)

Even when it comes to death itself (or, perhaps, especially when it comes to that moment), God is wanting to be involved – as the earlier reference to Psalm 23 shows. God's promise to the patriarch Abraham is to be appropriated by all: 'You will go to your fathers in peace and be buried at a good old age' (Gen. 15.15). 'I will ransom them from the power of the grave,' says God of his people, 'I will redeem them from death. Where, O death, are your plagues? Where, O grave, is your destruction?' (Hos. 13.14). Thus the Scriptures encourage the elderly to pray with the psalmist, 'Now that I am old and grey, God, do not desert me' (Psalm 71.18 JB). It is to be noted that this help from God is for all who age, not just a chosen few. As if to underline this, the book of Joel speaks of the way life can go wrong, like a land eaten away by locusts (Joel 1.4). Yet for those who will 'return to the Lord your God' (Joel 2.13), the promise is, 'I will restore to you the years that the locust hath eaten' (Joel 2.25 AV). As A. O. Collins puts it, 'On the basis of their repentance, God answered that he would show pity and remove their plague' (Collins, 1994). 'And afterwards, I will pour out my Spirit on all people. Your sons and daughters will prophesy, your old men will dream dreams, your young men will see visions' (Joel 2.28). Those who get old and look back on their lives with regret are thus invited to let God restore what seem to have been wasted lives. 'I am the Lord, who heals you,' God asserts (Exod. 15.26). John Taylor comments on Joel, 'The gift of the Spirit will be poured out upon all classes in Israel, irrespective of age, sex and status, and will no longer be the privilege of a chosen few' (Taylor, 1970, p.24).

Such a remarkably positive approach to old age is not reserved for the Old Testament, but is both encouraged and enhanced by the New Testament writers. The very first message of the emerging church, on the day of Pentecost, includes a reference by Peter to the Joel passage regarding old men dreaming dreams (Acts 2.17). As David Gooding remarks on Peter's sermon, echoing Taylor on Joel (above), 'The Holy Spirit was offered to all indiscriminately: men and women, young and old, without distinction' (Gooding, 1990, p.55). One of the early and most significant one-to-one meetings Jesus has is with an elderly leader of the Jews, Nicodemus. This man, a member of the ruling council, is challenged by Jesus as to his need to be 'born again' (an expression much maligned because of misuse in certain circles, but which did originate from Jesus himself), to which Nicodemus rejoins, 'How can a man be born when he is old?' (John 3.3–4). In a deep and complicated conversation, Jesus goes on to explain the need for a spiritual new beginning, and how he will die on the cross to enable this to be possible. However, the value of this whole incident for the current argument is that Jesus not only has time for Nicodemus, but is most interested in him, giving him new hope in his old age.

This approach to an older person is developed in the practical as well as the spiritual outworkings of the early church. As the work of the church grows, so it needs leaders, whose title is most significant: they are to be called 'elders'. At a very early stage such people are appointed and so named – as in the first Syrian churches (Acts 14.23), in the same way as the Jewish faith had 'elders' (Acts 23.14). As Howard Marshall explains, 'This appointing "elders" as leaders in Acts 14 sets the pattern for all the churches outside Jerusalem, to be repeated in several New Testament passages (a similar reference in Acts 20.17 refers to the Ephesian church)' (Marshall, 1980, p.241). Part of Paul's instructions to church leaders such as Timothy and Titus was to ensure that their churches were well led by 'elders' (1 Tim. 5.17; Titus 1.5). The very title shows that such people were not young, giving value and attaching importance to those who were older. As if to underline this, Peter not only tells the 'elders' to work well and caringly, but immediately says, 'Young men, in the same way be submissive to those who are older' (1 Pet. 5.5). Edward Selwyn, expounding on the Greek for 'elders' in verse one of 1 Peter 5, repeated in this verse, points out that 'The official "elders" of v.1 suggests those who are senior in years (v.5), ... and the thought of them suggests the duty of deference owed to them by the young' (Selwyn, 1947, p.233).

When older people are in need, they are to be looked after. In a detailed set of practical instructions, Paul tells Timothy how older men, widows and elders are to be cared for and respected. Families first, and then the church, are to look after those who grow older and need assistance, as Paul speaks sternly about those who fail to do so (1 Tim. 5.1–19). In this passage he does not allow those who can help themselves to benefit unfairly from his admonitions, but makes it abundantly clear that love and concern are vital. Paul speaks warmly of older relatives, making a charming reference to Timothy's grandmother, Lois (2 Tim. 1.5). As the apostle who founded a great number of early churches, Paul's teaching is clear: older people have a major role in leadership, must be treated with dignity and respect, and looked after when in need. Rightly, reciprocity is called for, as Paul urges, 'Fathers, do not exasperate your children; instead, bring them up in the training and instruction of the Lord' (Eph 6.4), echoed in Colossians 3.21.

When death itself comes, the New Testament re-emphasizes the eternal hope referred to earlier in the mention of Abraham, renewed through the death and resurrection of Jesus Christ. His words to the grieving Martha open many a funeral service: 'I am the resurrection and the life. He who believes in me will live, even though he dies; and whoever lives and believes in me will never die' (John 11.25–26). Writing on these verses, R. H. Lightfoot remarks, 'For those who believe in him, that is, who see in him the divine Word become flesh on their behalf, death has lost its sting; so far from having the power to destroy, it has become the gate of life' (Lightfoot, 1956, p.221). Jesus promised his first disciples, 'In my Father's house are many rooms ... I am going there to prepare a place for you .... I am the way .... No-one comes to the Father except through me' (John 14.2, 6). Even as people come to die, they can feel there is an eternal hope, echoing the words of Paul: 'For me to live is Christ – his life in me; and to die is gain – the gain of the glory of eternity' (Phil. 1.21 Amplified).

Whatever the age or condition of older people, the Bible treats them with respect, and gives them hope right up to death and beyond. Nor is this a mere theory, for the Scriptures are full of examples of those who epitomize this lifestyle.

The 'Golden Oldies'

From its first book to its last, the Bible details older heroes and heroines (with an occasional failure, too). Its personalities are not only the young, filled with expected zeal and energy: older people have a key role to play.

In the Old Testament

No one exemplifies this better that the patriarchs of the Jewish race, Sarah and Abraham. Prominent among the great people of faith in the New Testament's Hebrews 11, the narrative of their life only begins when Abraham is 75 and his wife 66 – hardly Spring chickens! Far from being at an age for settling down, this couple set out, at God's bidding, for a new land and a fresh beginning (Gen. 12.4–5). After various adventures, and a further 25 years, God meets with Abraham to announce that Sarah (aged 90) would have a child, through whom a great nation would arise. Not surprisingly, both of them laugh at such news (Gen. 17.17, 18.12). Perhaps it is incredulity, though some put a kinder interpretation: as one writer says of Sarah, 'Her laughter is caused by joy' (Lowther Clarke, 1952, p.348). But to these two with bodies 'as good as dead' (Hebrews 11.12) is born Isaac (from the Hebrew, 'one laughs'). Their faith in old age is held up as an example down the generations: 'Look to Abraham, your father, and to Sarah, who gave you birth,' God exhorts the people of Israel centuries later (Isa. 51.2). For a man whose biography only begins at 75, Abraham holds a unique place in religious beliefs. Not only is he a great example of faith for Christians (Rom. 4.13), but, as Wiseman comments, 'As a great prophet and recipient of the divine covenant Abraham plays a unique role in both Jewish and Muslim traditions' (Wiseman, 1962, p.7). All three religions would give to great significance of the expression 'Abraham, our father in the faith.'

This high regard for the old is taken up in the life-study of Moses, whose story dominates books two to five of the Old Testament. His life has a parallel with Abraham and Sarah, in that its major significance is in its last 40 years, as he leads the Israelites out (the 'Exodus') of Egypt to their 'Promised Land'. In his early days he is depicted as a killer (Exod. 2.12), a fleer from justice (Exod. 2.15) and a wandering shepherd in a foreign land (Exod. 2.21–3.1). In his late seventies, God calls him to lead the rescue of the people of Israel out of slavery, as he gives him instructions in the famous 'burning bush' encounter (Exod. 3.2—4.17). As an elder statesman, he, with his even older brother Aaron, challenges the all-powerful Pharaoh of Egypt, and for 40 years leads a disobedient and rebellious people to the very edge of their homeland. Perhaps his greatest moment is when he is given the ten commandments by God (Exod. 20). He is 120 years old when he dies (Deut. 31.1). In both Jewish and Christian traditions Moses is regarded as a remarkable man of faith, wisdom and leadership, not to mention courage. It was not in his youth but in his later years that he exhibited all these qualities.

One of the reasons for Moses' success was the backing he got from others who were themselves elderly. Mention has been made of his older brother Aaron, in his 80's when he became the first high priest for the Israelites. Even older was Moses' father-in-law, Jethro. He is pictured as a man whose wise advice and encouragement proved a strength to enable Moses to succeed with his most difficult work. Instead of trying to keep

Moses, his wife and family with him he said to Moses, 'Go, and I wish you well' (Exod. 4.18). Later, as Moses sought to lead and care for a disparate and difficult people, Jethro was able to advise him how he could govern more effectively (Exod. 18). It is clear from this account that a very elderly man was both listened to and respected to such an extent that his advice was followed – to the benefit of all. Thus the old are involved in the life of an emerging people.

Even in simple domestic stories in the Old Testament, the old have a place of value. Nowhere is this better seen than in the delightful story of Ruth. The Biblical book of the same name is a love story: how a young widow (Ruth) was able to find happiness with a leading Bethlehemite, Boaz, and became the grandmother of King David. The person who engineered the marriage was a woman who described herself as 'too old', the mother of Ruth's first husband Mahlon – the widow Naomi (Ruth 1.12). She is pictured as a generous, self-sacrificially caring mother-in-law, willing to release her daughters-in-law from any obligations they may have had when her sons died (Ruth 1.8). When Ruth pleaded to stay with her, she took her home, cared for her, and with no small skill led her to long-term happiness. Her self-effacing style is clearly portrayed, but her involvement is held up as an example of how an older woman can be a great influence for good. There is no suggestion that Naomi is either too old, or no longer of any use: the contrary is the case, and the grandson Ruth gave her is said by her neighbours to 'be a comfort to you and the prop of your old age' (Ruth 4.15 JB). The whole picture is of an old lady who both gives and receives love as a key figure in the family.

This valuing of older people in the Old Testament is picked up once again by King David in a delightful cameo portrait of an older man – one Hushai. David was on the move, and his friend Hushai was too old and ill to go with him. Far from being treated as useless, David found a special work for him to do, using his skill as an older statesman to thwart those who opposed the king. G. T. Manley in *The New Bible Dictionary* encouragingly says of Hushai: 'His devotion to his king, and his readiness to undertake a dangerous errand for him, affords a model for the Christian to study and follow' (Manley, 1962, p.548). For the current argument, it could be added that this man gives an Old Testament example of an older man who wants to be involved in the work of God and his people, and who is considered of value and importance despite, as well as because of, his age. His limitation of movement is turned into an asset. Adversity is not seen as a problem.

Nowhere is the problem of adversity being overcome in age better portrayed in any literature anywhere than by the man whose very name is proverbial – Job. As an older man, with grown-up sons and daughters (Job 1.2), he suffered the most terrible calamities of bereavement, ill-health and deprivation with such fortitude that 'the patience of Job' is an expression used by those who have never read his story. On closer reading, he appears occasionally extremely impatient, especially when asking the question, 'Why?' But the significance of both man and book lies in an older person who is brave enough finally to say, 'The Lord gave and the Lord has taken away; may the name of the Lord be praised' (Job 1.21). 'Job's exclamation is the noblest expression to be found anywhere of a man's joyful acceptance of the will of God as his only good. A man may stand before God stripped of everything that life has given him, and still lack nothing' (Andersen, 1974, p.88).

Here is someone who refuses to wave his fist at God when things go badly wrong. Sometimes older people – and the not-so-old – react badly when religion, the church or God appear to get it wrong: Job is the Bible's cautionary figure.

With such examples – a few from the many – of older people in the Old Testament, is it any wonder that the Jews have always respected the elderly and customarily wish them 'a long life'? This respect is often more open than that shown by the Christian church, and should rightly be seen as a challenge and a rebuke. Nor is this left behind when the Scriptures move on from the Old to the New Testament.

In the New Testament

The revolution is here – away with the Old, and the older generation! Is that the story of the New Testament? Emphatically: No. One of the major Gospel writers opens with two admirable old people, in a touching little family story. A priest, Zechariah, and his wife Elizabeth are described as 'both well on in years' (Luke 1.7). To them, 'barren' though

Elizabeth be, is born the forerunner of Jesus Christ, John the Baptist, through a miraculous work of God. One of the great hymns of the Church, the Benedictus (*Book of Common Prayer*, 1662), is taken directly from Zechariah's song at the birth of John (Luke 1.68–79). He speaks of God's 'rising sun' which will 'shine on those living in darkness and in the shadow of death' and 'guide our feet into the path of peace' (Luke 1.78–79). In some ways this beginning of Christianity mirrors the start of Judaism under Abraham and Sarah: older people having an unexpected and 'impossible' son. 'Abraham and Sarah are models for the story' (Montefiore, 1909, p.848). It is an indication of God's stamp of approval on older people.

As if to underline this, the very old are included in the greeting of the Christ-child, as Luke continues his Gospel. When the infant Jesus is taken to the Temple in Jerusalem for the ceremony of circumcision, two people are singled out for special mention. Simeon is described as 'a man in Jerusalem ... who was righteous and devout' (Luke 2.25). He is so old that he tells God, in a song, that he is now ready to die, having seen 'your salvation' in the person of Jesus. His words, like Zechariah's, have been used by the church ever since within worship: this time the Nunc Dimittis of Evening Prayer (*Book of Common Prayer*, 1662 and the Roman Catholic Daily Office for Night Prayer). With him, 'There was also a prophetess, Anna ... she was very old ... a widow until she was eighty-four' (Luke 2.36–37). She may have been even older. Montefiore, following the AV ('A widow even for eighty-four years'), says that the words 'mean that Anna was only once married, that she had lived with her husband seven years, and after his death had remained a widow for eighty-four years. She must have therefore been, if she married say at fifteen, one hundred and six years old' (Montefiore, 1909, p.862). She is the only other person mentioned as present at this key moment in the early life of Jesus, as 'she gave thanks to God and spoke about the child to all who were looking forward to the redemption of Jerusalem' (Luke 2.38). Not only are older people affirmed by these two, but their words and actions are shown to be both significant and important.

John, in his Gospel, also has an early meeting between Jesus and a man clearly described by himself as 'old' – the Nicodemus mentioned earlier. He displays many of the fears and hesitations of older people, and he does not come out of the encounter covered in glory. But his reply to Jesus' assertion that 'No-one can see the kingdom of God unless he is born again', 'How can a man be born when he is old?' (John 3.3–4) leads to a brilliant explanation by Jesus of the need for a spiritual rebirth. His concluding words to Nicodemus include what many see as the Gospel encapsulated in one sentence: 'For God so loved the world that he gave his only begotten Son, that whoever believes in him shall not perish but have eternal life' (John 3.16). Christianity has a diffident old man to thank for his courage in confronting Jesus and extracting from him such a spiritual insight. Nicodemus surfaces once more three years later, again in remarkable circumstances. After the death of Jesus on the cross, virtually all the friends and allies of Jesus have gone into hiding, for fear of the authorities. But Nicodemus joins forces with another older man – Joseph of Arimathea – to ask for the body of Jesus from the Roman governor, Pilate, to give it decent burial. Their action shows them succeeding where the younger disciples had patently failed.

This 'doing good' by older people is taken up in the account of the early church when Luke tells the story of Dorcas in the Acts of the Apostles. The only woman in the New Testament called 'a disciple', she is described as 'always doing good and helping the poor' (Acts 9.36). 'She was full of good works and the acts of charity which she did' (Lattimore, 1982, p.26). Her death causes great distress, especially among the other elderly in her town of Joppa, and Simon Peter – leader of the church – is sent for, and he miraculously brings her back to life. Her good works again show how God values the old in the New Testament, as she is commended by all.

The not-so-golden oldies

Happily – or unhappily – the Bible seeks to be an honest account, and thus it includes those who, in their later life, got things wrong. Not all older people are wonderful! Noah's story starts with a description of him as 'a good man, a man of integrity among his neighbours, and he walked with God' (Gen. 6.9 JB). He and his family were chosen to build the ark to rescue creation from the evil of humankind. When the flood had come and gone, God made a covenant with Noah, promising safety to the earth from a similar destruction. Despite this exclusive relationship with God, Noah proceeded, in his later life, to make a fool of himself, as he let drink get the better of him, belittling himself and spoiling his relationship with his family (Gen. 9.20–27). It is a sorry tale at the end of an otherwise exceptional life. However, both D. F. Payne and Derek Kidner caution against overmuch blame, the latter speaking of Noah's 'inexperience' while Payne comments: 'Noah's drunkenness is not openly reproved, and it may have been due to ignorance of the potency of wine; he was the first to attempt viticulture' (Payne, 1970, p.12; Kidner, 1967, p.103).

The book of Genesis contains a further story of a family being torn apart by an older couple losing their integrity. Isaac and Rebekah began so well, trusting God as he brought them together in a young romance, obedient to his leading of their lives (Gen. 24). In their inability to have children, they again trusted God as they prayed, and twin sons were born (Gen. 25.21). But, when the boys became adults, and the parents much older, the family took sides, as 'Isaac loved Esau, but Rebekah loved Jacob' (Gen. 25.28). This unnecessary division led to mutual antagonism and deceit, whereby Rebekah schemed against her husband to secure the firstborn's birthright for Jacob over his older brother Esau. Such treachery meant Jacob had to flee, and the deep division was never healed. This salutary story is a warning to all older parents who have favourites: God had to work despite them, rather than because of them.

It is not as if Rebekah and Isaac were not favoured – they were the next in line from Abraham and Sarah. Even the best can go wrong as they age. The tragedy is so often within the family, as the elderly impact their children: or fail to. Like Isaac, Eli, the High Priest at the beginning of the books of Samuel, fails to relate to his sons, to the detriment of all concerned. One wonders how his relationship with Hophni and Phinehas fell apart initially, because Eli is an old man when the book 1 Samuel opens. He must have been a very special person to have been chosen to lead God's people, but his lack of control over his wicked children, who seriously abused their position as priests, caused the death of all three. Eli was 'very old', and tried to admonish his sons for their immorality and misuse of the sacrificial laws, but 'they did not listen to their father's rebuke' (1 Samuel 2.22–25). Through the young Samuel, God had to admonish Eli because of failure to stop his sons' sin. In the end he died of shock on hearing of their death as they allowed the ark of God to be captured by the enemy. He had led Israel for 40 years, but his end is deeply tragic (1 Sam. 4.18).

Nor is this tragedy in old age limited to the priestly leadership: Israel's very first king went from good to bad to worse, too. King Saul began so well: 'There is no-one like him among all the people' (1 Sam. 10.24), was Samuel's observation as he introduced him to the people he was to govern for over 40 years. Despite a fine beginning, his life and reign went more and more downhill the older he got, as his headstrong personality led him away from obedience to God. Far from mellowing, he had to admit, 'I have sinned' (1 Sam. 15.24) and, in his old age, 'I have acted like a fool' (1 Sam. 26.21). Instead of praying to God, he consulted a medium (1 Sam. 28.7), and ultimately died on his own sword in battle (1 Sam. 31.4). His whole life is echoed in the song of Frank Sinatra : 'I did it my way' (whose own last words were, allegedly, 'I'm losing' as he died in May, 1998). God gave Saul every chance, and he failed to respond.

These cautionary tales from long ago in the Scriptures are a warning that becoming older does not mean becoming better, and old age can be a liability. By contrast, however, the Scriptures also contain stories of those who got it right from start to finish.

Golden from youth to old age

The best stories of all in the Scriptures are of lifelong successes – those who started well, built on their early achievements and went to a glorious old age. Is there a better example of this than Enoch, whose entire life history is contained in four verses, from Genesis 5.21–24?

> When Enoch had lived 65 years, he became the father of Methuselah. And after he became the father of Methuselah, Enoch walked with God 300 years and had other sons and daughters. Altogether, Enoch lived 365 years. Enoch walked with God; then he was no more, because God took him away.

What a great life! As the writer of Hebrews says of him, 'He received testimony (still on record) that he had pleased and been satisfactory to God' (Heb. 11.5 Amplified). Of course, most life-stories take up a lot more space, but none can better this man, one of only two people who did not die (Elijah is the other). Bowrie (1952, p.530) remarks,

> The description of Enoch shines like a single brilliant star above the earthy record of this chapter. The significance of many men may perish with their bodies .... But the man who towers in meaning above all the others is the man who walks with God.

As old age comes, the Bible shows how God wants older people to enjoy his help, presence and friendship more and more, and for this to affect not only the individual but those with whom he or she has influence.

Such is the story of Joshua, which spans five Old Testament books – Exodus to Joshua. As a young man he was a valiant soldier (Exod. 17.10) and a faithful assistant to the Israelite leader, Moses (Exod. 24.13). He stood against those who perpetrated evil (Num. 11.28), and was ultimately chosen to succeed Moses, and lead the Israelites into the so-called Promised Land (Num. 27.18–23). For the present purposes, however, his victories in battle in gaining the land can be passed over, even the famous battle of Jericho, until these words: 'After a long time had passed and the Lord had given Israel rest from all their enemies around them, Joshua, by then old and well advanced in years ...' (Josh. 23.1): what then? Had he stayed the course? By then he was 110 (Josh. 24.29). Had he failed, like Saul would later? What about his family life – was it chaotic, as Eli's would be? This is his 'last will and testament':

> Now fear the Lord and serve him with all faithfulness. Throw away the gods your forefathers worshipped beyond the River and in Egypt, and serve the Lord. But if serving the Lord seems undesirable to you, then choose for yourselves this day whom you will serve, whether the gods your forefathers served beyond the River, or the gods of the Amorites, in whose land you are living. But as for me and my household, we will serve the Lord. (Josh. 24.14–15)

Such was the testimony of an old man, who won through. The only person who could stand with him in all this was his friend and companion Caleb. With Joshua, Caleb had been among the twelve men sent in to spy out the Promised Land in Numbers 13 to see if entry was safe. Only these two spoke in favour, resulting in the majority winning the day and a further 40 years being wasted as the people wandered aimlessly in the wilderness. Because of their courage, both Caleb and Joshua were allowed into the Promised Land. Did Caleb rest on his laurels, basking in his glory? Far from it: in his old age Caleb sought another challenge. At 85, he asked for an area of hill country where a strong enemy still lived, so he could drive them out and live there with his own people. Indeed, as Richard Hess points out, this 'strong enemy' were the very same people who had terrified the majority of the spies originally. Caleb was as brave in his old age as when younger, and he drove them out (Hess, 1996, p.240). 'So Hebron has belonged to Caleb . . . ever since, because he followed the Lord, the God of Israel, wholeheartedly' (Josh. 14.14). These two – Joshua and Caleb – are Scriptural heroes from start to finish, proving that old age can be a great fulfilment of all the good that has gone before.

Other key figures through the Old Testament also bear witness to this attitude. Samuel began to serve God and the people of Israel when only a boy (1 Sam. 3.1–10), followed Eli as High Priest, anointed David king (1 Sam. 16.13), and went on right up to his death as one of the greatest men of God, to be mourned by the entire nation (1 Sam. 28.3). Jeremiah was called by God to be a prophet when he was 'only a child' (Jer. 1.7), and served as such during the reigns of no less than five kings of Judah. Did he give up? He wanted to! He was treated with great contempt by kings and people alike. His testimony was this: 'The word of the Lord has brought me insult and reproach all day long.' He then said, 'But if I say, "I will not mention him or speak any more in his name", his word is in my heart like a fire, a fire shut up in my bones, I am weary of holding it in; indeed, I cannot' (Jer. 20.8–9). These words in his mid-life went on, as his age increased, to be the story of his old age. Even when put down a muddy well, he refused to be daunted, continuing to speak out for God then, and into his latter years.

Daniel, a young man when Jeremiah was old, shows once again how a youth can stand up for God (Dan. 1) and still be faithful in much later life in the face of cruel opposition – even when thrown into a lions' den (Dan. 6). Not for him the easy way out as age advanced, but, rather, an even greater resolve not to capitulate. His apocalyptical writings are a foretaste of those penned by another person who succeeded from start to finish – the apostle John. Called to follow Jesus as a young man – probably still a teenager (Mark 1.19), and headstrong at that – he and his brother were nicknamed 'Sons of Thunder' (Mark 3.17); he went on to maturity as the close friend of Jesus (John 19.26), becoming one of the great leaders of the early church (Acts 4.3). It is in his later life that his greatest contribution is seen, as he wrote a Gospel, three letters (describing himself in the first verse of two of them as 'the elderly elder' (2 and 3 John (Amplified)) and the book of the Revelation – the apocalyptic conclusion to the Scriptures. Though many modern scholars dispute that the 'John' of Revelation 1.4 is John the apostle, the latter is identified throughout history as the writer of Revelation, going as far back as Justin Martyr (AD 140), Irenaeus and Tertullian (as argued in *A New Commentary on Holy Scripture*, Gore *et al.* 1928, pp.680–2). This is no place for a debate on the matter, but his Letters (and Revelation, if he did write it), show an old apostle who has triumphed through to old age as a constant follower of Jesus Christ.

If the dating of the Revelation is to be believed, John was in his 90's when he wrote it. One pictures him, sitting in exile on the island of Patmos, with the doctor Kynops (if legend is correct), an old man with a vision of 'a new heaven and a new earth' (Rev. 21.1). Such is the Bible's final triumphal story of old age.

To summarize

From cover to cover, the Scriptures reveal a God who is extremely positive about the very process of ageing, whilst being realistic about the problems and failures it sometimes brings. The vital thing to see is the key place older people have in God's thinking, and how they are treated with integrity and respect. Throughout the Old and New Testaments the old are socially integrated in a caring and respectful community. Though their failures are not hidden, their successes are lauded, and their contributions appreciated. The implications of all this for today's church are enormous, and will be considered in the following chapters.

8

What older people think of the Church

There can be a world of difference between saying what something is and then explaining how you feel about it. I have sought to show in earlier chapters how various people defined the word 'church'. Now I wish to explore how older people feel about the church: this is particularly apposite, a whole chapter having been devoted to the church's view of older people. In outlining my findings from research, I would refer to Appendix 1, Questionnaire 3, questions 1 to 13. The answers given by older people to those questions provide the basis for this chapter, together with specific research in residential homes for older people, as detailed in Appendix 3.

A very clear distinction became apparent between those who attend church and those who do not: hence the divisions which follow. As Appendix 4 shows in detail, over 50 older church attenders were interviewed (those going to church once a month or more), and 60 non church attenders were seen (either never going to church or only going for rites of passage or an occasional Festival).

Church attenders

The various questions asked in Appendix 1, as detailed above, gave answers which fall into four categories:

- How often do older people attend church?
- How long have they belonged to their current denomination?
- Why do they go?
- What is good and bad about the church, and its recent changes?

Attendance and Loyalty

The first two questions are easily answered: attendance is enthusiastic and loyalty often unswerving.

How often do older people go to church?

Figure 8.1 shows a great devotion on the part of those older people who go to church. Only four per cent go once a month and that (they said) because of needing to rely on transport. The 8 per cent who attend every day are Roman Catholics who attend the daily Mass, with Catholics also accounting for those attending four or more times in a week. Almost all Free Church attenders are once-a-weekers, as are New Church members, while the Anglicans vary considerably, from twice a week to once a month.

The significance of this is that older people can be relied on to be very supportive of their churches. It is rare for them to be absent more than one week in two, with Roman Catholics proving the most reliable. In some ways this is predictable, as attendance at a weekly Mass is an obligation about which many older Roman Catholics are punctilious, whereas other denominations do not have such an obligation. Specific denominational breakdowns are as shown in Figure 8.2: in each case, the message to the church is that older people are very regular attenders.

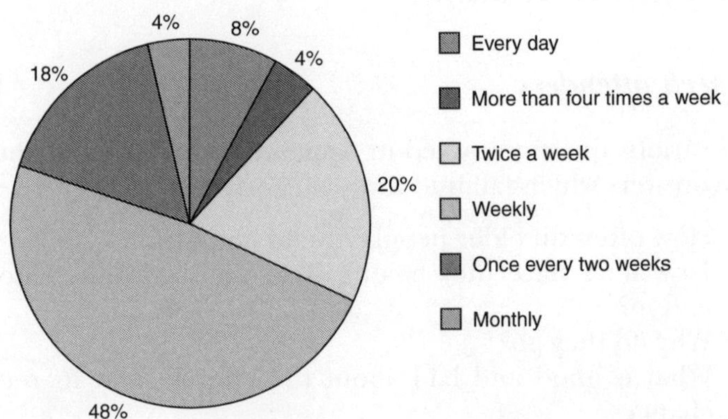

Figure 8.1 Regularity of church attending by older people

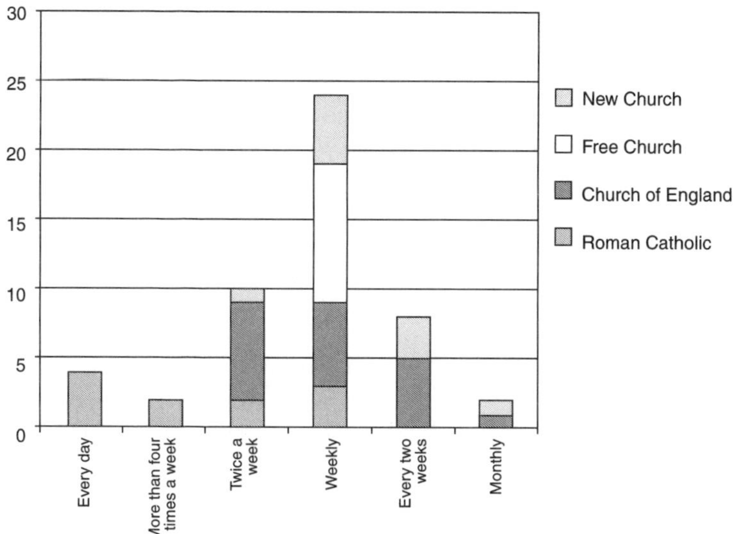

Figure 8.2 Denominational breakdown of church attendance by older people

How loyal are older people?

If the term 'loyalty' is used to refer to continuous affiliation to a given denomination, then these older people are also reasonably loyal. Sixty per cent have always belonged to the same denomination, according to my research results. This is especially so among Roman Catholics and Anglicans, though not so apparent among those who belong to the Free Churches. The latter have gained by people moving from another denomination to theirs and there seems to be considerable movement between the Free Churches themselves. Thus older people spoke of moving from the Church of England, the Quakers and the Methodists to the Baptists, while the United Reformed Church gained from the Church of England and the Methodists, for example. The Roman Catholics showed least movement in terms of both gains and losses, gaining just one Baptist and two Anglicans, while losing one older member to the Church of England. The New Churches, by very definition, are new, and consequently have gained more than others: only two of the six interviewed came from outside the church, the rest moving across from three other denominations.

This picture sounds confusing, because there was no consistency in the changes from one denomination to another: one went here, another there. The point worthy of note is the 60 per cent of older people who have been unswervingly loyal throughout their lifetime. No church can claim it has gained many, and any growth among older people would seem to have to come from the non attenders. If any church wishes to expand its older membership, it will have to proselytize: this will be explored further in Chapter 10.

Of those who changed denominations, their reasons were surprisingly pragmatic rather than doctrinal. This seems to suggest that the crucial divide is between attenders and non attenders as such. Where religion is practised appears secondary to the fact of its practice. Pragmatic ecumenism thus seems considerably to outdistance doctrinal ecumenism, people accommodating to doctrinal change for practical reasons. Apart from Roman Catholics there is little evidence that crossovers coincide with significant points in inter-denominational agreements (such as the formation of the United Reformed Church). This may indicate that attenders have certain basic beliefs which are relatively immune to denominational doctrinal differentiation.

Conversely, this pragmatic ecumenism may have been fostered by the growing collaboration between the Free and New Churches themselves and the more evangelical sections of the Anglican Church, with the erosion of the animosities between the old Establishment and traditional 'dissenters' (for example, the relatively common practice today of Anglican/Free Church shared communion services).

Some moved as a result of marriage. To preserve harmony, one partner would move across to the other's church to enable them to worship together. Others told me that a move to another town (or even, in a large city, a move from one area to another) gave either the excuse, the motivation or the necessity to change. The excuse, if they had not been happy in one form of church, was that a move had enabled them to get out; the motivation, if they wished to worship differently but had never quite made it; the necessity, if a particular denomination did not exist locally; all these happened as a result of moves. The latter was particularly the case for people I spoke with who had moved from (say) a Welsh or Scottish denomination to Central England where there was no provision for them.

One or two spoke of 'conversion': as Evan (78) said how he had 'converted' to Roman Catholicism from being a Baptist, when well into his adult life. However, as I will show shortly, quite a number changed for the simple reason of proximity. As people aged, it became physically impossible to get to their old church or denomination, and the church round the corner had to suffice, sometimes happily, sometimes with regret.

I turn now to a more basic and substantive question, that of the reasons for these older people attending church at all.

Why do people go to church?

The older people I interviewed had four major reasons for attending church on such a regular basis.

The value of church itself

'The church as a *whole* is good – not just the Church of England. I value it more as I get older.' Vic attends a city Anglican church, but expressed his happiness in all churches (though he gave the impression that he attended the one he preferred and would not necessarily transfer to another denomination). For Terry, it was his own New Church he liked. Asked what was good about it, he replied, 'Everything. I couldn't wish for a better church, spiritually and in the activities: they provide for everyone.'

The Roman Catholics, in particular, spoke of the importance of their churches. For Donald, 'It's a nice parish to be in because the people are agreeable.' For Catherine, at another city church, 'This is a lively parish. We support lots of causes and there is a good community spirit.' In a country parish, Betty said she liked 'The authority, the tradition of the church. We have got the truth from the horse's mouth.' 'The clergy and people are nice,' Michael told me, 'I'm glad the Monsignor was a sportsman!'

Older people value the church, its parish and its ministers *per se*. They also appreciate what goes on in the services, and in the worship. Maureen put it like this:

> 'In the Catholic Church we have the Blessed Sacrament and our Lord is there. I can sit in a Catholic Church when no-one is there and think. It feels lovely. I enjoy the peace. I love to go. There is nothing else left. If you have no faith then you've got nothing and all you can be is empty. If you don't believe then you are no better than an animal.'

That 78-year-old's comments were echoed by Liz. 'I feel I've got something. It helps me a lot. It's my life. I enjoy going to the Mass: I think about the way our Lord suffered – his death, the agony he went through – and the Resurrection.' Frank, an Anglican, likes 'The liturgical service compared with a hymn sandwich in the Free Church.' He said that 'Lovely Christian people are there – real stalwarts for the Gospel. I go because I love the Lord and meet with others who love the Lord.' The style of service clearly matters to Frank, as it does to Harold, who worships at a village Anglican church:

> 'I do respect most denominations, but the Church of England has a ritual. If you go to the Baptists or Methodists that's nice, but something is lacking – a depth of sincerity. The ceremony is lacking in the others.'

Doris goes to a Baptist Church because 'It's near. I'm not thrilled, but I go for the service, not to mix and see what others are wearing!' Others in the Free Churches spoke of the importance of worship. John and Ina go to a United Reformed Church because 'We go to the church which gives us worship'. Jean, having been Church of England, now in her older years goes to a United Reformed Church because 'It's the nearest. I go to worship, so it didn't matter changing churches because God is in all churches.' Although some of these comments are doctrinal, pragmatism is again seen to allow an ecumenical approach. There is not enough doctrinal difference to prevent attendance at a particular church which is, for example, nearer.

This positive and participatory approach is shared by some who appreciate the part they can play in the worship. Henry is able to 'Thank God for his goodness', and 'It gives me a lead as to how I should live my life'. Two older women, one a Methodist and one Anglican, love the 'hymn-singing', while Graham felt that 'You can pray to God in the Church of England'!

For many of these, one senses not only a valuing of the services but a real enjoyment of them. This leads to a second reason why older people attend church:

The 'positive' factor

This is best shown by my firstly quoting some replies to the question, 'Why do you go to church?' Older people said such things as:

> 'I love the church. I like the dignity of it all' (Ruby, Church of England).
>
> 'It's light-hearted and easy-going' (Bert, a village Methodist).
>
> 'I always have – it's part of my life. If I don't go to church on a Sunday I don't feel right. You need to get close to God and meet your brothers and sisters in church' (Dorothy, village Church of England).
>
> 'I love the liveliness and the life in it' (Mr A, a New Church member).
>
> 'Everything is good. You get out of it what you put in: it has been my life' (Hilda, also New Church).

As can be seen, different factors emerge: one likes the worship, another the company; one sees it as their very life, another likes the feelings church evokes. I was particularly struck by the reaction of two men who, on the surface, seemed very similar, but who gave quite different answers:

> 'I'm joyful: it's a good start to the day. We start the day with God's blessing' (Tony, who goes to a Roman Catholic Church in the countryside).
>
> 'There is a lot of love. It brings me together with other Christians – I feel their support. I like the fun and companionship. When I don't go to church I miss it immensely' (David, a city Anglican).

I spent a long time talking with each of these men. Probing more deeply into why they had answered as they did (though each was interviewed separately, came from different areas and do not, I am fairly certain, know each other), their differing lives seem to explain their answers. The God-centredness of Tony's answer came from his devotion to his church, and the particular value he placed on the Mass, which seemed pivotal to both his life and his belief. He had retired a few years previously: he and his wife spent a number of hours each day helping in and with the church. Their lives revolved round God and his work.

On the other hand, David had a busy life as a University Professor, working in a very secular world, with little immediate contact with many other 'Christians'. Thus his weekly church attendance meant meeting up with the Christian 'family', and gaining as much strength from them as from God himself. Neither man negated the other's view, but their emphasis was different because of the background from which they came.

Both men, and the others mentioned above, are all summed up in the simple reply of Evan, an older Roman Catholic. 'I always feel better when I have been'. Some seem to echo the prayer of Abbé Michel Quoist:

> It is nearly evening, and the day is almost over. Stay with me, Lord, for night has fallen and, too often, it is dark in my heart. (Quoist, 1973, p.24)

These expressed feelings do appear positive, and seem to make the church an important and positive place for some older people. To this can be added a third valued reason for going to church.

Friendship

I was impressed that this aspect of church-going was also to be found right across the denominations. Friendship is a major factor in social well-being and many churches provide a place of togetherness and care. Gertie, a Roman Catholic, told me, 'All my friends are there'. Katherine, from the Church of England, agreed: 'I enjoy my friends being there: they have helped me over tragedies and I wouldn't have liked to have been without the church behind me, especially when my husband died.' Jessie in a Free Church said, 'I feel part of a family. I look to them for support, and to help others as well.' Joyce and Doug in a New Church said they went to church because of the 'Friendship'. Joyce continued, 'No one has ever said "I have no time for you" in ten years.'

One interview stands out in this area. I visited an ex-Servicemen's Club to talk with men who no longer attended church. While there, a man overheard a conversation and called me over. He told me how he had not gone to church for many years, but that a particular city church had been most kind to him after his wife's death. The friendship and care he had received had drawn him back and now he worshipped regularly. It seemed a combination of a caring minister and a concerned congregation. Unlike others in this book, who speak of clergy who failed to visit, this vicar had called to arrange the funeral sensitively. The church members had not treated him as a one-off funeral attender, but as someone they could befriend and help. When he had gone to church the Sunday after the funeral, he had been given a real welcome. In his loneliness, this kindness had meant a great deal, and now he was glad to be back in his old denomination after many years' absence.

This was an interesting contrast to those who coupled the friendship aspect with the fact that they had always gone. Mary said she went for 'friendship, company, fellowship, comfort'. But she added, 'I was brought up to go'. Several others expressed a similar sentiment. It has been estimated that '96 per cent of the most committed adults had attended some church activity as children' (Finney, 1992, p.12).

On a lighter note, I interviewed two older men from the same Roman Catholic city parish (neither knowing I had seen the other). Frank told me, 'The community is good.' His near neighbour Ernest, asked what was wrong with his church (the one he attends with Frank), said, 'There isn't a sense of community in our parish. People feel they don't need the parish because of their affluence. We can't get help and there is no commitment to building the community of the church.' At this stage I realized how difficult qualitative interviews were in sociological research! In this particular instance, from the entirety of the conversations, it boiled down to personality and attitude: Frank was positive and enthusiastic about life generally and the church in particular; Ernest came across as more morose and a bit of a loner: hence his more negative replies. I will continue this contrast under the next heading.

However, the friendship shown within the church is clearly valued by many. There is a fourth major reason why older people go to church.

Faith in God

To continue the debate between Frank and Ernest (unknown to them), their variance on friendship and community continued into this reason for going to church – the value of being with God. For Frank, 'Enjoyment doesn't come into it. It is the right thing to do like eating, which you do whether you enjoy it or not.' By contrast, Ernest was positive here: 'The greatest benefit, which has been inculcated in me, is my faith, my knowledge and love of God and, to a certain extent, love for my neighbour.' In view of his previous remarks, his added comment was not surprising: 'But there are some people who I don't get on with.'

Despite their seeming differences, both men want the church to help them in their relationship with God, with which a number of older people would agree. Roger feels 'A sort of spiritual need. I am not looking for a community centre: I come here for me personally.' 'I want some connection with God,' Phyllis said. 'I want a relationship with God,' was how Betty put it. Winifred gave this thoughtful reply as to why she went to church:

> 'Because the Holy Spirit is with me, even if the service is dead, within myself I go to worship God, irrespective of who is leading and preaching. I go to get closer to the Lord and because we need each other and friendship.'

As these different comments come from members of three very distinct denominations, the reactions are more to do with the spiritual relationship with God, rather than a style of class or worship. Church attendance for them is not primarily doctrinal or pragmatic, but a deep, inner longing for spiritual satisfaction through a personal knowledge of God.

It is impressive to have so many very strong and positive reasons from older people as to why they attend church. There is keen support from many. It is therefore important that any negative feelings are taken seriously, because they come from a very loyal group of followers. To these negatives I now turn.

Negative views from older churchgoers

At thc outset it must be said that the positives far outweighed the criticisms which follow. As will be seen shortly, those who do not go to church were asked for their good thoughts about church, so it was only right to ask the churchgoers if they felt there were things wrong, both with their own church and with recent changes. The problems arose from only two or three sources.

The Minister

I use this term to describe a priest, vicar, or leader of a church, as several denominations are included here. Some comments were relatively innocuous, as with Doris, in her Methodist church: 'It depends who's preaching', or Roman Catholic Betty, who confided, 'Our priest is not a great preacher'. Others, across the denominations, regret the decline in the number of ministers – or their gender, as Barbara's complaint was, 'Only the disappearing vicar. I'm not in favour of lady vicars.'

There were those who had deeper concerns about their leaders. Frank felt 'Completely let down', especially by the changes the vicar had introduced. *Ageing* spoke of many older people feeling that their needs were disregarded by the clergy in favour of the young (Report of the Social Policy Committee of the Board for Social Responsibility, 1990, p.4). Ruby and Hilda, older members of a New Church, told me, 'Sometimes we are ignored because we are elderly'. Evan regretted a 'Lack of communication with the priest: he cannot manage the church at all, including the finances.' The strongest feeling was shown by Maureen, who said this:

> 'We shouldn't hide things under the carpet, especially sexual abuse. I'd kick them out – I'd show no mercy. The priests know what they're taking on. I would like to see more mature people going into the priesthood – they need to see the world first.'

It is possible that Barbara (above), complaining about 'the disappearing vicar', has put here finger on a reason for this problem: the less the clergy (as there are in almost every denomination), the more the spotlight is on those left. With several curates in a Roman Catholic or Anglican church, for example, one could counterbalance the shortcomings of another. Now one person on their own is unlikely to be able to please everyone.

If some see the leader being wrong, others criticized their fellow congregation members.

The people

There was no great consistency here. Some wanted more young people, or for the youth to do more. Winifred regretted the 'Lack of welcome', while Ina felt there was 'Not enough going on'. Pam disliked the 'Inefficiency', and Vic the 'Power struggles, especially as the vicar is leaving. I regret the fact that the church does not go out enough to welcome others.' Tony objected to 'The noise! There is talking in church and nothing happens until the priest is there – it's like a supermarket.'

To contrast this with those who had 'positive' feelings (above), it would seem that a contra-distinction can be made between those who seek friendship, and those who go 'to be with God'. The former want a greater welcome, the latter less noise. The balance which would suit everyone may prove impossible.

Perhaps this is a part of the changing styles within churches: the third ground for complaint.

The changes

It is hard for older people to deal with too many changes. 'Why should the style of worship be changed?' Dennis asked. Dorothy agreed: 'I am not keen on the updating of the Creeds, the Lord's Prayer and the Bible: they don't have the same ring in the new.' Is it because nobody wants to grow old (Grainger, 1993, p.23)? Richard Baker, the erstwhile newsreader on BBC television, tells how he was accosted by a small boy who asked if he was *the* Richard Baker. 'My Gran says she remembers you. She says you're historical!' (Baker, 1997). As we age, we forget that things must change and ageing becomes a repressed topic, even in our own thinking (Hiltner, 1975, p.97–101). This leads to frustrations and the dichotomy between annoyance and what we perceive as good. Mr A, an older member of a New Church, shows this well: 'I don't like the music when it is too noisy: there is no quiet to pray.' But, he added, 'I love the liveliness and the life in it.'

It was touching to hear Ruby's confession: 'I do not like the modern, "Shine, shine, shine", I am a narrow-minded old lady.' One wonders how the church can help 80-year-olds like her, especially when Graham, an older worshipper, complained that the church was 'Not growing up – still antiquated in its outlook.'

As I indicated, these negative views were in the minority: a considerable number, when asked what was wrong with the church, replied – '*Nothing*'.

For those who found no fault in the church, their answers were short and sweet. Typical of these were:

> 'No problems' (Mary, and Phyllis).
>
> 'Nothing really' (Harold).
>
> 'Not a lot – I don't try and find fault' (Terry).
>
> 'There's nothing wrong – I'm very happy' (Liz).
>
> 'I enjoy the changes' (Barbara).
>
> 'Changes have been done quietly, and we have moved a long way. An example is the more relaxed atmosphere; it is a friendly place, much more than it was' (Pam).
>
> 'I am enormously positive – I feel blessed up' (David).

I underline again that these comments all come from older people across the denominations. Churches may wonder how this goodwill can be harnessed and further helped. This will be explored but, before that, we need to consider the views of those who do not attend church.

Non churchgoers

Inevitably, the questions asked of older people who do not go to church were bound to differ somewhat from those asked of regular churchgoers. To paraphrase the appropriate questions from Appendix 1, the following were to further my research:

- When and why did you stop attending church?
- How often did you go before that?
- Were you always a member of the same denomination?
- What is good about the church, even though you yourself do not go?

These were to lead to what seemed most crucial:

- What is wrong with the church, as you perceive it?
- Why do you not go now?

Stopping and going

I intend, firstly, to deal with the top three questions, to assess the size of any problem which churches may feel they have in restoring any broken relationships with older people.

When and why did church-going stop?

There are times in a research project when a pie chart seems a certainty. For me, this was such an opportunity. But qualitative interviewing throws up its surprises and here was one of them. Despite the comment that 'Some persons drop their church membership in later life' (Gray and Moberg, 1962, p.53), almost everyone I saw had stopped going to church by adulthood, making any chart superfluous. It would only have shown a vast area of 'under-21', with tiny sections for any other grouping.

> 'I went till I was fourteen at school. I left school and the church on my fourteenth birthday. Before that you had to go every Friday to Confession and on Sunday to church. If you had not been in church on the Sunday you got six of the best from the headmaster on the Monday morning, because the headmaster saw that you were not there in church on Sunday.'

This story from Matthew may be more horrendous than others, but most of the men I spoke with left church after school or, at the latest, after compulsory church parades while in the Armed Forces. The Second World War was a turning point for some, even if too young to take up arms. 'I stopped because of the war when I was nine or ten,' said Ray (69), who had been to a Baptist Sunday school. Alan went to the Methodists until he was '21 or 22'. Gary 'Went as a lad,' while Bob and Roy went to the Church of England every week up to the age of seventeen. 'I took Communion,' Roy added. Charles 'Stopped after my teens.' They were typical of most men.

The years 1939–45 proved a defining time for a number of interviewees like Ray. With the enormous pressures exerted by the war, pressure on church-going either increased or decreased. It increased with compulsory church attendance in the Forces, causing resentment and an unwillingness to attend thereafter when back on 'Civvy Street'. It decreased for people like Ray because church workers, Sunday school teachers and the like were either called up or away to extra work, and the compulsion to attend church diminished.

The women, too, had similar early endings to their church attendances. Josephine went 'When I was young.' Pearl told me, 'I went to Sunday school. I was not forced by my parents.' For Winnie:

> 'I never went, apart from weddings and christenings. As a child I went to the Baptist Chapel and to its Sunday school. I've never been since childhood.'

Elizabeth went every morning before school and Mary went in her teens. But then they both stopped. For the rest, both men and women, church attendance is still a far-distant memory. Irene 'Went till my marriage forty-six years ago – I went every week.' Phyllis, now 86, went till she was married – but her husband would not go, so she stopped, aged 24. Hilda 'Stopped when the war came and our Congregational Church was bombed.' Maria went 'Every day till I was 40,' but that was 25 years ago. Flo has not been for twenty years and Angela for ten: 'I feel really awful about that,' she admitted. Only one person had stopped in the past year.

In three of the four cases of stopping attendance more recently, the interviewees were offended by a minister in their church. Maria felt her priest had lied very badly, Flo was aggrieved that her son was not allowed to continue in leadership in his Free Church because his fiancée was pregnant when they married, while the one who stopped a year before did so because her vicar made her feel left out in a youthful congregation. Each of these three was from a different denomination (Roman Catholic, Methodist, Church of England, respectively). Flo stopped because of her wish to see her family more often, coinciding with the arrival of grandchildren. Although I sensed indignation, there was also a clear feeling of regret in the first three and a missing of church in the latter.

The whole issue here is that older people either attend very regularly, or (with very few exceptions) have not been to church (apart from an occasional wedding or funeral) for a very long time. With a changing church (Chapter 5), any restoring of a relationship may, in reality, mean a starting all over again.

How regular was attendance?

Here is an even more surprising discovery. People who now do not go to church were once remarkably devoted. Maria went 'every day'. Wilf, who has not been for 30 years, told me:

> 'I went twice on Sunday, to the young people's group on Wednesday, the Church Choral Society on Thursday and church outings once or twice a week. It was our life when we were young.'

As will be apparent throughout this section, this was a sentiment shared by many. Until well into the latter part of the twentieth century many things now taken for granted simply did not exist for entertainment. Television was for the future; clubs for young people were concentrated in the church rather than city centre buildings built specifically as night clubs; pubs were much more taboo. Very often there was nowhere else to go. The church, and its hall, was coffee bar, sports hall, games room, dance club, outings, starting point and where-to-meet as well as a place of worship. It was invariably free, too, and parents were happy to see their offspring in a safe environment. Hence Wilf's comment (above).

I interviewed Wilf with his wife Elizabeth (aged 83 and 76 respectively). Their story is remarkable, because it covers questions not only of regularity, but of loyalty, reasons for leaving and for current non attending. Accepting that this may somewhat break the flow of my progressive argument, here is a large section of our conversation. Wilf's comment was backed by Elizabeth: 'I was brought up in church. Everything I did had to do with church. I went to church every morning before I went to school.' Both said they had been 'Church of Wales', the Welsh equivalent of the Church of England. Why, then, did they stop? Here are their replies, the one following the other without my intervention:

Elizabeth 'We had other things to do.'
Wilf 'Sunday was my main day off when I got days off.'
Elizabeth 'We worked on Sundays in the war, but they still took us to church.'
Wilf 'It became a working day.'
Elizabeth 'No-one wanted to go out in the war.'

There was a silence. Then:

Elizabeth 'We should have gone looking for a church when we moved, but we didn't. We needed friends to take us. I couldn't go now because I've had a stroke: I'm limited in walking. Now I don't feel part of it.'
Wilf 'It's an alien environment now. I don't know anyone who goes there – apart from a grumpy old man who lives opposite!'

Are some of these reasons and others excuses? It is noteworthy how frequent was their past involvement, and that their leaving was in one way slow, and another sudden (the move elsewhere). Why do they not go? They blame others:

Elizabeth 'Everything I did I did in the church. You don't see the vicar now. No-one came to our house to see about the funeral when my mother died. I was very upset because my mother was a real believer.'
Wilf 'The church is now very impersonal compared with before. You don't get a vicar even for a funeral.'

Would they go back now? Again, the answers were several and diverse:

Wilf	'No, we are past redemption now.'
Elizabeth	'I stopped years and years ago. You need something to draw you there. If you've got a car it's alright.'
Wilf	'It doesn't cater for people: it's too impersonal. They are not interested in the congregations. I don't even know who my vicar is today. I have to read the paper to find out.'
Elizabeth	'They should have visited us years ago but they didn't. We were not brought into it.'
Wilf	'No-one comes to see us. They know we're here but they're not interested.'

What complexity! There is so much to answer. Would Elizabeth and Wilf be willing to receive a friendly visitor from their local church? After this conversation I doubted it. It seems they and the church lost touch with each other, and reconciliation would be very hard, if not impossible. It is significant to note the passivity of Elizabeth and Wilf in all this. They would be proactive in many other areas of life, from shopping to visiting relatives: but when it comes to church, they are both unwilling and unable to make any move. One can only speculate, but I was left with the strong impression that Elizabeth and Wilf, along with other interviewees, felt that the church had a *duty* to approach them. This is of some interest, because if they had a physical need they would themselves make the approach to a doctor or a dentist. With further reference to shopping, this can be increasingly anonymous, especially in a supermarket, whereas going to a church could cause some embarrassment. Everyone must shop, and there is immediate help at 'Customer Services'. This universality and neutrality contrasts with the personal nature of being seen in church, making shyness something to be overcome. Long absence also leads to uncertainty as to what may happen in church.

After this diversionary interview, I return to regularity of attendance. Most used to go at least once a week. Louis now only goes to 'the Christmas Midnight', but went every week when young. Edna went 'Four times on Sunday – Holy Communion, Children's Service, Afternoon Sunday School and Evensong after I was confirmed at thirteen.' Gary went 'every Sunday', but only as a lad, 60 years ago. Flo 'Went to the Methodist Sunday school, and to church three times on a

Sunday when I was young. I walked a mile to Sunday school and a mile back.' Some were clearly under compulsion to go (as with Matthew, above). Peter complained, 'I went to Sunday school: I hated that. I went in the army because I had to.' John went 'Only because I was propelled.' Dennis 'Had to go to church parades in the war.'

This being forced to go was not the case of the majority: most seem to have been both voluntary and happy in their church and Sunday school attendance. But, once they stopped, there was no going back. I will explore in greater detail later in this chapter the reasons why people left and now do not attend, but it is appropriate here to consider denominational loyalty.

Loyalty to a denomination

A factor worthy of comment is this: I did not meet one older person who did not claim allegiance to one or another denomination. Even those who now would say they were atheists or, at least, agnostics, spoke of being 'Methodist', 'Roman Catholic' and so on. Kingsley Amis, speaking of *One Fat Englishman,* put it delightfully: 'He was of the faith chiefly in the sense that the church he did not attend currently was Catholic' (Amis, 1963, p.214).

The Roman Catholics agreed. Those who used to go were like Margaret. 'I'm a cradle Catholic': she has not been for ten years. Josephine has been 'Always a Roman Catholic – it's fifty years since I went.' Mr F has not only always been Catholic, but has brothers and uncles who are priests and even Bishops: he himself has not been for 30 years. Angela, another non attender, gave the reason:

> 'Once a Catholic, always a Catholic. It's your upbringing. It's instilled in you as youngsters. You go through baptism and first Communion and Confirmation.'

It is not within the ambit of this book to seek to answer the difficult question, 'What is a non-practising Roman Catholic/Anglican/Methodist and so on?' There may well be deep-seated beliefs even with total non attendance at a church (or little belief with regular attendance). My concern here is not so much with belief but with the relationship between churches and older people.

Those in the Church of England had a similar allegiance, even though more tenuous. This was exemplified by Doris. 'I'm Church of England. I've never been, but I consider myself part of the denomination.' Dorothy 'Was Church of England. Now I have no religion.' John was 'Always Church of England. I've not been since I was eighteen – you had to *conform* in those days.' Phyllis also has always been 'Church of England, but I've not been for sixty years except to the Ladies' Social Club.' The Free Church non attenders gave similar comments, of which ex-Methodist Gladys was typical: 'I've not been since the war'.

It is noteworthy how different some of the answers are. Doris is a loyal non-attender (not necessarily a contradiction), whereas Dorothy lacks any religion (she says). Gladys does not attend, but is not a disloyal Methodist (though the denomination may feel otherwise because of her non attendance). There is no monochrome picture here.

One or two had moved around, of whom Ken held some sort of record: 'I was Church of England, went to Chapel in the war, then to the Jehovah's Witnesses, then the Methodists. I'm now Methodist and Church of England on my infrequent visits.' Charles was 'Both church and chapel, but I stopped after I came out of the Navy at twenty.' Others moved with marriage. Lorna 'Was a Methodist but married into the Church of England.' Tony was 'Church of England but went to the Assemblies of God with my wife.' As I indicated, these were the exceptions. Older people feel a loyalty to the church of their childhood and youth, however long their absence has been.

Why is there this loyalty, particularly a desire still to be known as a 'Methodist' or whatever? It seems to be because of the commitment as a child or young person. The Jesuits' saying, 'Give me a child until he is seven and he will be a Catholic all his life', seems to work for other denominations, too. These whole generations of older people did feel a deep attachment to one church or another as children. Even though they have been absent for so long, there is a vestige of allegiance. Childhood memories seem to become more valuable and vivid in older age, and church is included in that.

If they have not been for such a long time, would older non churchgoers have anything good to say about their churches? Interestingly, a number did.

Remembering the good times

The BBC estimates that a million people over 65 who do not go to church watch Songs of Praise.

> That religion matters to a substantial minority of older people in Britain seems clear. Besides those whose religious allegiances are easy to identify, there is a group of uncertain size which would include older people who believe without belonging. These are people who have spiritual beliefs, but do not adhere to the practices or beliefs of any particular religious tradition. (Howse, 1999, p.103)

Among the non churchgoing older people I interviewed, a number fitted Howse's observation. Because of their long absences from church, none were able to speak of any good *changes* in the church. Their positive comments can be seen in their thoughts about church and the help it gives. These positives come before the negative feelings, which give reasons for non attendance, but the following indicate some to be believers, if not belongers.

The value of church

Despite non attendance, some older people were proud of their own denomination. 'The strength of the Catholic Church is that it is one church, holy church, universal church for any colour, devoted and well organized,' Daniel told me. Pam thought the Church of England 'Parish system is good – somewhere you can belong to'; while, for John, 'The Church of England is a lot less restrictive than the other denominations'. Ken likes 'The ancient architecture'. What the church teaches and believes is valued, too. 'The philosophies are good,' said one older man. Denis agreed: 'The principles of Christianity are good; for example, caring for your neighbour, not stealing, not committing adultery. But,' he added, 'even the church has a history of abusing these.' Margaret felt that the church 'Gives the children a way of life, which hopefully they will keep up if they grow older. It is a code to live by.' Thus some beliefs may have been diluted into a moral code.

As with those older people who attend church, there is a 'feel-good factor' here, too. Sometimes it comes from the music: 'I like traditional hymns,' said Ken. 'I like the singing,' Daniel told me. Angela enjoyed 'The peacefulness, the get-togethers and the prayers.' For Dennis, it was 'the solemnity and the sitting quietly to think' that he enjoyed. Marjorie, an ex-Methodist, appreciated 'Freedom. The Prayer Book of the Anglican Church is stilted. I love the freedom of the prayers and the services in Methodism with no set pattern.' One is left wondering why some of these people no longer attend because they themselves said they did not know when I asked. However, I will explore the reasons others did give in the next major section of this chapter. I felt that some agreed with the nostalgic ending to Pam's approval of her countryside Anglican Church: 'I always feel better when I've been. I feel good when I come away – I feel more fulfilled. I should make more of an effort to get there.' I was of the opinion that, with the slightest demonstration of positive friendship shown by a local church, some of these interviewees would love to return to enjoy these positive feelings once again.

The help from church

'They help a lot of people,' Lorna said. 'People in sadness get help from the church – if they are inclined that way.' Tom, with a trace of cynicism, agreed: 'It helps people with an unsophisticated background and people in distress.' Bob was pleased that 'The local church has good youth organisations: they keep the kids off the streets.' 'The church draws people together,' was Graham's answer to 'What's good about the church?', a remark echoed by others. Dorothy was pleased that 'Today more coloured people than white people seem to go – which is good.' Gladys liked 'The friendliness and activities'.

The significance of all this is that a considerable number speak highly of the church, even though they themselves have not attended for very many years. As Tony said, 'I can't think of any thing bad: I do think it's good.' Yet they do not go. Building bridges from the church to them would seem neither impossible nor even difficult.

All this must beg the more substantive question: What is wrong?

What's wrong with the church?

The answer to this question was again unusual: not for the consistency of the answers to 'When did you stop going?', but for the lack of any agreement at all. For the sake of clarity alone, I intend to group answers under the two headings: the church and the people.

The church is wrong

How is the church wrong? Saving my observations for the end, there is a great variety in the answers given: It is *inflexible,* according to Angela (ex-Roman Catholic): 'It could be more flexible. They could change things, especially priests being allowed to marry. Then there would be less scandal than now.' For a second, it is *intolerant.* 'The church is too rigid, intolerant of other religions. It is dogmatic and bigoted: if you were not a Catholic, that was it!' Daniel told me of his time as a youth. Bob (an ex-Anglican) feels it is 'too *pompous*: too much ceremony'.

For another Catholic, the church is *not holy.* Mary wishes 'It was more holy'. This latter comment may again be generational, but there are those who attend today who would wish for more dignity, a sense of preparing quietly for worship before and space to ponder after the service. Mary could not cope with the noise and the chatter, and she may well have a point. Even among those who attend regularly, there were those who told me that there is a contrast between preparing to be with God in a special way and getting ready for a party or a sports match. There is that sense of unworthiness, of approaching the One who is all-holy and all-powerful. Some quiet contemplation, even soul-searching, might be better helped by a more sober atmosphere. There will be room for joy, noise and celebration where appropriate in the service itself.

For some, the church uses the *wrong language.* 'The church has lost its way with the change from Latin,' one ex-Roman Catholic said. Matthew (also a former Catholic) sees the church as *hypocritical:* 'They are not practising what they preach'. *Boring* is another fault. 'It's boring,' complained Roy (ex-Anglican). 'It's worse than military service. It's a duty. Nothing appealed to me.' Phyllis (another ex-Anglican) found church *unenjoyable*:

'They talk long sermons which are not interesting'. (She has not been for 60 years: have times changed?) The reordering of some churches is seen as *destructive*. 'They've ripped the choir stalls out. It was nice years ago. I am shocked with the changes to the inside of the building.' Ex-Anglican Marjorie's views echo the delightful words of John Betjeman's 'Hymn':

The Church's Restoration
In Eighteen-eighty-three,
Has left for contemplation
Not what there used to be
(Betjeman, 1958)

By contra-distinction, the church is also '*out-of-date*' according to Dennis (also ex-Anglican) – and that includes the music. Finally, its beliefs are *mythical*. Two comments here are noteworthy:

> 'It's OK for anyone to believe. But for *me*, I can't believe what they say. The principle, and the Ten Commandments – you couldn't go wrong. But who believes it?' asked Cliff, from a Free Church background.

> 'Christmas, Easter, Communion and Angels don't exist,' said John. '"The Good Book" is only an historical document and is a series of deductions to keep the crowds in order. It is a myth invented for the priest to keep a quiet community.'

These varied objections to the church divide broadly into three categories: behavioural, subjective and beliefs. It could be possible for churches to change, or explain, for the first two. Learning to be flexible and tolerant are laudable goals in any event, and one would hope some churches are not boring or unenjoyable. A reaching out to those people who voice such objections should be feasible. For those who have difficulties of belief, and these were few (three or four in all), the answer might be in dialogue – if it were welcomed.

I now move to a second area of perceived wrongs.

The people are wrong

Sometimes it is the priest or minister. 'People who run the church are too staid. It needs loosening up,' Charles told me.

'The vicar doesn't care as vicars used to care,' said Edna. Josephine feels that 'The priests are doing wrong.' Some recall specific hurts from the past. Mavis was a barmaid when a priest called for several drinks, drove off on his scooter and caused a death and then lied about it. That, at least, was her view and she has never been since because of his dishonesty. Others are saddened by apparent lack of care; Margaret felt that her priests showed no concern when her husband died. May told me that her priest speaks of the 'dirty people' at her end of the parish whom he refuses to visit.

At other times it is churchgoers who are getting it wrong. 'It's what's wrong with the people,' said Ken. 'The decline of the church started with the rise of feminism and liberalization in the '60's.' 'The church doesn't cater for people,' Wilf felt, 'it's too impersonal.' For Tom, 'Those who involve themselves in the church are there for their own ends: people are "seen" to go to church and show off.' Or the church is seen to be for one group only. Pam sees her church as having moved from 'The Family of God' to 'The young people of God'. 'I feel pushed out,' she said sadly.

However, one or two accepted that the people to blame were – themselves! Louie put it well: 'There's nothing wrong: it's I who have changed.' Another man agreed: 'There's nothing wrong. My sister is a big believer and I respect her views. I'm a Charles Darwin fan!' Others expressed similar sentiments, echoing Dennis: 'Not being a regular, I shouldn't complain.'

It would appear that an occasional unqualified apology would not go amiss. Ministers and lay church members are going to get it wrong from time to time. However, if long ago a perceived wrong happened, it would be unhelpful to plead justification. Reconciliation may still be possible with the right approach. This may be the way to face the final major question: Why do some older people not go to church any longer?

Why do older people not attend church now?

American research 40 years ago identified various problems faced by older people in relation to the church:

- Some felt pushed aside by younger members.
- Some stayed away because they could not help financially.

- Some stayed away because they could not dress well.
- Some felt neglected, lacked transport, or were too ill to attend.
- Many were dissatisfied with changes in the church.
- Conflict existed regarding the role of older people in the church (Gray and Moberg, 1962, pp.96–117)

I would have to say that some of these do not now apply in the twenty-first century in Britain, especially those relating to finance and dress. But some are still an issue, as we shall now see. My research shows four major reasons for non attendance by older people: these are connected with disbelief, the church as an 'institution', other priorities and family networks.

However, an extract from an interview with Cliff, a 73-year-old ex-Welsh Congregationalist, gives an overview by way of introduction. The questions and answers are as they happened:

Me 'What about your early churchgoing?'
Cliff 'I was told to go as a child. I *had* to attend "Free Church" services in the Navy.'
Me 'But you don't go now – so why did you stop?'
Cliff 'When I left the Navy there was nothing then which was compulsory and so I didn't go at all.'
Me 'Why don't you go today?'
Cliff 'I have no answer as to why I don't go now. I'm cut off from my own denomination [living in England], my wife is not a churchgoer, and our social friends are not churchgoers. It's been more an erosion than a stopping.'
Me 'What would get you back?'
Cliff 'Nothing would get me to go.'

Although he has a denominational background, it would seem that Cliff never really formed an attachment to church: the opposite seems the case. He does seem to cumulate many of the reasons given by others for stopping, as will be seen in the next sections. There appears to be a mutual reinforcement of his comments, leading to his last reply. This overall picture is now followed by the four reasons listed above.

Disbelief

There were some older people who told me that their own disbelief kept them from going to church. Walter had been a regular attender until he left school, but then 'I worked with older men who were in the Communist Party. They swung me over as I read Marx, Engels and Lenin.' For John, the church 'doesn't fit a scientific chap'. One or two simply said they did not believe. Others explained their lack of belief in more detail:

> 'I don't believe in God and the Bible as it is written. The New Testament was written for people of the seventeenth century, people of the time of King James I and it suited the ill-informed of that age. I can't believe in an all-powerful God, or a power creating the world as per the Old Testament. I don't feel I could sincerely have anything to do with the church.'

So said Ray, whose Sunday school days at a Baptist Church ended when he was nine or ten. For Bob, formerly with the Church of England, it was more personal:

> 'In my teens we had a great youth leader who took us on bike rides after Sunday school. He was a real Christian: we worshipped him. The war came and he was one of the first who was killed in an air raid. I thought, "Where the hell is God?" After the war I didn't go: even the Germans thought God was on their side.'

There are remarkable similarities between Bob's sentiments and a number of the Psalms. The church has a delicate line to walk here: on the one hand it will wish to respect such views. Particularly for Ray, there would need to be a deep understanding. On the other hand, there will be those in the church who have faced such difficulties and come to a more positive conclusion. If someone like John, for example, were willing to meet with a fellow scientist who was also a Christian, dialogue could prove helpful.

I found it salutary to talk with a former Roman Catholic attender, who gave both a negative and a positive reply when asked about her not having been to church for forty years. She said:

> 'After I got married my husband was not a churchgoer. We had seven children and I had no time to go anywhere. I was with them and my husband was out providing for the family. But I still say my prayers, and believe in God.'

This lady (Mary, aged 63) should be an encouragement to churches to reach out with real understanding. She left for a practical reason, and still holds on to some kind of faith. Even 'disbelief' may only be in church attendance, not in the tenets of the Christian faith.

The church is an institution

'Why don't you go to church?' was the question to be answered here. An echo of some of the above reasons was given here:

> 'There's no appeal to me. I would rather sit in a pub' (Roy).
>
> 'All they want is your money' (Bert).
>
> 'The services don't relate to modern life and the life I lead' (Tom).
>
> 'I can't keep up with the modern times. Older people can't change that much' (Marjorie).

Others had similar comments and such diversity is difficult: one wants less change, another more. One man would rather spend money in a pub, another not give his money to the church. For a third man, there was 'Too much religion as I was growing up.' This latter reason, which we met earlier in this chapter, finds a pertinent comment in a recent book by Philip Yancey:

> I have a friend who tried to help a middle-aged man overcome his allergic reaction to the church, in his case due to an overly-strict upbringing in Catholic schools. 'Are you really going to let some little old nuns dressed in black and white keep you from entering the kingdom of God?' my friend asked. Tragically, for many the answer is yes. (Yancey, 1997, p.195)

Older people of different denominations criticized their church's ministers. I heard many comments, but one older lady appeared especially sad. Picking up Yancey's point, this is what Marjorie told me:

> 'I have not been since before the war. When I was fifteen my mother died and the priest said to me, "You've not been coming to church recently. That's why your mother died." I have never been since.'

There is no need to comment: *res ipsa loquitur*. However, in most cases, I gained the clear impression that a genuine apology would go a long way, if appropriate. Marjorie's was the deepest hurt, and I did ask her about someone offering her an unequivocal 'Sorry', but it would have been too little, too late. But, for the others, a genuine hand of friendship might reach across the divide.

Low priority

Phyllis spoke for a considerable number when she told me: 'I stopped going. I went cycling with a friend. I have nothing against the church, it is just my change of lifestyle.' Some older people want to do other things. 'I'm totally employed in things in keeping with my mind,' said Dennis. 'We had other things to do,' was Elizabeth's comment and she went on, 'We should have gone looking for a church when we moved – but we didn't. We needed friends to take us.' 'There was too much else to do,' Pearl said. For Nan, 'It's too much effort.' Peter admitted it is 'Just laziness'. One lady said, 'I just got older'. Pam leads too busy a life and would like to go to church, but 'It is a question of prioritizing'. 'I have many other things to do which are far more useful,' was Alan's feeling.

These last two, Pam and Alan, sum up most of the feelings and attitudes in this sub-section, with the specific words they use. Pam's 'prioritizing' included looking after a very elderly mother, as well as a lively family, their horses, and a husband. Alan included in 'things ... far more useful' a great deal of work in his retirement connected with projects and interests continuing from his working life and some hobbies which were very time-consuming.

For most of these interviewees, they do not have particularly negative feelings about church. There is simply no place in their lives for it. Some, however, would love to go, but their lifestyle has become one of being unable to go because of frailty, ill health, or getting too old. When I talked with Olive (82) and Evelyn (89), they said that they were now too old to go, but were grateful to various churches for conducting services in their residential home. Even more impressive was 88-year-old Marjorie, who had worked for the Methodists, but is now unable to go to church because of arthritis. Instead, she organizes the services in her Methodist Home for the Aged, including prayer meetings and hymn singing. She has no intention of letting her change in lifestyle affect her spirituality (Grainger, 1993, p.103).

Family networks

I asked Charles why he did not go to church. 'Apathy – that's the truth. My family came first.' For a considerable number, marriage replaced church, especially if a spouse was already a non attender. That was Emma's experience as a Methodist:

> 'I stopped when we got married – we went out on our motor-bikes. We went out for rides and to sport – I didn't go to the pub! I have been a widow for thirty years. After my husband died I went to church for a bit. I had friends who picked me up and they used to take me out rather than going to church.'

Her story is shared by several. Alan's wife 'Was not a churchgoer.' Nor was Mary's husband and they then had 'Seven children and no time to go anywhere. I still say my prayers and believe in God.' Partners are a cause of non attendance, as are children and grandchildren. One lady delightfully contradicted herself: 'I go to see my grandchildren. They only do Ring and Ride on a Sunday. At least they do it every day but I only use it then because my daughters are working in the week.' Gary did the same: 'I don't have time. Oh, I *do* have time, but I go to see the grandchildren.'

A deliberate choice has been made, or is being made, to be involved with one's own family, to the exclusion of the church family. There is no suggestion that it is bad *versus* good, but the choice keeps some older people from the church they once attended.

Why do many older people not go to church? For some it is a deliberate choice, while others have drifted away. Disbelief may contribute for a minority, but involvement with family, or doing other things, is a much more likely reason. If the church wishes to help, it will have to show that it holds even better reasons to enable older people to put it in their list of priorities.

In a moment I will look at the specific needs of those in residential homes. As a bridge, here is one meeting I had in such a home, run by the local authority. There I met Daisy, Marjorie, Bert and Lily, all in their 80's. I mention one or two individual comments from them elsewhere, but here is a part of our long conversation involving all of them. None was related, and they had only got to know each other in the home. All had once gone to church: Marjorie as a Roman Catholic, the others to the Church of England. We were talking at one stage about what was wrong with the church. The word 'All' indicates where the conversation was spoken in quick succession by each one, with nods of agreement from the others. I sat and listened!

All 'There's nothing the church could do to bring us in. They could try to make us feel wanted but they are too cliquey. We're pleased that the Assembly of God Church comes every nine weeks to take a service.'

(This contradiction between the church not wanting them, and their unwillingness to go, compared with their pleasure at a church coming to them, set the tone.)

Daisy 'I go when my back lets me!'

Marjorie 'I have not been since before the war. I was a Roman Catholic. When I was fifteen my mother died and the priest said to me 'You've not been coming to church recently, that's why your mother died.' I have never been back.'

Bert 'People only go to church to see what other people are wearing.'

Lily 'A lot depended on your parents – we were made to go. You must have some faith because you pray when you go to hospital "O God let me get better".'

(It was encouraging to have such individualistic comments.)

All 'Nothing could take us back. We are as good as those who go. We would appreciate a visit by the vicar or minister – that would help us. We would like the church to come and hold a service in here.'

(Here again is the passivity; they do not want to go to church, but welcome the church coming to them.)

Lily 'We don't want to be the forgotten lot.'

Such diversity, and so many different experiences: yet there is a happiness at the nine-weekly service, and an openness to visiting. I shall explore this more as I consider residential homes.

Residential homes

As Appendices 3 and 4 show, I visited a number of retirement homes for older people, in particular those with denominational affiliations or connections. Every home, without exception, wanted some church input and involvement. The senior member of staff I saw would reply with a simple 'Yes', or 'Definitely' to the question about church involvement in the home. They also indicated that the majority of their residents wanted such participation. One answer was unintentionally quite amusing: 'Fewer than in the past, because fewer go to church: thirty out of thirty-eight.' With such a large number wanting to be involved, the tongue-in-cheek comment proved the point.

In these days of older people getting even more elderly in years, those who live in residential homes tend to be quite limited in their physical ability to get out and about. Consequently, not many can get out to church. In all homes connected with a denomination, residents are encouraged to go to church if they can. A home may help with transport, or the local church members collect their friends. Methodist homes say, 'They feel welcome'. An interdenominational home sees residents attending church outside 'Rarely, because we have services here'. One Roman Catholic home takes one resident to Mass every day.

Similarly, denominational homes all have services within the home and regular visits from their chaplain, who is a local priest or minister. Methodist homes seem to manage something weekly. One told me of a service monthly, a Bible Study monthly, hymn singing monthly and a visit from the chaplain, all combining to make an event each week. A Church of England home has its own chapel with five services each *day*! The Roman Catholic homes have a weekly Mass.

The problem lies in two areas. In homes which are not associated with a specific church or denomination, it is becoming increasingly difficult to get a group of churches to feel committed and volunteers get less in numbers. By far the greatest need is in homes which are secular. Even among those with churches literally a few yards away, many feel neglected, or forgotten completely. Residents of these homes, especially those run by the local authority, felt isolated from the church. Very often they had moved to the home from some distance away, so the local church was not their own, either of the same or a different denomination. Heads of these homes were more than willing for priests, ministers and laity to visit and, if the residents requested, take simple services in a communal lounge. Time and again I heard pleas for church involvement. The failure may be one both of not asking by the home and not bothering by the church. I was left with an impression of needy people and opportunities to help being unheeded.

It could be said that some heads of homes were merely being pragmatic in their willingness to let the church come in, a 'keep the customer satisfied' approach. This was not the impression I gained in the homes I visited. Staff were aware of many of their residents praying and valuing a spiritual input into their lives. If there was a cynical, 'It will do them good and keep them happy', I did not detect it. The staff did want their residents to be happy, and felt church visits would help. Even if non religious themselves, they showed a willingness to make a room available. I will consider this further in the concluding chapters.

Final thoughts

A word rarely heard these days is 'cherish'. The *Chambers Twentieth Century Dictionary* defines it as: 'To protect and treat with affection: to nurture, nurse: to entertain in the mind' (Macdonald (ed.), 1972, p.224). It is a word which churches of every denomination would do well to adopt as the one which expresses their attitude to older people, whether attenders or not, able-bodied or unable to leave their own or a residential home. Some of those older people have been hurt by a church or its leader. Many have drifted away, often for reasons which appear realistic.

Yet two things are clear. All those I spoke with feel an affinity, however distant, with a denomination. And among the vast majority there is a degree of goodwill towards the church, which church leaders may want to explore. I sensed that some complaints were more a *cri de coeur* than a shutting of the door. Those older people who attend church are, on the whole, loyal. Of those who do not attend, a proportion would value renewed contact. Wrongs can be addressed. Churches may wish to consider the appropriateness, in certain cases, of a reconciliatory approach. I will consider how older people can help the church, and *vice versa,* in the final chapters. This chapter has revealed that there is great hope for continuing and renewed relationships.

9

What can older people do for the Church?

Are older people and the church together or apart? A book committed to this question could end with a simple answer one way or the other, including the sociological and religious reasons for such a conclusion. But such an ending would be less than helpful and these final chapters will seek to suggest ways in which a greater togetherness may be possible. In this chapter I will explore how older people might be encouraged to be involved in the life and work of the church, on the basis of the evidence which they supplied.

My research, both in reading and in the interviews I conducted, would suggest that older people have a much lower opinion of their value and the contribution they can make, than those who lead and share in church life feel about them. The majority of older people seem to feel they have retired *from* something, not *into* a new role (Burton-Jones, 1997, p.7), whereas many church leaders and members are optimistic in their hopes for older people having a positive part to play in a variety of church activities.

Where can older people fit into the life of the church? I will consider this under five areas: nowhere; in the church itself; privately; in the fellowship of the church; in the community.

Figure 9.1 shows the views of my interviewees who do not attend church, describing what they feel they can do for the church. It is to be expected that Figure 9.2 would have more positives, being from those older people who attend church – as indeed it does.

Working from these charts and from the many and varied answers from these older people, plus leaders and members of churches, where do older people fit in to church life?

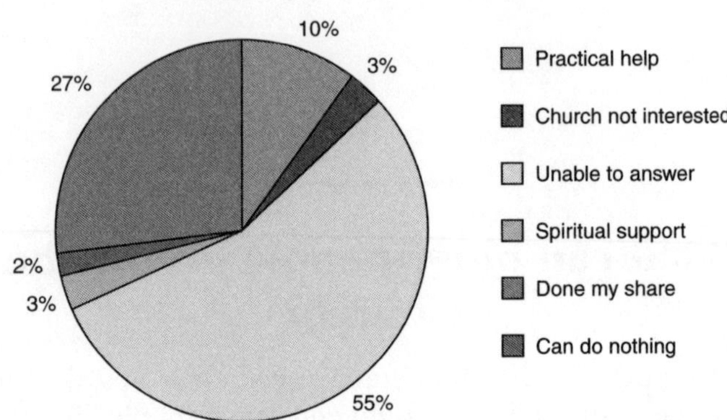

Figure 9.1 Views of 60 church non attenders as to how they could help a church

Nowhere

Most negative answers came from people who do not attend church. Figure 9.1 should give serious cause for thought among those who would wish to recover long-lost members. But Figure 9.2 shows that a significant 38 per cent of older churchgoers also have an inability to respond, or a feeling that there is nothing they can do. Why is this?

For some, attenders and non attenders, understandably it is *old age* which prevents involvement. 'What could you do for the

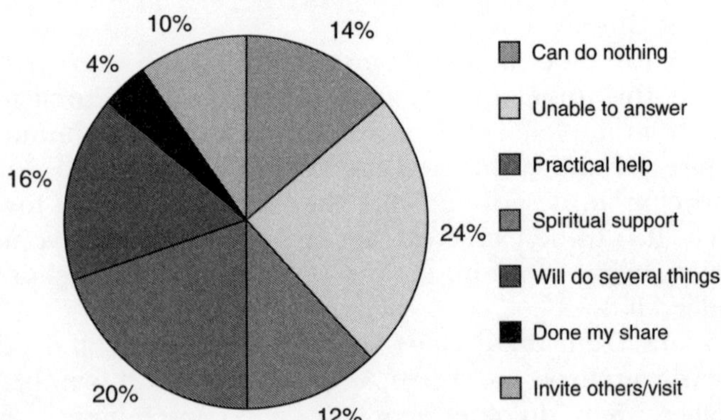

Figure 9.2 Views of 52 church attenders as to how they could help a church

church?' I asked Angela (77). 'Not a lot really – I'm a pensioner.' May (80) said she was 'Too long in the tooth.' Marjorie (87) pleaded *health*: 'I can't help with anything: it takes all I have to keep *me* going.' None of these attended church at all. Elizabeth (76), a non attender, responded: 'I've *done my share* – I've looked after my mother.' Apart from health, it could be possible for these and others to be involved. A Roman Catholic priest said this: 'Many are retired and *could* help, but very few are willing to commit themselves to any church work.' Ernest (68) was willing to admit to a degree of *unwillingness*: 'There's a lot I could do but, *mea culpa*, I share a common reluctance to get involved.' A younger member of a Roman Catholic church told me, 'They *should* fit in anywhere, even in the children's liturgy. Their own inhibitions and our putting people into categories sometimes prevents this.'

Others simply *do not know* where they would fit older people into the life of the church. This was conveyed with some sorrow from the two Pam's, the first 23 and the second 60:

> 'I don't know where they fit in. I know where they should fit in: places on the Parochial Church Council, having their say, being catered for in the services – but I don't think they are.'

> 'I've thought about this long and hard. I can't think of anything. The vicar said he'd think about where I would fit in but he has not come back. If you're over twenty-five, my church does not want to know.'

These two Church of England members, one who is young and goes, one older who does not now attend, share the same puzzlement as well as the same name. There is a feeling of being *not wanted*. Evan (78) felt this: 'It depends on the Minister: he won't let me do anything.' Non attender Wilf (83) said, 'They know we're here but they're not interested.' Marie (48) was concerned for her mother:

> 'My mother doesn't fit in now. She used to be in the Union of Catholic Mothers. A few older ones organize the church with the priest: they are very cliquey and my mother feels shut out. She is not as involved as she used to be. She feels she is taken for granted. She goes most Sundays, but doesn't feel involved. You are either "in" or "out" as an old person.'

This all has such a ring of sadness about it. A great deal which follows in this chapter is very positive, and sometimes appears as a *cri de coeur.* Leaders may feel there is a place for older people, but many of them do not seem touched by, or aware of, such concern.

In the church itself

I turn now to the positive. In all my survey, this far outweighed the negative comments. Both leaders and members of churches, along with many older churchgoers, believe that older people can and must play an important part in church life. Even more, one of the real surprises to me during my research, in interviewing those who do not attend church, was to meet some ten per cent who not only want to help, but some who actually do help. My preconception would have been that those on the outside might appreciate some support, but would universally think that they have nothing they themselves could contribute. As I will seek to show, preconceptions may be erroneous, and mine proved to be. One point is worthy of mention: it was more in the rural setting, where the village church appeared more as the centre of the community life, that participation by the non attending older person was being volunteered. The church seems closer to village life than in a town or city setting.

I now look firstly at the church as a place of worship and an organization. Four key areas need mention.

1. Worship

The Church and the Older Person, published 40 years ago, puts 'Participate in worship services' as the first thing older people can do for the church (Gray and Moberg, 1962, Chap. 9). The Bishop of Warwick agreed, putting 'Presence in worship' as his top priority for older people's contributions. A Roman Catholic priest said they helped by 'Just being there, especially at Mass in the week, because they are retired.' A countryside Church of England vicar said they were important 'By turning up. I need them to come on board'; while a United Reformed Church leader said that older people were the regular attenders every

Sunday, compared with young families coming twice a month: 'They have a real sense of commitment.'

In some situations, if older people were not in church, there would be no worship. 'They keep the church going at the moment,' one leader told me. 'The churches I go to in Coventry tend to have congregations with a majority of elderly women,' wrote the Secretary of the Inter-Faith Consultative Group of the Church of England General Synod (Lamb, 1998). As we have seen, older persons participate more in religious activities than any other age group (McFadden, 1995, pp.161–75). 'If the elderly weren't there, there wouldn't be a church,' was how Natalie, a sixteen-year-old Roman Catholic, put it starkly. That is not necessarily a negative comment, however. This sharing in worship, 'The testimony of a life of faith' (Whitehead and Whitehead, 1981, p.135), encourages the young. Nick (22), in a New Church, spoke of the older people as not being 'boring': 'They are normal people who come to church,' he said. 'I've seen an old lady happily clapping, compared with younger people who don't,' commented Odie (24). 'Visitors see them and enjoy their friendliness. Their very being there is important – their presence,' a Church of England vicar told me.

Hence there is a great deal of thankfulness for the mere fact that older people come to church at all. Yet here is the anomaly: not one older person spoke of this. They do find religion very important, as even secular surveys show (Matheson and Summerfield, 1999, p.40). They may realize the value of faith to their own well-being (Chester and Smith, 1996, p.47), but do *they* see their value in worship as simply being an *act of presence*, rather than because they might be 'useful' (Grainger, 1993, p.12)? I take this expression to mean doing something *active* by way of helping, rather than only *being* in the congregation. Perhaps an occasional affirmation of older worshippers would not go amiss. They are important worshipping members of the church.

2. Spiritual help within Services

The previous point can be taken further: older people can bring a vital contribution to the services within the church by their active involvement. In certain circumstances they can run whole services – especially ones for themselves (Stafford, 1989, p.52), as I discovered in more than one residential home run by the Methodist Homes for the Aged. Whole new services can arise if an older person gives a lead. 'We're going from a fortnightly to a weekly service because I got it going,' John, a United Reformed Church member in his 70's, told me. 'It's amazing, we can run services ourselves without a minister. I organize the services.' How sad that he was one of only three older people who spoke to me of things they could do in helping with services. Perhaps they have been scared off by remarks such as, 'In some churches, the leadership team bears a passing resemblance to the old Soviet Politburo: no one knowingly under the age of sixty' (Warner, 1999, p.9)! But ministers value older help: 'An elderly man runs the choir, organizes the readings and prayers, which means I only need to preach at Evensong. They run things because they have experience,' a city vicar said. Older people do not need to be discouraged into assuming merely passive roles (Chester and Smith, 1996, p.49). In this twenty-first century, this possibility is increased by growing lay activity in all denominations. As clergy numbers decline, even Roman Catholic lay people can (and do) run Eucharistic Services, as has been the case in the Free Churches for some years.

Participation in organization may include leadership of the services – even younger people told me this. Older ones have the experience and wisdom (Harris, 1987, p.110). As Rob (17), a town Church of England young person said, 'What people can do depends on what they are able to do, not their age.' Older people can possess a tremendous spiritual legacy (Fischer, 1992, p.1–15). 'While the physical body decays with aging, the soul or spirit may yet grow' (Lyon, 1985, p.59). The very vulnerability of an older person can be a blessing within the worship of the church, as when this vulnerability is viewed as 'a positive thing ... a place where you can become fruitful' (Nouwen, 1995, pp.1–8). If churches affirm the dignity of older persons, those churches will discover their own calling more completely (Paul and Paul, 1994; Hird, 1995, p.viii). Every older member of a church should be seen as an active member of the Body of Christ, with gifts to contribute (Harris, 1998a, p.2). I asked one Church of England vicar in a city parish church how older people could help. His reply was:

> 'As every Christian can: full commitment of gifts God gives them as members of the church. Active participation – prayer activities, fellowship, worship, sharing their story or testimony. They provide the maintenance of continuity and history.'

Pope John Paul II, in his *Christifideles Laici*, encouraged this approach: 'The expected retirement of persons from various professions and the workplace provides older people with a new opportunity in the apostolate' (Pontificium Consilium pro Laicis, 1999, p.20). Many want to be involved (Richter and Francis, 1998, p.72), and young churchgoers want them to be. 'They have an awful lot of experience and knowledge to share – it would be nice to see them share this. We don't see them at the front any more,' Sue (a young, countryside Anglican) lamented. She went on, 'It's almost as if the vicar has found a formula he is happy with which works. He has a basic core group to do everything – prayers, lessons and so on.' In other words, by including some, the vicar is excluding others, especially the older congregational members. Her husband Mike agreed: 'The elderly should be more active in the service. The young people wouldn't turn their noses up if the old people did things.'

To revert to Pope John Paul II, he believes that 'The elderly . . . themselves have a valuable contribution to make' (Pope John Paul II, 1995, p.2). They should not feel redundant or marginalized in the congregation (Appleton, 1998, p.2.01) but, rather, valued for their current contribution (Coleman *et al.*, 1993, pp.1–18). As David (15) told me, they can do 'The readings, participate in the congregation, lead the prayers, sing.' When things go wrong in services, older people can help to steady the ship (Friedman, 1985, p.208). They have a 'quiet, unassuming presence' and their gifts should 'not be left unnoticed and unused' (Webber, 1990, p.27), even when health is failing (Metropolitan Anthony, n.d., p.9). Examples can be drawn from Caleb (at 85 asking Joshua for a fresh challenge of building his new home on a mountain still occupied by an 'enemy') (Beasley-Murray, 1995) and Moses (Howell, 1997, pp.34–8) of older church leaders who have blessed congregations. Amy (14) told me that 'After the young people go out to their activities, the older ones shine.' A prospectus for a residential home in Coventry says this: 'At St Andrew's we see the life of the resident here as a constructive, positive and important period in their Christian life' (St Andrew's House, 1999). Should it not be so in church services also?

3. Commitment to church organization

It is not only in the services, but in the service of the church that older people can shine. They have been described as 'The most recruitable people in a church' (Warren *et al.*, 1997, pp.103–5). Compared with the rest of the population, an increasing proportion of older people volunteer to help with religion (Matheson and Summerfield, 1999, p.7). They can form the basis of the leadership: 'Churches are held together by older folk when the work and pressure is on younger people which prevents them from being as active as the older people are able to be,' a Baptist minister said. A Methodist minister valued 'Their commitment and their responsibility.' Rachel, a 25-year-old, from a country Methodist church, told me that 'One or two of them run the church – the rest are willing accomplices!' For some denominations this is a problem, with Cardinals in the Roman Catholic Church being in their 70's and 80's and forming the power-base (Hornsby-Smith, 1999). Others appreciate the roles they have as treasurer, Elder, or as other types of leader locally. The Church of England, in particular, has valued much greater lay leadership in the last few decades (Warren, 1995b, p.10).

As such, older people can be part of the welcoming at the beginning of a service and the making of tea and coffee at the end: at least, that is how Steve (20) sees them. A city centre church uses older people to keep their church open and welcome through the week. A United Reformed Church minister sees his older people as 'The powerhouse of the church.' He told me how he wrote to one man who took early retirement, 'Your minister needs you': he is now 'Totally involved in our work.'

That man has, among other things, mended the church organ. His minister is tapping this 'unrealized potential' (Apichella, 1989, p.10). Even those who do not attend church would be willing to help here. 'I'd mow the lawn and help in practical ways' said Alan (70), a Free Church non attender.

Dennis (73), a Church of England non attender, was the same: 'I'd help with the building. I do support the church. I help to run the fete, I promote the raffle for funds.' Older attenders agree. 'Since 1962 I have done bazaars and fetes: I think I need a rest this year!' Frank (65) said. 'I clean the church now, I help at bazaars, garden fetes, I sell raffle tickets and visit the sick' (Liz, 78). 'I'm the church cleaner' (Maureen, 78). 'One elderly man cleans the church' (Tracy, 19). In other words, much practical as well as spiritual work is available for older people, who can be 'The engine of the church', as a town vicar put it. This 'potential contribution' (McFadyen, 1997, p.12) is wanted by senior leaders. The Roman Catholic Archbishop of Birmingham wants churches kept open through the week by a rota of older people and for them to help in the priest's house by being secretaries, door-keepers, phone answerers, diary keepers and (with training) counsellors.

4. Finance

One other area is worthy of note, that of finance. 'Their financial contribution is huge because of the numbers,' a Roman Catholic leader said. A Black Church minister agreed: 'They are the financial backbone and give more, relatively, than those who are working.' Older non attenders also help here, sometimes with a wry smile: 'I gave them a subscription a fortnight ago – they were pleading poverty!' Mr B (72) remarked.

More than that, older people's expertise in financial matters is appreciated. The Archdeacon of Coventry spoke of this gift to the church. Non attending Pam (70) said how she helped the village church give a card and £5 to each elderly villager each Christmas.

In this whole area of work within the church itself, whether it be worship, spiritual or practical help, so much can be done by the older person. Throughout, one is left wondering whether these older people are led to believe in their potential, and whether such potential is ever fully realized. But if the more public arena is not for some, perhaps there is another sphere. It is to this I now turn.

In private

Very many of the older people detailed in Figures 9.1 and 9.2 at the beginning of this chapter had no answer as to what they could do for the church, or felt there was nothing to be done. There are two matters which might be worth raising with them.

Prayer

Gray and Moberg (1962, Chap. 9) give, as their second and third answers as to 'What older persons can do for the church': 'Engage in their own personal devotional activities' and 'Pray'. A number of church leaders and members put this to me as the first thing older people can do. 'Pray,' was one vicar's one word answer. 'Their ministry of prayer at home,' said another. 'We undervalue prayer by the elderly and housebound' was the Bishop of Warwick's opinion. 'When it comes to prayer there is an army of pray-ers when you count all the elderly who are praying,' said a Roman Catholic lay leader. Some see the value of this, with their own prayer groups. Ina (71 plus) told me how she runs a 'Prayer Link' of older people from her United Reformed Church:

> 'I run it in our home. We pray for the people in the village, for the churches in the village and for things to happen. We have had strong answers to prayer. We meet every Monday morning.'

This has a real impact on others in the church. John (53) told me of older people having 'A lifetime of prayer behind them,' and how 'They exude a serenity which is uplifting.' At least, he added, 'Some of them do!' With the housebound, one Roman Catholic priest told me, 'They pray for us all. I tell them, "That's your job". They get newsletters to help them to pray.' A Baptist leader spoke of his members: 'Some have a well-developed intercessory prayer life and can tell you of answers to prayer.' The Bishop of Coventry told me his story:

> 'The elderly in my last church prayed for the youth group before it started and then for the people in it. We involved the elderly house-groups with prayer requests for the young people. Youth groups started with one and went up to twenty-five and then to a hundred plus because the old

prayer partners were involved in praying and also involved in supporting the young people.'

When older people say things like, 'All I can do is pray,' some of the above should give cause for encouragement rather than for bemoaning the situation. The church values its older people praying, perhaps much more than they realize.

From all the above comments, it is clear how much older people appreciate being kept informed about specific matters for prayer. It is less easy to pray for more anonymous situations – the homeless, the poor and so on. If the older members of the church were aware of what the more active members were doing, specifically to help in these areas, or of individual needs, there could be a deep, prayerful involvement. The youth group of a church, for example, may have a project on the go (as the Bishop of Coventry said, above), and it would give a real sense of partnership, as well as of being part of the church community, if this project could be part of the prayer life of older caring people.

Time

Linked often with prayer is the time older people have. The Archdeacon of Coventry put it this way:

> 'The old have time: the challenge is that the Christian servant does not retire – they have the ministry of intercession and time to be used that way and they can be caught up in that opportunity and see the crucial nature of it.'

This great gift of time can be of real value to the church. A Roman Catholic leader told me that he values 'Their fellowship – they contribute because they have time to talk.' They have time for friends and families (Appleton, 1998, 2.06). There is time just to 'be', rather than having to 'do' all the time (Katz, 1975, p.146).

> In the mellowness of maturity, they have time for the leisurely pursuit of their own interests. Older people – at least some – can savor the wisdom that comes with age and come to terms with their Maker. (Cosby, 1987, p.18)

This view by Bill Cosby agrees with the comment that 'Old age should not be seen as a problem but a time of life with fulfilments of its own' (Sutherland, 1999). Older people have time to be involved (Thomas Berry (in Tiso, 1982, p.5)). This includes time for the church. A Church of England vicar told me, 'The newly retired are God's gift to the church because of their energy and time.' It is important to note that this group of 'early retired' is demographically often younger than my older interviewees, being aged from 50 or 55 upwards. As other responsibilities fall away, there is more 'Disposable time on their hands' (Regan and Smith, 1997, p.25). They have 'hours of time', said a Methodist senior leader. He was backed by a Baptist leader: 'Many have the time and space to do lots of routine jobs to help the cause.' They should not be viewed as 'passive, dependent and withdrawn', but as having time for active involvement (Creber, 1994, p.5).

I am not wanting to give the assumption that this view is universally the case; Cosby's opinion would not find an echo in some of those I interviewed. Many feel old, lonely and useless. Cosby and the others quoted above are setting an optimistic goal which is not always achieved. I can only refer back to the earlier section in this chapter for the large number who feel they have 'nothing' to give, fitting in 'nowhere'. These older people have the time, but as I have already quoted, feel 'Too long in the tooth', or too ill, or too old. One older person is left feeling that 'My church does not want to know'; another does not 'Fit in'. This whole section on time, with its optimism, needs to be balanced against that previous section, without repeating it all again here.

However, in the ministry of prayer and the use of time, church ministers do see great value in older people. Here again, positive affirmation would be needed to realize this potential. The problem is about turning theory into practice. A Church of England vicar explained it this way:

> 'In theory there is a ministry of prayer, when at home Communions we talk about the problems of the church and get them to pray for us. They probably feel passive recipients.'

It is in this last sentence that the key to the problem is seen. Could there not be an encouragement to move these parishioners to become active participants? I asked a Baptist minister what older people could do for the church. He answered:

> 'Time, energy, wisdom. They have a lot to offer. The churches are held together by older folk when the pressure is on younger people which prevents them from being as active as the older people are able to be. The older people do help.'

It leaves me with the question, Why is there an apparent breakdown of communication here? Since church leaders affirm the value of the time older people have to offer, then they could be more involved in the next matter to be considered.

In the fellowship of the church

Earlier chapters have shown how the word 'church' has various connotations. The one which received the greatest support was that which meant 'people.' It is necessary to consider how older people can be valued within the fellowship of the church, the body of people. A number of matters are pertinent.

Wisdom and understanding

There are certain things which only time can give. The wisdom of years is one. When I asked Pam (72) what she could now do to help the church, her reply was slightly hesitant, but very positive:

> 'My wisdom with the years may be of interest and help. I help the church through my background of social work and am able to help folk through crises.'

Pam was the only older person who mentioned the value of life's experiences. I do wonder if older people realize the value of their contribution of wisdom and understanding. Many have a great deal to give in this area. The corollary is that the church must also provide learning opportunities for older people, as Chapter 10 will show (Sutherland, 1999, 1.14). This wisdom of the years is meant to be a blessing to the wider community (Carey, 1997, p.5). 'They have tolerance,' a Roman Catholic priest told me, 'Are wiser and more understanding. It is the wisdom of years. They are positive people.' Older people have

'A wealth of life experience, a breadth of experience which those who are younger don't have' (Pascall, 1999). To quote again from the elderly Pope John Paul II, 'Elderly people help us to see human affairs with greater wisdom, because life's vicissitudes have brought them knowledge and maturity' (Gledhill, 1999b, p.5). Dame Cicely Saunders, founder of the Hospice Movement, said (at the age of 81), 'The spirit of a person can be more powerful and giving when the body is weaker' (Saunders, 1999, p.19).

There is particular value in this wisdom reaching across the generations, which is itself a vital part of Christianity (Harris, 1987, p.104). Church leaders see this. A New Church minister told me: 'Wisdom is what we need them to share, and they have a good role in praying and helping the younger people who are starting out on the road of life.' Rachel (15), from a town Church of England church, agreed: 'They can give advice about Christianity and how to approach life. It's not that they should simply say "Don't do this", but they should give positive help. They can talk about your problems.' Older people are points of reference in the struggle young people now have in leading Christian lives (Jerrome, 1989, p.783).

Others agreed, feeling that their example is huge to younger people. Two younger New Church lay leaders, Brian and Christa, told me, 'They [older people] can encourage us through their experience and their helping.' A Black Church minister agreed:

> 'Their experience is very useful. They have a wealth of knowledge which is valuable in any discussion. They affirm the traditional side of the church and bring a balance between the traditional and the modern.'

It is not insignificant that '69 per cent of elderly people are in contact with at least one of their children at least weekly' (Report of a Working Party of the Board for Social Responsibility, 1995).

Recent writings on intergenerational relationships speak of the great value of the grand-parental generation for children and teenagers (King, 1999). That younger generation agrees. 'They can give invaluable advice,' Simon (19) told me, 'They have seen the progressions within the church and we can use this to make the church better.' As a major American report put it, 'Congregations should recognize that their elder members are often specially endowed with gifts of wisdom, serenity and understanding' (White House Conference on Aging, 1961, pp.122–5). Older ones offer the younger church members a sense of secure and lasting wisdom, treasured by the young (Morrison, 1998, pp.43–5).

It was amusing to have Rob (15) say that 'They stop the church changing completely and going mad. That's good because they are more sensible and more traditional – but we don't want a complete change to all the modern stuff.' I say, amusing, because the retired Bishop of Coventry did the opposite: 'Genuine wisdom perceives and encourages new things and brings the experience and memory to bear in a creative way.' If it had been the other way round – it may not be too strong to put it like this: 'Our first and most important task is to help the elderly become our teachers again and to restore the broken connections among the generations' (Nouwen and Gaffney, 1976, p.17).

As I commented in the earlier section on prayer, a caveat is needed here, too. Several bridges need to be crossed if these 'broken connections' are to be restored. In a rapidly changing society, older people may not speak the same language as their grandchildren's generation. As society makes major advances, interests may well not be the same. In a twenty-first century world of IT (Information Technology), there are those who are older who know little of this, or of a new century's working conditions, changes in gender roles, or alterations in family situations: these are not easy divisions across which to bridge the generational gap. The comments of some of the young people in the earlier chapters concerning what is an older person (Chapter 2) and what the church thinks of older people (Chapter 6) are apposite here. 'Change disempowers some long-term members', was how the Baptist General Superintendent summed up the situation.

However, there *is* a wisdom in age, and from this wisdom comes a second major contribution older people can make within the fellowship of the church:

Care and encouragement of others

Young people do not just value wisdom, they need the care and help which older ones can give. 'I value their friendship. A role model is important for younger people by people much older,' was how Charlie (26) put it from her perspective as a youth worker. A Roman Catholic priest agreed. 'We have older people who become prayer companions for children making their first Communion. They talk to the children about their faith, one to one,' he told me. Ann, a lay worker in a city Roman Catholic church, put it this way:

> 'The young people need an understanding of living in the community. We must set up situations where people do things together. We are trying to create a social awareness, to show what people can do, and need. There is a fear in the old people about the young people, and at church we are trying to break down this fear.'

This working together is valued across the denominations. A Black Church minister told me that his older ones 'Look out for the younger ones,' while a New Church minister said that 'The elderly help the young people, especially the small children.'

Even when ill or very old, a person can give and receive love (Rosewell, 1987, p.163). It may be that the responsibility to care actually grows greater as people age (Laslett, 1989, p.196). There is a proverb in Mali:

> A young man's gait is rapid, but he does not know the way
> An old man's gait is slow, but it made the way.
>
> (Patterson, 1999, p.1)

This is why, when an older person who is a member of a church is bed-bound in a nursing home with no short-term memory, they are still able to be an encouragement, both in and through their suffering (Elliott, 1995, pp.22–4). Someone like that is a demonstration of dignity and enrichment (Pope John Paul II, 1982, p.1). Do church people rather view such individuals as social problems? We think of caring, not of receiving care. Right up to their last days, older people can minister to others, as well as receive ministry (Collyer, 1997, p.1). Even those in main church leadership can discover this, as their values are re-affirmed (Peter Coleman, in Foreword to Howse,

1999, p.iii). A New Church minister said, 'I have a couple in their seventies I see as my spiritual parents. They have a lot to offer and we have a lot to learn from them.' A town vicar told me of 'One man in particular who at Christmas gives me a letter to say all the things he has appreciated about my ministry during the year.'

Almost every denomination had someone who spoke warmly in this way. A Roman Catholic priest said of his older people, 'They give warmth and affirmations.' A Methodist minister told me of her people: 'The older ones open the door, give me a cup of tea and understanding and support.' It is significant that only one older person spoke of their value in this way, and he was a non attender. Tom (65) was asked, 'How can you help the church?' Here is his answer:

> 'Apart from raising money, I try to give moral support to the vicar from outside. He and I exchange problems: for example, the people around him.'

Are older people aware of their value in this whole area? They certainly did not tell me so.

Within this whole area of care, there is also the mutual care older church members have for each other. It has been said, in sharp terms, that 'Before the elderly await help from others, they must help themselves, if they are at all solicitous not to reinforce the popular view of old age as decrepit and helpless' (Pereira, 1982, p.156). However, another way of looking at this was as a lay leader put it to me:

> 'They have time, patience, experience and they have grown up with the notion of being neighbours. They enjoy talking about nothing over a cup of tea, having a grumble and a laugh, which is wholesome. They have history.'

One priest said how this is especially valuable after bereavements, when they give each other informal care. 'Older people are irreplaceable apostles, especially among their own age group, because no one is more familiar than they with the problems and the feelings of this phase of life' (Pontificium Consilium pro Laicis, 1999, p.19). Older people know how the human body fails. Thus Harold (83) said he could 'Help people. I still drive and I help at a stroke club.' They realize that their contemporaries will need a visit. The Roman Catholics lead the way in organized visits. Bishop Pargiter spoke warmly of the Legion of Mary, the Union of Catholic Mothers and the Society of St Vincent de Paul as means by which the young-old, in particular, visit the old and housebound. Some older Roman Catholics have been members of one of these Societies for many years and younger ones appreciate the work they do: 'They know how to deal with problems,' Paul (23) said.

Other denominations spoke of their older members 'Caring for each other. This extends outside the church walls,' a Methodist minister commented. 'They have a paternal attitude to the other older folk in the church and visit,' a Baptist leader told me, adding, 'They care for each other very well because there is no patronizing.' A Church of England lay leader spoke of taking older people to help him with Communions in older residential homes: 'One woman in her seventies did this for the first time last week and wrote to thank me for giving her the opportunity.'

In passing, I mentioned the joy older people find in chatting. An observation needs to be made on this specifically.

Telling life-stories

I was looking at the value of a cup of tea and a chat as a way older people encourage each other. Sharing in their own oral histories is a boon both for the teller and listeners if both are older (Clements, 1979, pp.24–5). A Baptist minister told me, 'We get them to tell their stories. We have to build their confidence in speaking in front of people and learning to laugh and share.' A Roman Catholic priest agreed, taking the story-telling a stage further: 'The elderly have a story to tell – the church community is doing this. Each story is individual, but the stories coalesce to make it part of our faith.'

Older people, therefore, do not only enthuse each other with their life-stories but, as members of a church fellowship, encourage faith in others. A lay leader suggested this be taken further, by older people going into schools to talk of their lives and their faith and what that means to them. 'Unless the children meet elderly people they are missing out,' was how she summed up her feelings. These older people have a background and knowledge which will equip the next generations (Howell, 1997, pp.34–8). John, in his 50's and thus approaching his older age, put it this way:

> 'We need to hear how they have come through so much. We would then admire them even more: for example, those whose husbands were killed in the war. They have accepted hard times. You can only find this out in individual conversations.'

Although Frank's book is about interviewing techniques, the title *The Wounded Storyteller* is wonderfully emotive and descriptive: that is what an older person telling their story is (Frank, 1995). Their stories matter so much, because life is 'biographical as well as biological' (Cole, 1992, p.21) and science cannot replace the mystery of life (Phillipson, 1998). As Jean Tritschler argues, our society seems to value only things which are 'Productives, utiles et visibles immédiatement'. But there is, in the midst of these, 'l'ordre de l'invisible', including 'des souvenirs que l'on ressuscite' (Tritschler, 1991, pp.77–88). How can following generations be helped? By these 'souvenirs'. Not one older person felt this worthy of mention. How much may be hidden away within those whose lives are marked by a walk of Christian faith? Story doors need unlocking, for the benefit of all. As Frances, a lay worker in the Roman Catholic church put it, 'They have history'.

It is not only the past which would bring value: I come to three special areas where the older generation can be of help.

Showing old age is good

In all my research through interviews, I set my face against leading questions – those where an answer was stated in the question itself. Surprises arose, not only from what people said, but from what they did *not* say. Perhaps my questions were too much related specifically to the relationship between older people and the church. That was inevitable, considering the parameters of this book. With a considerable amount of literature on one area where older people are of special value, it may be of significance that no one told me how older people can affirm the value of old age itself. Despite their reticence, I would wish to suggest that older people in the church can be of great help here.

> Both the teachings of America's religions and the values of her social scientists include the goal of making old age a time

> of happiness and joy, a stage of good personal and social adjustment, an age of high morale and a time of life satisfaction, rather than a period of mental anguish, social maladjustment and dissatisfaction.

Gray and Moberg (p.188) set this benchmark in 1962. Is that the message we are receiving from older people today in the church? Do we think of age as growing older, or a disease (Age Concern, 1994, p.7). Those who reach retirement are often badly affected by the adjustments needed (Grainger, 1993, p.6). There needs to be a reversal of the desire to be forever young, as Chapter 3 sought to show.

Although I said that no one had spoken about this area specifically, a United Reformed Church minister was strong in his contrasting of older people with younger ones:

> 'The sixty-fives to seventy-fives are the powerhouse of the church: I want to state this is a real positive for your research. The young ones run around like headless chickens because of society: there are two workers in the family; they keep their children running to avoid mischief, and there is a mortgage to pay. When that finishes there is a great pool of still water: this is a tremendous challenge for the next thirty years. Committees are made up of older people and they can be a very positive workforce on a practical level. If the older ones care, visit and do DIY around the church the young ones don't complain about that!'

Georgina Bray refers to a favourite film of mine, *Arthur*, where the title character asks his butler, 'Hobson, do you want anything?' 'I want to be younger.' 'Sorry,' replies Arthur, 'It's your job to be old' (Bray, 1991, p.5). Accepting this as true for all of us when we get older, what is our attitude to be? Can older people in the church help us here? Do we fight old age, or accept its growing limitations gracefully (Anke, 1993; Wainwright, 1999)? Will we, like Agatha Christie at 75, thank God for a good life and love received (Johnson and Slater, 1993, p.31)? However much the pain and awkwardness of ageing takes its toll, will we still feel that life is not long enough (Yaconelli, 1998)? The contrast has been expressed in this way:

> Ageing is seen as loss, decline, a downhill course. But while there are losses in aging, there are also gains and empirical

> observations show that many persons enjoy getting older. From a psychodynamic viewpoint the losses in aging, though painful, are made bearable by considerable gains that afford new pleasures. (Pruyser, 1975, p.102)

We need our older people to give us this contribution; to be able to say with Maurice Chevalier in the film *Gigi*, 'I'm glad I'm not young any more'. Old age can be portrayed as an opportunity (Sutherland, 1999, 1.10). Whether that necessitates following the lead of John Glenn to go back into space at 77 to demonstrate 'Grey Pride' is a moot point (Whitworth, 1998), but his trip did show that older people are often alert and active and can indulge in extreme physical endeavours (Brooke *et al.*, 1998). That may be for the few. For others, like 63-year-old Barbara Macdonald, 'I'm growing old disgracefully and enjoying each step along the way' (Johnson and Slater, 1993, p.11).

This positive attitude is borne out by statistics: the over-60's have a greater expressed life satisfaction than any other age group with all aspects of life, apart from health (Hunt, 1978; Bond *et al.*, 1993). Times have changed and there is now a freedom to develop and grow in later life (Guillemard, 1983b, p.82).

Demonstrating that old age is a fulfilment

Older people can show that, as they age, this process is not only good, but a fulfilment of all that has gone before: there is something missing without it. My office wall calendar (one which never gives its sources!) told me, one February day, 'For the ignorant, old age is winter, for the learned it is a harvest.' The Royal Commission on Long Term Care included in its values that 'Old age represents an opportunity for intellectual fulfilment and for the achievement of ambitions put on hold during working lives' (Sutherland, 1999, 1.18). The last two or three decades of life are to be ones of development and growth (Coggan, 1997, p.1). All of life's experiences can come together, bringing meaning to the whole of life (MacKinlay, 1993, pp.26–70).

In the lives of those older people who are part of the fellowship of the church, there is a particular role for them here. Great interest was aroused by a Report which *The Times* summarized: 'Religious belief can make people happier and healthier as they enter old age' (Gledhill, 1999a, p.10). Its writer did not exactly go so far, but said: 'It is not implausible to suppose that religious belief, by helping people to preserve their sense of the meaning and value of life, might contribute to the prevention of physical disease' (Howse, 1999, p.72). The *Lancet* was not happy, describing the link as 'at best weak and inconsistent' (Sloan *et al.*, 1999, pp.664–7). However, older churchgoers can show that, whether well or ill, life is being fulfilled for them by their religious values.

These older members of churches can give a vision and a hope to those who follow them that life has meaning and purpose (Koenig *et al.*, 1997, pp.3–4). This 'Zest for later years is . . . upheld by an indomitable faith' (Dobbins, 1977, pp.9–10); the fullness and deepening of earlier stages of growth, with confidence and hope in God (Rainbow, 1991, pp.195–204). 'The underlying testimony of our religious traditions [is] that aging . . . can be a time for the positive actualization of the human spirit' (Le Fevre and Le Fevre, 1981, p.1).

Janet, a Roman Catholic lay worker, told me, 'Their example is huge to the young people. If they have lived fulfilled and faithful lives it shows the young people what life is all about.' Even when an older person stops specific activities, their continuing more passive enthusiasm can show the fulfilment of old age. Barbara (69), a Church of England member, put it like this:

> 'I've done it! I've run the guides, been on the PCC, been the co-ordinator for social events. Now I can be sociable and support things and events. But I don't want to run it.'

It does seem, from all this, that older churchgoers can give major encouragement to younger generations that life gets better with age. Otherwise, where is the Christian hope? The poet W. B. Yeats put it well:

> An aged man is but a paltry thing,
> A tattered coat upon a stick, unless
> Soul clap its hands and sing, louder sing
> For every tatter in its mortal dress.
>
> (Yeats, 1956)

There is one final way (in more senses than one) in which older people can help the fellowship of the church.

Helping a good approach to death

The actor Kirk Douglas had a stroke in 1996, when 80. A year later, he was interviewed for the *Sunday Times*. He said this:

> Most people are resistant to thinking about God and especially death. They behave as if it's the one thing that will never happen, when it's the only thing that's guaranteed. Everyone should think about death. It makes life more precious. (Goldman, 1997, p.82)

It is possible that only an older person with religious beliefs could say this. Mark Twain encouraged us to 'So live that, when we come to die, even the undertaker will be sorry.' Henri Nouwen has written that 'Aging is to befriend your death' (Nouwen, 1995, pp.1–8). With Walter Gaffney, he wrote that 'Aging is not only a way to darkness but a way to life' (Nouwen and Gaffney, 1976, p.17).

I talked with 62-year-old Graham, a young-old churchgoer. While not speaking specifically about death, there was an implication within what he shared with me. How could he help? He replied:

> 'I'm disabled. But when I'm in hospital I speak to people to help them. I go round the hospital to help: I talk to people in trouble. I help friends and colleagues when they want to talk about God.'

My experience has been that the quiet peace and confidence with which older Christian people approach their own and their loved ones' illnesses and deaths is a tremendous comfort and encouragement. I am convinced that older churchgoers today have much to give the rest of their fellowships in helping them, not just to age well, but to face death well, too.

I now turn to a final area of service which is possible for older people to give to the church or, rather, in this case, to give *from* the church.

Into the community

There is sometimes a dilemma within churches as to whether their members should give all their time to church matters, or if they should be involved in a wider work beyond the church walls, as it were. Older people can give a lead here, to show that a 'both/and' scenario is possible. I have tried to show how a great deal can be done by older people within a church. There are at least two areas outside the church where they can be of real service.

The community as an area of service

The United Nations has drawn up a set of Principles for Older Persons. Under a sub-heading charmingly entitled 'To add life to the years that have been added to life,' one of the principles says this:

> 8. Older persons should be able to seek and develop opportunities for service to the community and to serve as volunteers in positions appropriate to their interests and capabilities. (United Nations, 1991)

Government figures show that 80 per cent of people in the 65 to 74 age group volunteer to help in some way in the United Kingdom (*Social Trends 24,* 1994, p.141). For older churchgoers, this can be seen as an opportunity to represent the church in the community (Gray and Moberg, 1962, Chap. 9). An Anglican vicar in a country parish told me about the older members of his congregation:

> 'A lot do community things in the village. The church has to have a strong vision in the community: the elderly do this and run the Over-Sixties Club and so on. An elderly couple from the church make tea at the Monday bingo. Support and visits to the elderly are done by the elderly from the church.'

I felt, as he told me, the sense of everyone benefiting: the vicar, his load being shared; the rest of the church, aware that they had a positive presence in the community; the village, knowing there were those who cared in spiritual as well as practical ways; and the older people who did these acts of kindness, knowing that they were doing something of real value. One hears of adverse criticisms of the church: when older Christians use their talents to help their peers it gives a counterbalance (Koenig *et al.*, 1997). This can also be seen in the way older people from different churches work together in these projects. A Methodist minister said that his older people not only 'Help in the local community' but also 'Have ecumenical involvement'. On an estate suffering from social deprivation, a vicar spoke of her older people trying to bring old and young together to create social awareness and to break down fear. I gained the impression that they may be the very best people to do this brave but vital work.

Some are doing this, however old they are. Doris is a 90-year-old Methodist, who told me, 'I help to visit people on the sick list.' Others are not, as Vic (70) admitted: 'I could do sick visiting – I should give more that I do for myself.' My interviewees overall gave positive indications that older church members are playing a real part in their surrounding communities. Frank (65), a Roman Catholic attender, spoke of what he does:

> 'I am a minister of the Blessed Sacrament. I do a lot of voluntary work visiting schools [he is a former head teacher]. Since 1962 I have done bazaars and fetes: I think I need a rest this year! I do work at Christmas.'

A Methodist minister enthused about what his older people did, speaking of their

> 'Caring for one another: this extends outside the church walls. The fellowship is growing because new people are coming in. They help in the local community and have ecumenical involvement.'

Frances, a lay worker in a Roman Catholic church, told me of the older people in her county parish:

> 'They have time, patience, experience and they have grown up with the notion of being neighbours. They enjoy talking about nothing over a cup of tea – having a grumble and a laugh – which is wholesome.'

Many older people from churches are working within the community. Perhaps it is modesty which prevented their speaking of this. I sometimes wonder whether churches more easily praise work done within their ambit, not always giving credit for work done in a wider society. It certainly is an area where much can be done by older people.

The community as an area of mission

A number of older people told me of their quiet commitment to the mission of the church in spreading its Good News. Speaking to older people in 1984, Pope John Paul II told them, 'You still have a mission to fulfil and a contribution to make' (Pope John Paul II, 1984, p.74). Terry (65), from a New Church, agreed with this: 'I go on Mission and do evangelism and do work wherever the church leaders say.' David, from a city Church of England church said, 'I would love to do activities to encourage people to come closer to Jesus. If that means sweeping the floor, that's fine.' However, he added (from past work experience, I know), 'I don't want to be part of the committees!' Both men said these things with no sense of being pressurized into having to go out, but with a great willingness to be involved. 'Senior adults in missions are natural combinations' (James, 1996, pp.66–76), which seems to be true. Harris speaks of the particular difficulties retired ministers have in knowing what to do. 'Yet every retired minister is still a member of the Body of Christ and has distinctive gifts which the whole church needs for its missionary task. All too often they are unused' (Harris, 1998a, p.2). It may be that this is true of many very able older people.

Old age does give an opportunity for sensitive evangelism (Beasley-Murray, 1995, p.182). Within the Church of England, the Church Army is trying to use those aged between 55 and 70 in this way, 'Remaining as they do a largely unused resource in the local church' (McFadyen, 1997, pp.11–12). A leading Methodist minister spoke of the 'Bigger networks of relationships,' which his older people have, 'Which is very valuable for pastoral care and evangelism.' A Church of England Bishop said that older people have a 'Mission to their friends and by their life'. Even those who were in the 'old-old' category told me how happy they would be to do this.

That age group also said that at least they could invite their friends in. Jean, in her late 70's, when asked what she could do, laughed as she said, 'Helping and encouraging Doris who doesn't come!' Doris was sitting listening at the time! Mary (90) gave a similar answer: 'I could ask others to come, as the church people invited me.' Steve (20) related how 'One old lady goes round the roads and asks at houses for children to come to the Sunday school.' Rachel (25), a younger Methodist, when asked what their older people could do, told me what they were already doing: 'They do bring their friends to the Women's Fellowship and to Alpha. They are keen to do outreach. They have ideas to get their friends and neighbours along: they want tea dances!'

Here then, is another great area for older people to be actively involved, by lovingly and caringly being committed to the community in which they live, by deed, life and word.

Words into actions

This has been a chapter which has raised a number of questions for me. As I conclude it, I would wish to draw attention to several in particular.

The first is, what can older people do for the church? A leader within the Free Churches gave a one sentence answer to me: 'There is nothing they cannot do'. Kofi Annan, UN Secretary General, in his 1998 World Day of Older Persons message, said: 'A society for all ages is a society which, far from caricaturing older people as retired and infirm, considers them on the contrary as agents and beneficiaries of development' (Pontificium Consilium pro Laicis, 1999, p.12). I have tried to show that within the life of the church, its services and its people, and into the wider community, there need be no limit to opportunities.

Secondly, do older people realize this? The vast majority of quotations in this chapter are from textbooks and church leaders. My older interviewees were, on the whole, very reticent in speaking of what they could do for the church. Their ambitions were almost all lower for themselves than those their leaders had for them. I am left with overriding questions: do older people realize how important they are, how valued they are, and how much they have to give? It has been my concern throughout this book to let the people speak. Their very reticence in this area of what they can do causes me to voice my concern.

I therefore raise these further questions. Do the words of the experts and leaders need to be turned into actions? Have some leaders grown up with the notion (enforced perhaps by their training) that they have to do almost everything? Are they not particularly good at networking and delegating? Are they willing, in reality, to let lay people get on with aspects of work and ministry off their own bat? People increasingly have great and varied skills: are they allowed and encouraged to use them? Would it not be possible to use the skills of those who have been managers, or teachers, or carers, for example, in the life of the church? Is the church aware that those in the 55 to 65 age group especially are looking for something to do, and are well qualified to help?

It is a fact that there have never been so many fit and able older people. My research would suggest that huge, untapped resources are there, available to the church. With numbers of clergy and ministers in almost every denomination falling year on year, it would seem that a solution to 'Who can do the work?' is ready at hand. Where is the answer to all these questions? Let 87-year-old Phoebe have the last word here: 'I would do anything I was asked – I don't mind what I do.'

10

The Caring Church

'8 p.m. Special Youth Service. Be there or be square.' So runs many a poster on a church notice board. It begs the question: What about, '4 p.m. Special Older People's Service. Be square and be there'? It is quite understandable that churches should place an emphasis on attracting new generations. The responses examined in the last chapter indicated that many interviewees believe that older people also need their own niche and must not be excluded by virtue of other emphases. If there are 'Youth Retreats' and 'Youth Camps', should there not also be 'Age Retreats' and 'Older people's Camps' (though not necessarily of the tented kind)?

This chapter aims to give positive suggestions as to what the church can do for older people, be they current church attenders or not, as derived from responses received from leaders and lay people. My concern is to suggest specific future openings by synthesizing the expressed aspirations of different categories of interviewees, especially those who have not themselves been in dialogue. Partly this is 'market driven', in that I emphasize what older people themselves have told me they want from the church. I have also gone somewhat beyond that by researching in some detail what others believe is possible, both in further interviews with church leaders and members and by considering appropriate writings on the subject. The two sets of responses have then been synthesized.

As I will seek to show, the church needs to see itself as a community which will care, listen, explain its changes and respect the feelings of older people. It needs to provide good activities, visit on a regular basis, give vital spiritual help and be the sort of environment where, in the eyes of the interviewees examined, older people feel comfortable. These issues will each be explored in some depth. But I begin with the views of older people and some general observations.

What older people want

All the questions asked of older people in my interviews (see Appendix 1) led up to 'What can the church do for you?' As might be expected, Figure 10.1 shows considerable differences between those who attend church and those who do not.

It is important to keep the chart in Figure 10.1 in mind throughout subsequent pages: is the church meeting these needs? In reviewing each of these, two or three are immediately significant. For both churchgoers and non attenders, visiting them in their homes was a high priority. Practical help and transport are needed. A welcome and friendship would be appreciated.

Those who want no help

The considerable number (38 per cent of those who do not attend) who say that nothing can be done, should lead the church to be under no illusion that many of them would return, nor should it leave the church complacent about its

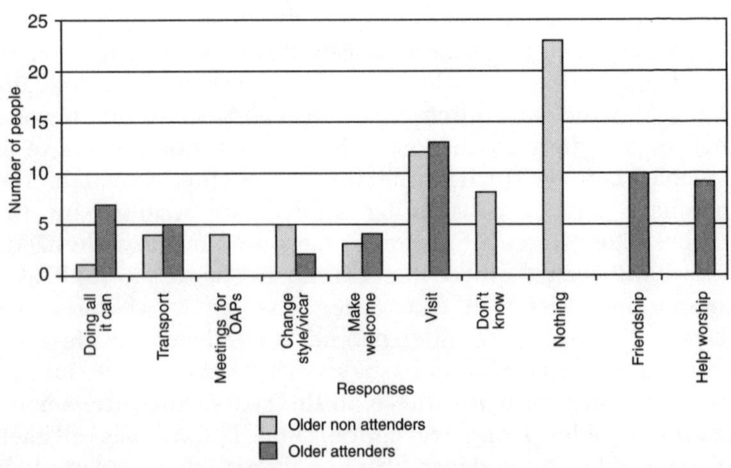

Figure 10.1 What can the church do? The views of all older church attenders and non attenders

need to reach those who are younger: it may be too late when people are older, although Chapter 8 indicates that there are those who would value contact and invitations.

I am about to look at all the areas where the church can care and share, but it is appropriate to deal first of all with this group who feel the church cannot help them. The problem lies in their diversity. I have examined and re-examined all the responses given in interviews, and no real pattern emerges as to why they do not want any church involvement in their lives.

The majority of non attenders had no outstanding social characteristics in common. 'There's nothing now for me,' I was told by 74-year-old Lorna, whom I interviewed with her husband. Was it significant that she was married, and thus did not need the church's help? It did not seem so, and she indicated her willingness to help if the church were 'doing anything'. By contrast, and yet in agreement, 70-year-old Pam said the church could do 'nothing' for her – yet she is a widow. In a similar vein both married and widowed men gave responses which agreed with each other (though seen separately).

If marital status and gender made no difference, neither did their circumstances. Some were surrounded by family, others were not. Ray (69), when asked if the church could do anything for him, told me, 'No. I'm independent and life is good to me. I'm happy with my situation.' On the other hand there was Maria (66). Her reply to the same question was: 'The church could do nothing,' and then added, 'I'm very alone.' Roy (64) told me the reason the church could do nothing for him was that he was 'Reserved, lonely and shy'. These answers were echoed by others. The church could do nothing for the active or passive, the fulfilled or lonely.

Was there a reason for all this? Again, the answers were so diverse as to lead me to the conclusion that there were always reasons, but not one which stood out for large numbers. Jack (76), the husband of Lorna (above), did not want the church's help because he did not like the vicar. Daniel (79) felt the church could do nothing for him because he had lost his faith: 'If you lose your faith then you believe it is a con,' he said. In reviewing the answers from all my interviewees, 74-year-old Josephine put things succinctly:

> 'The interest has to come from the person. It has to come from you. The church can't do anything unless you want it to.'

I felt that this reply summed up the answers given by many of those who did not want help from the church. They each had their individual reasons, personal to themselves. There was no overall pattern, nor situations which recurred frequently. But there was this 38 per cent who did not want the church's help.

I turn now to the other 62 per cent of non attenders, and the 100 per cent of church attenders, who would value help, looking firstly at the views of writers and those who are giving help.

Sociological writers

Considerable thought has been given already by sociologists (and others) as to how the church can help older people. Where they deal with specifics, they are included under the appropriate sections which follow. A number have given overviews. I will seek to follow their ideas where relevant, but it may be helpful to set out some observations here.

One of the earliest to study the relationship between the church and older people was Robert Gray, whose Ph.D. research culminated in an unpublished thesis in 1953, parts of which were later synthesized into 'A Study of the Personal Adjustment of the Older Person in the Church' (in Gray and Moberg, 1962, pp.68–95). He suggested that the church helps older people to adjust to circumstances by alleviating anxiety concerning death; providing companionship; providing opportunities to participate; helping adjust to the death of one's spouse; giving support in dark days and crisis; coming to the individual in need; and satisfying basic socio-psychological needs.

I find the order of these interesting, and wonder if some, at least, are what the church should be doing for everyone and why the church implicitly does not do these for its older people. With his co-writer David Moberg, Robert Gray, in their 1962 book, in Chapter 8, 'What the church can do for older people', looks at ten areas: my comments, where appropriate, are in brackets:

1. Help meet their spiritual needs. (This should be obvious, but is importantly made a specific first need.)
2. 'Educate'. (Gray and Moberg use this to mean the education of the rest of the congregation to show up what could be construed as inappropriate attitudes.)
3. Help develop individual personalities. (It is often forgotten that older people can still develop and move forward.)
4. Help meet physical and material needs.
5. Help meet social and recreational needs.
6. Help older people solve their personal problems. (This repetition of the word 'Help' gives it the emphasis which my interviewees sought.)
7. The church should adapt its physical facilities to the needs and problems of older people.
8. Co-operate in research studies. (This would seem vital, but seems rarely, if ever, done between churches.)
9. Use its influence in civic and political affairs. (Has the church in Britain responded to this?)
10. Study its community. (Of key importance: I did not find evidence of many churches doing this.)

Moberg himself, ten years later (Moberg, 1972, pp.47–60), was still urging action, but in more practical ways: senior citizens' clubs, meals-on-wheels, telephone reassurance, counselling and referral services and friendly visiting. I will look at these in detail later. Gray and Moberg's seminal works wait until 1980 to be joined by others. Kerr's *How to Minister to Senior Adults in Your Church* (Kerr, 1980, pp.85–9) shows the need to balance activities and content, with spiritual enrichment and special services going alongside learning opportunities, socialization and opportunities for service. Tobin *et al.* (1986, p.32) identify four broad roles for churches and synagogues: providing religious programmes; serving as a host; providing pastoral care programmes and providing social services.

Through all these, a pattern emerges: the need for both spiritual and practical help, the one balanced by the other. Carlson and Seicol (1990, pp.65–6) put it thus: 'Congregations need to examine their programs and policies to determine how elder-friendly they are.' Bruce Rumbold said, from an Australian viewpoint, 'While some specific concerns of ageing people differ from those at other stages of life, the fundamental issues are the same: to belong, to find meaning in life, to participate and contribute, to grow in grace and hope' (Rumbold, 1993, pp.20–25).

Gaynor Hammond has done some recent research in the North of England and states that certain things are vital for the spiritual well-being of older people: to have a sense of identity, as unique people; to feel valued, having self-worth; to be able to offer skills, life experience and wisdom; to be part of the community, not just as a burden. This final view (Hammond, n.d., p.2) leads me to an even wider perspective.

Authoritative statements

Two key official organizations have, recently, published statements giving their views on the rights of older people. It is not inappropriate that the church should have these keenly in mind when looking at its own approach.

In the 1999 'Year of Older People', the United Nations set out five Principles for Older Persons, which deserve to be repeated in full here:

> *Independence*, including being able to reside at home as long as possible.
> *Participation*, including opportunities for older persons to share their knowledge and skills with younger generations.
> *Care*, including benefiting from family and community care and protection in accordance with each society's system of cultural values.
> *Self-fulfilment*, including access to the educational, cultural, spiritual and recreational resources of society.
> *Dignity*, including being treated fairly regardless of age, gender, racial or ethnic background, disability or other status.
> (United Nations, 1999)

Of course, these principles are for governments and society generally: but surely the church can have no lower standards. These principles have been endorsed and expanded by the 1999 Royal Commission on Long Term Care (Sutherland, 1999, 1.18). The whole Report needs to be read by those who have any concern for older people. It speaks of older people as

'A valuable part of society'; old age being 'A natural part of life and not a burden'; as 'An opportunity'; and that 'To compartmentalize old age and to describe old people as a problem is intolerable – morally and practically'. The Report is primarily about long-term care, but these observations are key to all the thoughts which follow.

What is happening

I want to look briefly at three areas of current work which either influence, give advice to churches, or provide support.

Charities and organizations

There is no sense in the church trying to reinvent the wheel, as it were. Britain is blessed with several excellent organizations which are already working with older people. These organizations would appear to be more than happy to help churches in their work among older people, but I have not found very much co-operation by churches, and a working partnership would seem mutually beneficial.

It is invidious to suggest that one particular organization is doing more than another, but Help the Aged and Age Concern each have a high profile and are working hard to encourage and support older people. The former encourages every church to have a 'church friend' (a volunteer from the church who keeps in touch with Help the Aged) with whom it will liaise. The latter's report *Claim to be Heard* (Age Concern, 1980) speaks of churches and church members giving 'imaginative friendship', help from a Transport Officer, speaking up for the elderly and helping with bureaucracy, hospitals, death and bereavement. Writing for Age Concern, Donald Bell gives practical ideas such as making it easier to join in worship; including the elderly in as many church activities as possible; adopting lonely people, and for churches to work with the local authorities' Social Services, as well as with Age Concern. He suggests that a local home for elderly people could be adopted by a church and that the mentally confused should also be helped (Bell, 1980).

All sorts of help are at hand. Nationally and locally there are provisions from Social Services and health care. Some churches may turn to specifically Christian organizations such as Outlook, Faith in Elderly People (Leeds), the Christian Council on Ageing (Derby) and Methodist Homes for the Aged. I am of the opinion, based on my interviewing research, that some of these are unknown to many churches or, even if they are known, are little used. Add to these Counsel and Care, Research into Ageing and the Association of Retired Persons, to name only a few, and churches can find much support for their work with older people. In the area of care, there are (*inter alia*) the Alzheimer's Disease Society, The Association for Pastoral Care in Mental Health and the Carers' National Association.

I mention these *en passant*, not as an attempt to give the whole picture, but to indicate the breadth of work already happening. Friends of the Elderly, in their 1998 *Annual Review*, speak for themselves, but their words would find an echo in many of those organizations mentioned:

> Friends of the Elderly is committed to enhancing the independence and quality of life in older people, both in their homes and on their own, through the provision of a continuum of care in a local setting. This can include (inter alia) befriending, respite care and volunteer support.
>
> (Friends of the Elderly, 1998, p.1)

International work

It may be helpful for local churches to consider the world scene when seeking what can be done to help older people. I cite only one of many examples: research done for the *Journal of Applied Gerontology*, where a survey covered 1000 churches in an American state to discover how many visited older people, and why. The findings included some very encouraging statistics: 80 per cent of the 1000 churches visited the housebound and nursing homes and 70 per cent those in hospital, 44 per cent provided transport, 37 per cent gave telephone reassurance, 32 per cent had social and recreational facilities, 25 per cent education and discussion groups, while 16 per cent delivered meals to homes (Sheeham *et al.*, 1988, pp.231–41). Here may be ideas for churches nearer home and an area for further research.

Some work and research is already going on internationally. Again, to mention but one, Opera Pia International works as a religious, non-governmental organization at the United Nations. Working with the UN, it is looking for religions, governments and non-governmental organizations to work together in 'a co-ordinated effort to develop new approaches and programs for and with aging persons'. It seeks to care not only for the physical and mental necessities in older age, but the psychological and spiritual needs too, to find 'the often latent riches and resources of their age' (Hore DiFilippo, 1982). Are the churches attended by interviewees seeking to realize such aims? I will try to give an answer shortly.

The National Situation

I will also consider what individual churches are doing. Again, to prevent the reinvented wheel, denominations may benefit from what others have done and are doing at a national level. The Presbyterian Church of Ireland has an Advisory Forum on Human Rights, which has produced a Senior Citizens Policy Document, showing the need for its church to speak to Government, not to duplicate existing services and help, but to get involved and share when it can (Lampden, 1989). Such an ongoing organization within a denomination may be able to help. Reports have a practical impact. The Church of England has seen its own Reports on older people largely shelved: *Ageing*, *Happy Birthday Anyway* and *Something to Celebrate* (Report of the Social Policy Committee of the Board for Social Responsibility, 1990; Board for Social Responsibility, 1990; Report of a Working Party of the Board for Social Responsibility, 1995). However, they are all worthy of dusting down and reconsidering in detail by all denominations.

The Free Churches have also done some serious work on how the church can and does help older people. Methodist Homes for the Aged have given a remarkable lead in the provision of residential facilities for older people and produced guidelines, through the Christian Council on Ageing, on many aspects of ageing (Christian Council on Ageing, 1998). The Baptist Union surveyed its churches in 1992 to see how much work was being done with the elderly. They found that 14 per cent ran luncheon clubs, 11 per cent provided transport and 15 per cent had specific meetings (Jackson, 1998, p.3). The United

Reformed Church has produced a Report, *Respecting the Gift of Years*, aiming to lead that denomination to a strategy on ageing (Appleton, 1998). It is interesting to note that they intend to co-operate with both Help the Aged and Age Concern, as well as formulating their own plans.

Thus some work is being done from which individual churches can draw. But I now turn to substantive suggestions as to how the church can relate well to older people. I begin with the church community.

Building a community

By far the greatest number of people who defined the word 'church' in Chapter 4 spoke of it as the people who constitute its members. How can churches provide a community for older people?

The caring family

As people get older, family life for many starts to disintegrate through bereavement, separation, children moving away and an inability to travel too far, or too often. When the local church provides what could be seen as a substitute or alternative family, it meets not only a spiritual but a social need. This can be seen in several ways.

Friendship

'We suggest that there is much scope for more imaginative friendship within the bounds of many congregations and that attention to this simple point would bring an increase in the well-being of many old people and enrichment to younger members' (Lampen, 1989, p.25). It is sad that the Irish Presbyterian Church has to state the obvious, but they are admitting shortcomings at this basic level. New Church lay leaders told me about the older people they help: 'The greatest need is befriending,' they said. This view is borne out in a survey carried out in three areas in south Coventry by a local New Church. Among their findings were two of significance here. In answer to, 'What do you feel is the greatest need in this community?', 25 per cent answered 'Community spirit' – the highest of any response. The question, 'If you were looking for a church to attend, what kind of things would be important to you?' was answered, 'Offer friendship' by 33 per cent (13 per cent higher than the second answer), 'Warm, welcoming', followed by 'Sincere', 'Good atmosphere' and 'Sense of community' (Jamieson, 1998, p.9).

People in this church's neighbourhood want the church to befriend them, says the Report. 'Whether we are solitary or gregarious, introvert or extrovert, we depend on networks of other people in order to maintain our basic humanity' (Grainger, 1993, p.7). Beckford put it thus:

> Considerable importance is attributed nowadays to the role of informal networks of social relationships in religious organisations of all kinds. Beginning with Gerlach and Hine's (1970) investigation of the reticulate character of Pentecostal groups, a large number of studies has confirmed the point that social networks are essential to the life of religious groups.... This has been found to be true not only for marginal movements but also for mainstream Christian churches. (Beckford, 1985, pp.125–38)

My findings would agree with this, where such networks respect older people for who they are (Howse, 1999, p.107) and where the approach is, as Becky (14) told me, 'Being friendly and considerate'. A New Church minister said that the way the church could help older people was by 'Being friendly, talking to them, giving them value and hearing what they have to say. We are fighting the breakdown of our Society which segregates out old folk. The church is in danger of doing the same. The church is about community.'

Twenty per cent of older church attenders told me that 'friendship' was what they wanted and/or being valued in the life of their particular churches. Their answers were summed up by 83-year-old Harold.

> 'What can the church do?' I asked him.
> 'Be friendly, help people,' he replied.
> 'What is good about your church?'
> 'Our church is a friendly body of people and it's a nice

> comfortable church. My wife and I came to [another village] in 1982 and we said, 'There's something lacking.' There was no choir, it was dark and remote. We came over to [this village church] which was bright and cosy. We got to know the people who were so welcoming.'

I encouraged him to pursue this theme, as a result of which he added:

> 'Most of us have our problems and depressive moments and I get support from these people. I can talk and they listen. I can share my problems and they are willing to listen to me.'
> 'So, what do you enjoy?'
> 'Friendliness. I like to see what goes on.'

As can be seen, this was Harold's constant theme: he wanted friendship, and had finally found it in this particular village Church of England church. Dorothy was another who said that what was good about her Anglican church was the 'friendliness'. Phoebe, 87 years of age, said she felt 'at home' in her church, with people being 'approachable'. Although she had some reservations about her church, including not being 'fond of the vicar', the overall friendliness underlay this answer:

Question: 'What can the church do for you?'
Answer: 'No more than it's doing. I think it's wonderful.'

To summarize this sub-section, both church leaders, members and older attenders see the relationship between members, especially older members, as being of key importance. Friendship, as Harold showed, can be lacking, and thus missed. Where a friendly atmosphere exists, it is greatly appreciated by older church members. It was, as Figure 10.1 shows, second only to visiting in order of priorities for older attenders.

Love and care

'TLC' (Tender Loving Care) is something one's mother was supposed to dispense. For older people, who dispenses it now? The Coventry Community Plan is an example of efforts being made by local government to give a lead. Of six stated priorities, one is entirely devoted 'To meet the needs and aspirations of

Older People' (Fletcher, 1998, p.9). The Diocese of Rochester in South East England has provided a church leadership initiative by appointing its own 'Older Person's Officer': reference will be made to this later (Hooker, 1998, p.5).

The Brethren in Christ (an American denomination) say that younger people especially should show a real care to their elders because so much has been done for them by the elderly and that so much can be learnt by such caring. They also point out that a reciprocal arrangement will work as the younger ones age and they are helped by the next generations in turn – an interestingly selfish sociological premise (Brensinger, 1996, pp.461–73)! A more positive hope was expressed by a younger church member when Jez (26) told me: 'I want to bridge the gap: we can make it together.'

Certainly some church leaders seek to show this latter approach. One country vicar told me that his aim with older people was 'To love them to bits: if you pour love in, you get love out.' His Archbishop agrees. 'We shall remember that we human beings are interdependent, not independent of each other,' said Archbishop George Carey. He went on to speak of meeting the particular needs of the poor, weak and afflicted, as he addressed the needs of older people in the twenty-first century (Carey, 1997, p.9). The Irish Presbyterian Church says how 'The elderly are to be respected and honoured and are to be cared for by the Church family' (Patterson, n.d.). This responsibility is a basic tenet of the Christian faith (Apichella, 1989). It does not matter whether the reason for giving this love and care is from the somewhat selfish notion that it may lead to others caring for oneself in one's own later life, or the more altruistic motive of love for love's sake (Regan and Smith, 1997, pp.10–11). Nor is there unanimous agreement on this, even in helping one's own parents. Gill uses the British Household Panel Survey to show that, even among churchgoers, a considerable percentage do not feel they have a duty of care in this way (Gill, 1999).

I asked Freda, who told me she was 'over 76', what was good about her church. Her reply is significant.

> 'Comfort, support: there is love and Christianity there.'

I found it interesting that she put 'Christianity' last of the four. She was not alone in this, as others also implied the presence of the Christian faith, but emphasized the value they placed in the love and care they found in their particular church.

Again, then, there is agreement between leaders and older attenders: the love and concern which a church can provide is much appreciated by older members.

Value

The Rev. Jackie Treetops has carried out some excellent research into the church's ministry with older people. In her book *A Daisy among the Dandelions* (Treetops, 1992, p.3), she relates a meeting with 'one old gentleman' who told her, 'I'm on the rubbish heap!' He had been an army major, and a churchwarden for many years, 'But nobody cares, nobody comes. I might as well be dead.'

How does the church react to this salutary story? Gaunt says that the church ought to be able to emphasize the uniqueness of every person (Gaunt, 1998, p.1). It need not be difficult. A Roman Catholic priest said, 'We could give a presentation which would be of value to them [older people] and show them how valuable they are.' It is simply the problem of making this happen: the good feelings are there, but may not be being expressed. Pam (23) said of older people, 'They matter because they are people, not because they are old.' What is needed is a positive affirmation in a community which celebrates wholeness (National Interfaith Coalition on Aging, 1975), valuing the contribution of older people: that is what church leaders told me.

What of the older people and their views? They agreed that, in the role of the church providing a caring family, there was a need to make older people feel they belonged, and had value.

> 'What can the church do for you?' I asked 65-year-old Frank. 'The church should give me the opportunity to feel needed – active not passive.'

I encouraged him to go on with this thought, and he gave a poignant follow-up:

> 'Loneliness is hardest when no one wants you.'

In similar vein, Pam (60), replied to the same question this way:

> 'I want the church to make me feel that I belong and

challenge me. There has to be a way of making everyone feel valued.'

Pam had complained to me that her church had now over-emphasized the place of young people, and her position in the church had not only become insignificant, but untenable. The significance of Frank and Pam's answers is that Frank still attended regularly, whereas Pam does not now go. Yet there is a common *cri de coeur.* Terry, 65 years of age, speaking of the relationship between the church and older people felt that the latter 'Are neglected a bit'.

This is a real challenge to the local church (Grainger, 1993, p.9). Perhaps that is why the Diocese of Rochester's 'Older Person's Officer' (above) cites 'To encourage the Church to value older people' as her first priority (Hooker, 1998, p.5). Whilst older people spoke openly about this need of being valued, only one leader (the Roman Catholic priest (above)) mentioned this as a problem, or a priority. There would seem to be a need for dialogue here.

Pastoral care

A particular way in which this 'valuing' can be expressed is by providing good pastoral care for older people. Beginning with the major transition which retirement brings, sensitive pastoring will be of continuing value (Butler, 1998, 6.7). The whole church can share in this particular way of affirming God's presence through older age (Lyon, 1985, p.118). This is particularly essential for those older church members who have little or no contact at present with their ministers or congregations (Harris, 1998a, p.3). Care being required in this way should induce a sense of urgency on the church's part, as well as the need to bring a loving, understanding approach (Jordan, 1996, pp.43–54).

However, churches are well placed to give pastoral care, helping people to age well and seeing them through the difficulties of growing older (Haswell and King, 1997, p.9). Some churches do work hard on this. A Baptist minister put it this way: 'The pastoral care is something which older people receive more because they are quite ill and therefore they receive a priority.' I regret not asking him if the able-bodied were given the same attention! One such (Dennis, 81) told me, 'We need pastoral care because it is greatly missed.' If churches and their older people are to relate well, both the Baptist minister and Dennis must find a meeting point.

This leads to the second requirement of the church as a community. As well as providing a caring family, there needs to be 'a listening ear'.

A listening ear

'They forget what it was like to be young,' Natalie (16) complained and continued, 'We do nothing for them.' But older people told me that they do not forget and do want to talk about it! These older people have a *Claim to be Heard,* as Age Concern (1991) called a publication. 'We don't want to be the forgotten lot,' pleaded Lily (89). Little is written about this deep-seated need (Tinker, 1997, p.27). I found in my interviewees that it is a need. Dennis, in his 70's, told me:

> 'It's nice to talk with your contemporaries about when you were children. The church needs to provide a community for this – that may get more old people in [he himself does not attend church]. Old people need to be educated as to what the church could do. They should advertise to local people about joyous occasions when they can talk.'

Is the church doing this? A Black Church minister said, 'I find some people who are backwards looking and I realize that I need to listen to their views and be a more caring pastor.' As an old lady said to Mary Morrison (1998, p.107), 'Do not deprive me of my old age, I have earned it.' Certainly some of the younger church members I met felt listening and talking was a part they could play with older people. Ruth (44) said that 'They enjoy talking with me. I am happy to spend time with them.' Several in their teens and 20's agreed, one saying that 'The old chat better'; another, 'They are nice to talk to'. This bridging of the generations is of such value to both. For the older ones, it allows them to share their life-story and, for the young, it is a discovery of history. On a personal note, I recall my grandmother (born 1887, died 1989), telling me of her great-grandfather telling *her* of the

Nation's rejoicing at the victory of the Battle of Waterloo in 1815: now that *is* history!

More than that, it is not the history of textbooks, it is the history of the family, of the church, of the hidden social nuances which make up the real story of life, spanning many years – maybe a century or more (Hammond, n.d, p.2). It gives the next generations the chance to hear what Rhena Taylor (1996a, p.3) calls 'Their faith-story' – how the Christian faith can last from Sunday school to old age. This sense of dignity in sharing a valued life (Wilcock, 1999, p.75) is seen by some to be *the* major need of older people: Bray sees 'Presence' and 'Listening' as the first two requirements of the elderly (the third being 'Corporate Worship') (Bray, 1991, pp.16–17).

Would it not be appropriate for churches to establish specific groups (even if ad hoc) to enable this 'listening ear' to open? Who knows what might result as joys and sorrows are shared – even the problems of faith in later life (Coleman *et al.*, 1990, pp.10–14), in all-age groups where ideas and activities are shared (Gaunt, 1998, p.1)? Of course, such a group could be for the older ones alone, as we shall see later. As Barbara (69) told me:

> 'We need a group system of people of our own thoughts and age to share our thoughts and problems. I don't want it to be like a homegroup where the problems are about children. We need a group to pray for aches and pains and loneliness.'

It all comes down to a willingness to hear. In the community of the church, both leaders and lay people told me that there must be 'a concern to explain'.

A concern to explain

Listening is one thing: explaining is another which I was told is often left undone. As this book has earlier sought to show, major changes have taken place, and continue, in the lifetimes of older people in the church (and those who do not now go). 'We need to reassure them about the changes and the role they can play,' a Roman Catholic priest told me. It is costly to let go of 'inappropriate structures ... to develop fresh contemporary and appropriate models of mission for today's setting' (Warren, 1995b, p.47). While this may be vital if the church is to survive

(Warren, 1995a, p.11), there are going to be both positive and negative reactions to changes especially in the liturgy (Hornsby-Smith, 1989, pp.95–114). Is sufficient time and effort given to do this, particularly for lifelong churchgoers, whose older age may make them wary of too great a change undertaken at too fast a pace?

Progress may best be made by including these older ones in the changes, even if it means inviting them 'To come and have a moan,' as one priest put it with a smile! The church should be able to offer a 'context for dialogue' (Harris, 1987, p.3). Do churches, especially their ministers, rush ahead regardless? The following is worthy of serious and positive consideration:

> Religious organisations can change too quickly for some older people and this needs to be born (sic) in mind by ministers. Religious organisations should consult older people as closely as other groups in their communities about the need of change, explain it well to them and involve them closely in educational initiatives .... Older people benefit greatly from feeling they have a role within their church. They are thereby assured of their place within a developing community and the danger is minimised that they are left behind in the process of change. In return, they are able to offer valuable witness of the church's continuity, its 'memory of faith', to younger members. (Coleman *et al.*, 1990, pp.10–14)

One Church of England vicar said that he has 'To authenticate what I have done and move them on gently. They respond to love and good humour and not being told what to do.' Another succeeds 'By including them in the forward thrust of the church.' However, this positive attitude was not always perceived by older people themselves. Older people told me they felt left out and left behind. One specific issue was in the area of the change from Latin to English in the language of the Roman Catholic Mass. Betty is a regular attender at Mass, but told me how she struggled with the Mass being in English, and said that 'There should be a Latin Mass for those who want it.' No-one seemed to have given her a good reason why this was not now available everywhere. Her husband Tony looked for another kind of help:

> 'The priest ought to explain the scripture readings because some of them are hard to understand,' he told me.

This couple, aged 65 and 70, attend church daily, but lack the help they need to understand changes and difficult doctrines. An older attender at a Church of England church in the city told me how her vicar had said that 'It was necessary to change services for the young,' but she still could not understand why. 'Why ruin something that has been stable over the years?' she asked me. No-one had properly explained this to her. Echoing comments in previous sections, she summed up her feelings in these words: 'The church could be more gracious and kinder to us.'

In a similar way Roger, another older member of the Church of England, was asked, 'What do you most dislike about your church?'

> '"Things ain't what they used to be",' he quoted in reply, and went on: "We try to pander to the lowest common denominator. People should be educated to understand what is going on. Some of the congregation are alienated." Then he added, "I realize I am extreme in my views!"'

But, from what others have said, he is not extreme. There does seem to be a plea from a number of older people, as I have sought to show, for 'people' to 'be educated'. In one city Anglican church, I was told by Pam (72) that 'Changes have been done quietly,' thus avoiding this need to explain all at once, explanations having been given along the way, as it were.

There does seem to be a degree of agreement between leaders and older people on this concern for explanations as to what is going on, especially where and how older people can fit in and cope with change. If this concern is expressed, it seems to have positive and productive consequences.

At other times the community of the church needs to give very specific help, as explained in the next section.

A comfort at times of death and bereavement

Society seems at last to be emerging from that era when death was a taboo subject for conversation. Older people have to face death in two ways: others, and their own. The church should have a significant place in helping with both.

Bereavement

Four initiatives, often interlinked, can be pursued by churches where a bereavement occurs. Of course this applies to people at all ages, but the elderly inevitably face more contemporary bereavements, and coming to terms with the subsequent adjustments may be more difficult.

First is love and friendship – one form of help which all can give. Older people 'Appreciate friendship, especially the bereaved and lonely,' was how Sue (in her 30's) put it. A city Church of England vicar said that 'There is comfort being among people, particularly if there is a bereavement.' Another told me that older people come back to church at these times. Secondly, it is my experience that an occasional church service specifically for bereaved people is much valued, especially by older people. I am often invited to speak at such, perhaps as a result of my writing the book *Bereaved* (Knox, 1994), and the sense of gratitude is deeply moving.

Thirdly, older bereaved people have expressed to me the worth of being visited. A Roman Catholic lay person said, 'The priest visits when he can, especially at bereavement: he is very good with funerals.' Two or three older people were strong in their complaints to me about ministers and churches which did not visit at these times. Jack (76) used to attend the Church of England. He told me this story:

> 'I knew two old ladies who lived a few houses apart in the same road. One died in her nineties, leaving the other in her eighties. The vicar didn't even go to see her, though both did a lot for the church. So she didn't go into the church again because she didn't like the rector.'

Whether it would have made any difference to Jack himself if the rector had visited, the rest of my time with him led me to doubt. But clearly he expressed a concern at a perceived lack of attention at a time of great loss. Another couple felt let down when their minister failed to visit when they suffered a bereavement. However, as they did not attend church, a degree of telepathy may have been needed by that minister to know he was needed.

Even if a church does work out a bereavement strategy, it may not get it right. Maureen (78), from a Roman Catholic Church, told me:

> 'They formed a Bereavement Society – it was so awful because the people who were in it could not be of much use because they hadn't come through bereavements themselves.'

Maureen may well have struggled with this because of her own experience. I asked her what the church could do for her. Her reply was this:

> 'Talk to me. When I lost my husband the parish priest came and I asked him to say a Mass. The priest said he couldn't say my husband's name in the prayers because my husband was not a Catholic. I thought that was very odd because God knows his name.'

There was also some positive feedback on this issue. Frank (65), another Roman Catholic, said that 'The community was very supportive in grief.' He went on, 'When my wife died three years ago the church played its part in every regard.'

Bearing in mind the comment of Maureen about the Bereavement Society the church had set up, it may be that here is a role the church's older people can fulfil. A Church of England vicar said how she needed 'The active elderly to do this. Some have done bereavement visiting – I need to make sure they can cope with doing this.' She added the caveat that 'They do not need to be too close to their own bereavement.' In other words, those who help should not be carrying grief from their own bereavement too closely, or they will not be able to give the objective help needed.

Whilst many can help with friendship and visiting, the final area is that of bereavement counselling, which needs at least some training. In a survey in the Leeds area, only a third of Urban Priority Area churches there offered bereavement counselling (Burns, 1991, 5.19). The Presbyterian Church of Ireland has acknowledged the need for more of its clergy, ministers and parishioners to be trained in this area (Lampen, 1989). My conversations with church leaders suggests this is needed in all denominations, though some are working at it. A Black Church minister said that he had just launched a bereavement ministry, especially applicable for the elderly. This whole area of bereavement would appear to need some more work and training to be done by churches, as it is both valued and needed.

Facing death

I felt it significant that no church leader or member spoke of helping older people to face their own death. Only one older person spoke of it: Edna said, 'We need reassurance that something is there and there is somewhere we are going as we get older and face death.' It would seem unusual that others did not make the point, as I will now seek to show from the writings of others.

Many writers speak of the importance of a church's willingness to give support and comfort as death approaches. In research in the 1970s, it was found that those with strong religious beliefs were rated lowest on death anxiety. Interestingly, those with confused religious beliefs were rated higher than agnostics or atheists (Kalish and Reynolds, 1976). How can a church help? Feeling inadequate should be no cause for paralysis; the founder of the modern hospice movement has said that 'The fact that you can't do everything doesn't mean you should stop doing something' (Saunders, 1999, p.19). Some dying people do come back to 'their religious and cultural observances', though there is no clear reason why they do (Neuberger, 1995, p.9).

The community of the church can help its older members to be prepared for death. It is wise to see that 'Preparedness is not just about making a will and setting one's house in order; it is about having found meaning in one's life as it comes to its end' (Siddell, 1995, pp.28–9). Is the church helping dying people to 'enter things eternal' (Metropolitan Anthony, n.d, p.11)? This will give hope, not just for the future, but could improve the quality of life now (Runyan, 1989, p.59–60). There can be a vital ministry as death itself approaches, perhaps with a special service with Communion and helpful prayers (Siddell, 1993, pp.151–79). Bible readings of the crucifixion and resurrection of Christ and the rites of confession and absolution may be appropriate (Peberdy, 1993, pp.219–23).

In the meanwhile, there can be time 'To pack your bags and say goodbye, and sorry, and thank you' (Saunders, 1999, p.19). The Church needs to ensure its fear of breaching an area rarely discussed does not prevent it from caring for its older members in this way.

Now to happier matters! Outside the community of the church are those who may well wish to share its life.

The desire to invite

Very many older people do not attend a church regularly. Yet, as my research reveals, virtually every older person associates themselves with a specific denomination. If there are unseen barriers, can these be removed? Irene (67) said that 'If the vicar could talk to me, it might get me back. I need the vicar to make the move.' I contrast that with a vicar who said, 'We don't know how to reach them. We know there is a need. There are those who give us dirty looks, but there are those who give us kind looks – they are longing to find the way.'

It may be a case of finding where they are: not just an address but in their hearts and minds. Is there a halfway house? One vicar answered her own problem when we talked about this. She said:

> 'I don't know how to get them back because of their prejudice or apathy. They won't cross the threshold – but a few meet in home meetings which can be home churches. They need stepping stones. One of our church wardens is nearly 80 and lives in the sheltered flats. She organizes a sitting room meeting for all those in the flats with the warden and organizes trips and so on. Between seven and eleven meet for Eucharist once a month – some have never been before – even to church. They may come to the church barn dance in the church on Shrove Tuesday and get to know each other.'

As churches go out to invite, they will meet people described here, who will come so far. There are those who care about the church: is the church aware of this? Tom (65) told me that he did not know what the church could do to get him back, but, 'I'm not against it. I'd do everything I could to make sure our 900-year-old church in my village stayed open.' One could conceive of several practical ways of making Tom feel part of the church community. If the barrier is spiritual, a visit from the minister could well be of benefit. No one put it better than Monsignor Tom Gavin, when he told me:

> 'The district nurses tell me who the Catholics are! Then I go and see them. I sweep in and pretend I've known them all my life. I go and say "we all make mistakes" as if they'd been in church last Sunday. They don't need to beat their breasts –

> they fear a "rollicking" so I don't give them one. I ask them if they've got anything special on their minds that they want to confess then I give them absolution and tell them to come back to church. I make it easy for them to return.'

If the converse is true and the church has been wrong (or seen to be, even if it was not), would an apology hurt that much? Clergy have admitted to me that their predecessors may have acted badly, frightening people away. They agreed that others left the church because of 'hypocrisy', or the church being 'wrong, unpleasant and stupid': these are words actually used by ministers. The Archbishop of Birmingham acknowledged, 'Somebody may have been offended by Father so-and-so, but that may have been forty years ago. It is time to forgive and forget and return to church.' One of his priests took this a stage further: 'We need to apologize for wrongs, especially if a priest got it wrong.' The old saying about a soft answer turning away wrath is apposite here.

As a further help, one church leader I met spoke of a return to faith programme in her church called 'Journey of Faith'. This, or an invitation to a special event, does draw older people back: that is what ministers have told me. The Bishop of Warwick spoke of 'pick-up points' from where people last were to get them back to something which is not totally unfamiliar.

There is one final area I wish to refer to in the life of the community of the church, without which all the above can seem manipulative at least, if not coercive.

The willingness to let go

'The interest has to come from the person,' Margaret told me, 'It has to come from you. The church can't do anything unless you want it to.' There must be a willingness to respect the word 'No', however much a church may wish to proselytize, or recover its lost flock. 'If they don't want to go back, we have to respect their privacy,' Bishop Pargiter told me as he spoke of 'A lot of lapsed Catholics.' One of the oldest people I met was 96-year-old Robbie. I asked her what the church could do for her. The church may not care for her answer, and feel saddened by it, but here is what she said:

> 'I don't feel they could do very much and I don't feel in great need. Perhaps I'm very wicked, but I don't. The church could do nothing to attract me. I have no need, not now. The church could not get me back. I am one of the wicked ones of this world – though I don't think I'm wicked. People are just as good who don't go as those who do go.'

Figure 10.1 at the beginning of this chapter showed a number of non attenders who bleakly said that nothing could be done for them by the church, or to get them back. 'We're past redemption now,' one older couple said. Roy (64) is 'Too shy to go. I don't expect the church to make an exception and come to me.' Matthew (72) will go 'Only when they cremate me.' 'If you lose your faith then you believe it is a con,' was Daniel's (79) comment. 'I'm too far gone,' said Mr F (70). Although most of these examples are from men, women did make similar remarks. There was no denomination or area singled out, nor a particular history to lead to these remarks. It boiled down to personal choice.

Similarly, almost every denomination had leaders who felt *they* could do nothing, either. A leading Roman Catholic priest said: 'We can do nothing to attract back the older people. They need to be convinced of the need to save their souls.' The Methodist Superintendent put it delightfully: 'We are the church they decide not to come to.' The Bishop of Coventry spoke of his personal experience:

> 'They won't come back because it is not the church they left. There has been a huge cultural change. I don't think there is an answer to getting them back. My father left when the robed choir went! After a lot of persuasion he did come back in the end, but I think this is exceptional.'

A Church of England lay leader confessed 'I don't know what would make people get out of their chairs and come to our church.' A Salvation Army Captain agreed: 'At the moment I can't see what we can do. Unless something happens we will die.' Perhaps most significant of all was the observation of a Baptist Church secretary, himself over 70, with 90 per cent of his congregation over 65: 'We ask how we can get the elderly in. There is no easy answer. I don't know any answer.' One is tempted to say that if he and his church cannot do it, who can?

All this negativism needs to be seen in the context of the positives in the rest of this chapter. However, it serves as a cautionary note, both on the size of the church's task, and on its need to respect those who stay away and wish to remain that way. For the community of the church there is still a great deal to do, as I have sought to show.

Specific activities

> The church today ministers to the physical, social and economic as well as the spiritual needs of man because of the recognition that all areas of life are intimately interrelated. (Gray and Moberg, 1962, p.118)

As I read these words, I wondered two things: is this true in many churches in their relationship with older people, and are those on the outside aware of such help when it is? My query is because in various surveys, including *The General Household Survey* and *Population Trends,* older people were asked about their various 'Activities'. They answered about 'Watching TV', 'Dressmaking', 'Going to the Library' (*inter alia*), but there was no reference to any church-based or religious activity. Despite a further search, church-going and church activities were not mentioned anywhere else either (Askham *et al.*, 1992). Tinker writes about 'Community care – support from the wider community' in her *Older People in Modern Society* (Tinker, 1997), but makes no reference to the help the church can give, nor does she suggest that older people can help the church. Even her index has no reference to 'church' or any religious activity – an odd omission. What could be done by way of activities for older people?

Meetings

I mentioned earlier in this chapter how older people value the chance to meet together. May (80) put it like this: 'They should have a gathering for older people once a month for coffee or tea.' May is not a churchgoer, but it is clear she would welcome such an activity. Ernest (68) enjoys church, but still wants 'Social gatherings'. In providing for the spiritual, churches need to include others' concerns, too. Where they do, they are appreciated: 'It does a lot,' Maureen (78) said of her church, explaining, 'There are clubs for older people.'

The church is aware that it must do this. Coventry Cathedral's Precentor told me that 'The church has to offer things to people to draw them in, as the world offers things like a bus pass. We need to offer a lunch club, which is often a lifeline.' He added an interesting rider: 'The church will be well thought of when we do.' Even the provision of care is of mutual benefit. Lunch clubs, coffee and tea gatherings would not take vast effort, and would be so appreciated.

If the church wanted to add a spiritual dimension beyond the fellowship aspect (one would imagine it would!), that also can be easily done. Regular attenders at such clubs may well be surprised if there were *not* an occasional service, however informal, not least because this common interest helps to break down relationship barriers (Litwak, 1985). This 'religious' side may take the form of a discovery group (rediscovering faith), or, as one Church of England leader said, a 'Friendship Club' with an occasional speaker. I understood the caveat from a Methodist minister: 'We have got to be practical and not too "religious", so they do not feel they are "being got at",' she said.

These groups can be a key link to society in general (Pieper and Garrison, 1992, pp.89–105). Marjorie (88) wanted the church to visit her, but still felt that 'This is not as good as a fellowship in a group because many old people are lonely': a very key sociological observation. As the older age group grows, it may become worthwhile having groups within the age-groupings: young-old and old-old (Lesher, 1996, pp.525–38). There can certainly be a place for single-sex groups for older people, particularly for men (Thomson, 1998, pp.12–13), who are sometimes less gregarious and social than women (though women's groups are popular, too). The types of clubs differ between the sexes, even in older life (Victor, 1994, pp.185–6). Churches like Dorothy's (69) have a Ladies' Fellowship and a Men's Fellowship. Because of the larger number of older women in many churches, 'The older men especially are left out' – or so David, in his 60's, told me.

Clubs tend to meet occasionally. But there are those who want more.

An open church

Why is the church not open all the time? I was asked this several times. 'There's a church hall – why is it not used three times a day?' non attending Alan (66) wanted to know. Frank (82) does attend, but observed, 'We could provide a meeting place for old people. Now most of the people don't know the church is there.' The Central Methodist Church in Coventry does open every day for light refreshments. 'It is good to see the minister walking round,' Pauline (76) told me. I know this to be a much-valued meeting place, especially for older people in the middle of their shopping. With the young-old being so mobile, many would like to visit churches, both in town and country. Older people could keep them open, which is rarely done at the moment (Laslett, 1989, p.169).

The Area Baptist Superintendent agrees that there should be daily activities in the church building, which includes the ability to talk about problems and difficulties: 'The old folk do not just want us to jolly them along, they want us to take them seriously,' he told me. 'They face death, illness, friends facing illness, and fear. The intelligent older people need to relate to those with whom they can talk sensibly.' Several writers in gerontology back his comments enthusiastically. Garner (1996, pp.77–84) believes that a church's older adults become 'more productive, active and healthy' through education, nutrition seminars and physical activities. Jordan (1996) also urges continuing education, including courses on grand-parenting. Recent gerontological surveys suggest that such education even helps brain cells regenerate (Crompton, 2000, p.39). Yarborough (1996, pp.85–89) says that these educational activities have 'Met with unqualified success,' and goes on to say how music can play a big part here, including the formation of 'senior adult choirs'.

Daily education groups could work well. For fear that 'all work and no play makes Jack a dull boy', other specific activities are possible, which I group together under a single heading:

Places to go

I met Dorothy (80) in her Home for Older People. She does not go to church and felt that 'The church could do more for the elderly – it could organize a trip.' But her needs were small, as she added, 'I would be happy if they wheeled me out from this Home occasionally.' One Roman Catholic church would meet her needs well. The priest told me, 'We have Tuesday Society weekly for the over-55's. There are 40 or so who come. They have concerts, talks, whist and go to shows in London and Birmingham and holidays to Tenerife and so on. We have pilgrimages to Walsingham.' For someone like Dorothy, 'We arrange lifts'.

If this is all too much for some, particularly Dorothy, what about a 'Holiday at Home' (Spriggs, 1998)? The idea is simplicity itself, because anything is possible. There can be outings, meals, entertainment, quizzes, videos, talks: anything goes. Others in the church can help, especially the young. A well-presented epilogue each day may be valued, with one of the Sunday services being incorporated in the holiday week: 'Songs of Praise' could be popular, judging from my interviewees. The older people will be good in planning it, too. They may suggest a tea dance or even aerobics (or so Spriggs suggests).

Entertainment at other times could be part of the activities for older people, at home or away. Games like indoor bowls, outings, including rambles: so much can be done (Creber, 1994, p.19). Churches often have the facilities: but are they made available? Evan (78) told me, sadly, 'We could organize entertainment: we have no whist drive or anything in the school hall for the elderly. We have our own swimming pool, but it is rarely used.' If all else fails, a Christmas party would be a start (Treetops, 1992, p.6).

Finally in this section on activities, I will consider the locality of the church.

Activities in the area

Activities in the geographical area covered by a specific church can be either by or for the older people. 'A large proportion of older people have enough physical, mental and spiritual energies to devote their own time and talents in a generous way to the various activities and programmes of the volunteer services' (Pontificium Consilium pro Laicis, 1999, pp.11–24).

Much help is needed in every neighbourhood by older people: who better to give it than their contemporaries (Clements, 1979, pp.64–5)? Here is an opportunity for what has been called 'a second career' (Freeman, 1996, pp.31–41). It is a chance to use what is approximately one-third of a lifetime positively, as part of lifelong education and service (Sax, 1993, pp.12–19).

This is a major area where the church can help older people in practical ways. 'I go and visit and keep them company,' Steve (20) told me and went on: 'I do decorating for them. I am more able to do this than they are.' Church members can do shopping and find furniture for those in need. Harold (83) told me that his church helped the elderly with their fuel bills. I was astonished with a recent figure: in 1997, for persons of pensionable age, 250 million medical prescriptions were issued (*Regional Trends*, 1999, fig. 7.16, p.100). Is this not an area where a church (especially its young people) could help by collecting prescriptions for its older people? Practical help like this can mean so much. The area Methodist Superintendent spoke to me of access to help, such as finding a plumber or making a doctor's appointment, where the church could assist. Finally, the church can alert the authorities where there are needs and speak up where there is apparent injustice (Heinecken, 1981, p.85).

In trying to answer the question, 'What can the church do for older people?', I have considered the caring community, with the need for family, a listening ear and a willingness to explain, invite and let go. Then there are many activities I have suggested. As Figure 10.1 shows, some serious consideration must also be given to visiting.

Visiting

The whole of what follows can be summed up in one straight answer from 90-year-old Doris, when I asked her what the church can do: 'Visit. Just get on with it: half the ministers don't even bother to visit.' Many seem to agree with her. The South Coventry survey I have already referred to asked the neighbourhood how they, as a local church, could be more useful in the community. Twenty-four per cent said, visit and help older people – the highest response received (Jamieson, 1998, p.11). When it is realized that 51 per cent of those 75 and over live alone (Families and Communities, 1997–8, p.16), Doris's plea is important. A Roman Catholic lay leader told me, 'We need to visit sheltered accommodation, blocks of flats where old people are – they would make us welcome. It needs not to be a one-off.' A priest regretted that 'The lapsed are not seen.' An older couple who do not now attend told me, 'They should have visited us years ago, but they didn't.' How and where can the church help here in a practical as well as a spiritual way?

Phyllis (86) no longer goes to her Church of England church. 'The church could visit us occasionally,' she told me, as we sat in her home. 'They should have done that all along.' A lay leader from her denomination agreed: 'Those at home could have more done for them, particularly by us visiting them.' Primarily, the need is to get to know who needs a visit, assuming a church feels it has a responsibility towards its frail and housebound members (Age Concern, 1980, p.15). Marjorie (88), said, 'The church must be on the look-out to hear about "the old lady at No 11 who never goes out" and therefore the church must set up pastoral visits.' Winifred (80) put it to me strongly: 'The church should go and talk and see why people don't come. They should sort it out one to one. The personal touch is what is needed.' Despite her own church attendance from her Old People's Home, Winifred added that 'Months go by for me without a visit. Visiting keeps people in touch.'

Does the church know such people? Is it willing to befriend them in their need? Who will hear what Ruby (80) told me?:

> 'The church could be more gracious and kinder to us. They could visit us a bit. I am a lonely old person: I can go four or five days and not see anyone. I do phone. There are lots who are lonely and no-one bothers with them. Someone should call. The old are ignored.'

Happily, I did find another side when I met Mary (90). 'If I'm not there on a Sunday,' she said, 'someone always phones me on the Monday to see if I'm alright and the vicar comes if I'm not well.' It was clear how grateful she was for these acts of friendship. An article in the *Church Times* pointed out that providing a service like Meals on Wheels was good, but simply arriving and departing could exacerbate the feeling of isolation. The article pointed out how tremendously important it is to build and sustain caring friendships with older people in their homes, so they feel valued and supported (Parkinson, 1999, p.18). The danger is, for those unable to leave their homes, that they fade from their church's attention (Stafford, 1985, p.155).

The problem is how much may arise from this visiting a person who is completely or semi-housebound. There may be money and health matters to sort out, sleep problems, depression, memory loss, spiritual needs – the list goes on (*Caring for the Elderly*, 1997, p.3). John, in his 50's, explained the dilemma:

> 'Everyone loves children and would be happy to be friendly, because they are not threatening. If you visit the old, you might have to spend time waiting in hospital if they collapse. If they are ill you are duty bound to visit them. I used to visit an old man next door when we lived in Birmingham every day and that was a burden. As Christians our first priority is to help people.'

I accept the need for visiting, the lack of it and the problems from it. However, many do want the church to visit them at home, so what is possible? The church has a specific spiritual role to play here. If visitors are from the church, they can (perhaps, *should*) pray with and for the older person. With permission of the church leaders, a simple service could be helpful, including Communion if appropriate. 'I take the Eucharist to the elderly,' Martin (33) told me.

Churches can work out who is best to visit, to share the load. Organizations like the Roman Catholic Legion of Mary are able to keep in touch with many. Here is a real opportunity for the young-old and the newly retired to bring much blessing and to receive it, as the Baptist Area Superintendent told me. Young people in the church can help here, too, as I have already shown. 'I want to be there in support,' Matt (28) said: 'I spend time with an elderly couple and see that they are alright.' It was clear that there was reciprocal appreciation. Gill (27) told me how her old parish had an 'Adopt-a-Granny' scheme (though her eyes twinkled as she admitted that it was not called that!). She had been friends with an old lady and often popped in to see her. As long as care is taken under the Child Protection Act, this sounds an excellent intergenerational scheme.

Inevitably the most appreciated visits tend to by the minister of the church. However busy ministers are, this is what older people told me they wanted. Even the Archbishop of Birmingham volunteered that 'The older people are glad to see me when they are visited.' One of his priests did point out that 'In a large parish the priests could do nothing but visit,' so that 'The elderly members need to reach the elderly,' but his colleague in a country parish said that 'If they [older people] are ill in hospital and the priest comes to see them then they may return to church.' Visiting by clergy is, in every church, a bit hit and miss, I discovered. Even in a New Church, with few older members, Ruby (62) 'Would like the pastor to visit me.' She added, 'If you are not in a home group you get no visits.' But in a Church of England country church I heard that the vicar did do home Communions whilst, in a city church, Greg (74) told me 'The local vicar does visit,' even though Greg is a non attender. But how clergy cope when they have a parish of 11,000 (as one city clergyman said), is impossible without massive lay help. So when Liz (76) says that older people 'Enjoy the clergy visiting,' but 'They don't get enough visits,' one understands the sense of tension.

The forgotten people

In three specific areas I was left with the impression that people felt neglected, marginalized, even ignored, hence this heading.

1. In residential homes

In looking at churches visiting residential homes, I use this term as shorthand to include other communities such as sheltered accommodation and warden-assisted flats. Almost every church has one or more such home in their locality. I did not visit one single home for older people, whether it was denominational, charitable or local authority owned, which did not say how its members would value visits. What can churches do? A model system exists in the Eastbourne area of Southern England, where a large number of churches have joined together to provide Pastoral Action for Residential Care Homes for the Elderly (PARCHE), whereby homes are ensured visits and care from one or more churches (Reeve, n.d.). It takes an enthusiast to get such a system going, but helps to meet the longing for help and visits which I heard in several homes, especially those which are specifically secular.

How can the church share in the life of a residential home and with those who live and work there? The following suggestions include the answers I received from key staff in several homes, when I asked them how the church could help them, spiritually and practically (Appendix 3, question 10), as well as answers from church leaders, members and older people resident in homes.

Presence

> 'People need human contact. While the staff are doing their chores, our residents need someone to talk to: the TV is not for old people. There is so much value by befriending these folk, especially those with dementia.'

This plea, from the head of a leading denomination's home, was being met in a simple yet effective way in one inter-denominational home I visited. I saw Ruth (14) throwing a ball to a number of residents in turn. When she stopped, I talked with her and she told me:

> 'I am doing my Duke of Edinburgh's bronze award and my church is linked with this old people's home. I visit once a week in my own time, especially during school half-term, for a period of three months. I play ball with them and chat. They like me playing. I help with keep fit.'

The joy on the faces of the people was obvious. Everyone benefited, including Ruth on her way to a nationally prestigious award. The constant plea from several homes was, where are there more like Ruth? Ted (81) told me that, when his church asked, 'I was the only one to volunteer to help at an old people's home up to road.' I was left wondering whether only the adult congregation had been asked, as I suspect was the case. Perhaps one of the children's or young people's groups could have been encouraged to have adopted the home, visiting from time to time, even with entertainment.

Practical help

The term 'Christianity in Action' might have been coined for this situation. Church volunteers could do so much helping in practical ways in and with a home. One home manager said, 'We need people to pick up the residents who want to go to church both Sunday and midweek. I have to take a lady to the midweek meeting because there is no-one from the church who will do it.' I felt the pressure of this lady's work as she told me. Another manager said that church people 'Practically could assist with the voluntary work: talking and befriending. They could take some of our residents out locally to the pub or the café. They could help with feeding. There are,' he said, 'all sorts of simple tasks.' He was not asking for trained, skilled carers, but 'We have not seen anybody. There is lots to do but no-one is doing it in old people's homes.' The phrase 'more in sorrow than in anger' seemed to sum up his mood.

There is no shortage of what can be done in a practical way. In an American survey, specific help was indicated by homes as being needed in such diverse areas as transportation, co-ordinating 'creative ministries', giving legal and financial counselling, encouraging, conducting special birthday and anniversary celebrations, helping in the home's garden and playing games (Peifer, 1996, pp.489–90). One home told me they would like help with money-raising. Another home told me, positively, that 'The church is doing what is needed.' One home manager went so far as to say that the church was doing too much! It provided the home's treasurer, money-raisers, helpers and chaplain, in what was clearly a happy and much-appreciated balance.

Spiritual involvement

Here is the unique contribution a church can make to a home. My research would indicate how much this is both wanted and appreciated. Three or four possibilities need a mention here: services, informal spiritual help, chaplaincies and visits by clergy and help to get to church.

Services. Edith is 78. She used to go to church, but cannot now get out, living in a home which is local authority owned. She said rather wistfully, 'I would go to a little service if they organized it.' Nan was the same, in a similar home: 'We would like the church to come and hold a service here,' she told me. It would be invidious to have services which were anything other than completely voluntary. However, my research and my own experience in helping residential homes is that many residents really value a caring, informal, not-too-long service, with well-known hymns (large-printed), thoughtful prayers, a Bible reading and a talk. Here is an opportunity for a cross-section of the local church to help. Amy (15) was happy that she and her friends could do this: 'We play music in the nursing homes when there are services there.' A church lay leader from a New Church said, 'We do mini-services in old people's homes on a Saturday night: we do five homes like that. We give a word and we share.' I personally have seen great joy on the faces of residents as a hymn from childhood recalls happy memories.

Informal help. A great deal more can be done on an informal basis, especially if a service would be either unwelcome or inappropriate. The head of one denominational home told me, 'Spiritually, people could come and assist with prayers, meditation and Bible reading and talk about God and what he can do for an older person, especially to talk about death.' To some that may sound 'heavy'. I am simply quoting him verbatim. In my conversations with residents in all types of homes I found many to be deeply spiritual: considerable numbers prayed privately every day and would have really valued such informal help and encouragement. The complaint is not one about spiritual work being done, but its *not* being done.

The head of a secular home said this:

> 'I would like the people who come from the morning service [at the local church] and bring Communion, to stay for a cup of tea and have time. I wish they had longer time, particularly when they visit once a month. The vicar could bring lay folk to chat with people after the service. We would value prayer groups, an Alpha course and a Bible study if volunteers would come in. It would have to be *here*, and in the *afternoon*.'

There is no suggestion here of the church's intrusion: the very opposite. Her views were supported by the head of a Roman Catholic home in these serious terms:

> 'If we do not care for the spiritual, then caring for anything else is useless. It is my experience that if a home of any sort [she had worked in secular homes, too] persists, then they can get church help both for Sunday services and privately. As people get older they become more religious. People turn to God.'

One cannot deny the deep feelings expressed here. Time and again I found them echoed by heads of homes and by residents. There is a difference between unwelcome proselytization and ignoring perceived spiritual needs and requests. A head of a Methodist home gave me another all-embracing plea:

> 'The church needs to think how it can involve our tenants in its life. Churches tend to be good and supportive to people who've always gone. The church should not forget the older ones. The church should help the lapsed, for example by lifts. They could run a little Bible study here.'

I have to say how struck I was by the strength of feeling from so many who, far from wishing to exclude the church, deeply regretted the lack of spiritual help. There was a wide expression of feeling that so little was done in informal pastoral care of a spiritual nature (MacKinlay, 1993, pp.26–30).

Help from ministers. A further specific spiritual help, sought by both heads of Homes and residents, was the involvement of local clergy in informal visiting and in the role of chaplain to the home.

> The need for chaplaincy in aged care will continue to grow. At one level, this is a fact of living in an ageing society. At another level, it must be recognised that society is once again beginning to acknowledge the spiritual dimension of human beings. (MacKinlay, 1993, pp.26–30)

This observation from Australia is supported by Tritschler (1991, pp.77–8), who delightfully speaks of the chaplain from a French viewpoint: 'L'aumônier n'était pas là pour ramasser les cendres, mais pour souffler sur les braises de la vie' [The chaplain is not there to collect the ashes, but to blow on the embers of life]. Some homes have such a chaplain, as a Methodist minister told me she was such in her local Methodist Home for the Aged. Roman Catholic priests would almost certainly do this for their denominational home. The problem arises more in non-denominational, inter-denominational and secular homes. My research shows that some homes would value a formal link with one or more members of the clergy.

Others would want the clergy to help informally. As Edith (78) told me, 'I would like it once a month if a minister, priest, leader of the Salvation Army and so on, came into our sheltered complex.' She was not alone. Nan, in a residential home, agreed: 'We would appreciate a visit by the vicar or minister – that would help us.' However, I did meet one minister – of a Black Church, who was going the second mile: 'We are seeking funding to build a residential facility,' he said. When in doubt, build your own!

The overall and overwhelming view I have found is that almost every residential home of every sort and owned by whomever, would value the church sharing in its life in one way or another. There are open doors, waiting for church folk to walk through.

If some homes and their residents feel forgotten, there is another group of people who share that problem, and I now turn to them.

2. Carers

As people age, the vast majority of those who need to be looked after are cared for at home. According to *The General Household Survey* 1990, there were then 6.8 million carers in Britain and such a figure is bound to have risen by now. Of these, 79 per cent were looking after someone 65 plus, 18 per cent themselves being over 65. What help do churches give to the carers in their congregations? 'A few churches, too few, have made an effort to identify the carers in their congregation, to ask them what support they would appreciate and to organize the necessary help' (Burns, 1991, 5.27). In my own research, no-one mentioned carers at any point. I cannot recall hearing church prayers anywhere for the carer, though the old and frail would themselves be prayed for every week in a church. This is a major area for further research and for greater action.

What can be done? There is help from local authorities and from organizations like the Carers Christian Fellowship in

Cumbria and the Jubilee Centre in Cambridge. Locally, it is to the church that a carer may look for support. A church needs to discover who the carers are and aim to support them not only spiritually but in practical ways, too. Carers are likely, at various times, to feel sheer physical tiredness. Speaking with one carer over 70, she related to me how relieved she had been the previous night to get four hours uninterrupted sleep: the norm was being awoken every hour by her cancer-ridden husband. She was clearly drained emotionally and struggling spiritually, not being able to get out to church. She was not part of my specific research; I was visiting as a friend the weekend before writing this.

The church can help simply by befriending both cared and carer, pastorally visiting them, praying and 'cared-sitting' to enable the carer to get out for some respite (Harris, 1998b, p.13). From my recent visit, the problem seemed to be a lumping together in the minds of outsiders of cared and carer as one person because they happened to be married, not realizing that each had different needs. If babysitting can separate mother/father and child to give relief to the parent, why not elderly-sitting? This would be of especial help in the final 'sharing' I wish to consider now.

3. Dementia sufferers

The relationship between the church and those suffering from dementia could provide a basis for an entire book. I deeply regret giving this vital subject what will appear to be a cursory glance. I also regret that no-one spoke to me about this problematic relationship, although I met a number of dementia sufferers in my visits to residential homes. In Great Britain, there are 220,000 men and 450,000 women who suffer from dementia in the 65 plus age-group, with nearly 30 per cent of all those in the 85 plus group (*Population Trends*, 1998, p.27). The subject is well dealt with in the ground-breaking research by Petzsch (1984) and more recent works by Treetops (1992 and 1996) and Goldsmith (1996).

Alzheimer's Disease (after Alois Alzheimer, the German neurologist who first described this physical disease in 1907) is the most common form of dementia, a progressive disease causing inability to reason, think, learn and remember. My aim in this book is to see how older people and the church can relate to each other: what then of the hundreds of thousands who suffer from dementia? How can the church share with them? Treetops (1992, p.7) makes the telling comment, 'It is interesting to see how children crying or wandering can be tolerated and even accepted by congregations whereas confused people and their carers can be shunned.'

Here is an opportunity for churchgoers to treat with dignity older people suffering from any form of dementia (Report of the Social Policy Committee, 1990, pp.93–4).

> Since productivity and attractiveness were not conditions of God's love, volunteers in a nursing home will treat the disorientated and unkempt with the same courtesy and consideration as the alert and pleasant. For the love experienced depends on the nature of the giver, not the deserving of the receiver. (Cartensen, 1983, pp.30–8)

This must be true in *every* situation. Dementing people should be valued for themselves, not shunned (Petzsch, 1984, p.26). With a little training, volunteers can help greatly, as long as they are prepared to work 'on a generous time scale' (Goldsmith, 1996, p.83). This is where an Older Persons Officer can give guidance (Hooker, 1998, p.5). Do churches value the uniqueness of people, whatever their condition (Brain, 1998, pp.16–17)? If so, simple things can help dementia sufferers. A 'memory box', full of photos, diaries, music and so on can be excellent for sight and touch (Treetops, 1996, p.11). A theatre in South London tours with an Edwardian shop to help those with memory loss recall what they were doing in childhood (Naish, 1999, p.14). A garden designer in Edinburgh, Annie Pollock, has created a 'forget-me-not' garden with an old-fashioned washing line, a bird table and memories to stimulate dementia sufferers (Elliott, 1999, p.9).

It is a case of making the effort to communicate, sharing feelings and relationships (Jewell, 1998, pp.4–7), listening, being calm, having time and not being embarrassed (Goldsmith, 1996, pp.58–9). This is particularly so in sharing in worship. 'Religious people need to worship God. People with dementia who have a faith have the same need' (Treetops, 1996, p.6). There is a need to maintain 'spiritual connectedness', especially as no-one can know 'another's relationship with a Higher Power' (Richards and Seicol, 1991, pp.27–40).

One to one, there can be prayer, singing and reading. In a group situation, dementia sufferers should be included in worship, whether it be in a home or a church. Dementia sufferers could be encouraged to share with others in Communion, join in the singing and in no way treated as a 'problem'. As I indicated, this is a huge area for work and Treetops' *Holy, Holy, Holy* (1996, p.6) is an excellent guide for churches who wish to shoulder their responsibility to share with dementia sufferers.

As I have been considering how the church can share with older people, I have deliberately left the church building itself until this point, in order to stress the vital place it plays in sharing its spiritual life and what needs to be done in practical terms.

The church itself

Spiritual life

How can the church share its spiritual life with older people?

Be there. When I asked Betty (65) what the church could do for her, she replied, 'By having Mass every day. By being there.' The very presence of the church was important to her and to others whose comments have been recorded earlier. Even non attenders value the church's existence. Boswell wrote of one Dr John Campbell in these terms: 'I am afraid he has not been in the inside of a church for many years; but he never passes a church without pulling off his hat.' Boswell concludes that 'This shows that he has good principles,' but it also shows that Dr Campbell was glad of the church's very existence, as are many today.

The spiritual dimension is very important for many older people (MacKinlay, 1993, pp.26–30). 'The church is there to facilitate my worship,' Ernest (68) said. The Archbishop of Canterbury pointed out in a speech that many older people wrote to his headquarters saying they wanted a more effective ministry from the Church for their 'spiritual reflection, discussion and worship' (Carey, 1997, p.5). As David (63) told me about his church, 'It makes sure I don't lose sight of Jesus.' Michael (84), from another denomination, agreed: 'It looks after my soul.' The church needs to address spiritual development (Rainbow, 1991, pp.195–204), particularly for those older people who have experienced going to church since Sunday school long ago (Howse, 1999, p.27). Research in the United States shows that people world-wide cope with their problems more through God and the church than by going to the doctor (Koenig, 1993, pp.195–203).

The church must, firstly, be there to give spiritual help. Its proximity also helps make for easy attendance. Wakefield's research indicates that 'The two most common specific reasons for adults [attending church] were the nearness of the church and style of worship' (Wakefield, 1998, p.133).

Good leadership. John (65) does not go to church. When would he go? 'Only if they put a good vicar in the village,' was his terse reply. Of course, there are good ministers. A Roman Catholic priest told me he tried to help older people by his 'availability', his 'constant physical presence in the building', greeting the congregation at the Sunday Masses, and every day at the lunchtime and evening Masses. A Church of England vicar made a point of caring for the elderly disabled, by taking the Communion to them *first* in the service.

A good leader need not be the minister. Large parts of a service may be better led by people who themselves are older (Brookfield, 1996; Jordan, 1996, p.54). The emphasis is on *good.* 'Meager and shallow worship for the aging is not a "gerontological problem", it is a human problem, and cannot be solved by liturgical gimmickry at the nursing home' (Holmes, 1983). What should be done with bad leadership? May (80), who does not attend church, was clear: 'Change the priest!' she said – with feeling.

Something in the service for older people. A good leader will think of *all* the congregation when planning a church service. The head of one home spoke of her church-going residents: 'They feel forgotten because no-one has thought about them in the main services.' The only appropriate service was the early Communion, and 'It is very hard to get them to the eight o'clock because of the time.' There is the danger the other way, too, however. A Free Church Area Secretary said that 'There is nothing to worry about in the service because it has an older style. Most preachers are sixty-plus: in this District there are only three preachers under sixty.' One wonders about the young people's needs here. The Bishop of Warwick sought a balance: 'We need a broad menu – something for everyone, which includes services where the elderly feel particularly at home.' The church should be an 'all-age community' (Report of the Social Policy Committee, 1990, p.116), where the whole church family meets (Harris, 1998a, p.2).

Ministers told me, 'We need to keep up some of the older hymns,' and an older liturgy sometimes. The latter gives a sense of order, which older people value (Hughes, 1999, pp.6–7). I was not sure I recognized the sort of service Peter (74) envisaged, as he did not go to church, but I got the general drift. He would go 'If they had a Sunday service as the old services used to be, without hugging, kissing, banjos and jumping up and down. Then I might go.' I wondered where he had got these images from, but decided to leave well alone. However, a sense of quiet and reverence is valued, with some aspects which are known and loved.

An opportunity to respond. Although it has been said that there is no evidence that non-religious people turn to religion in old age in large numbers (Johnson and Mullins, 1989, pp.110–31; Harris and Cole, 1980, p.296), nevertheless churches may wish to give older people the opportunity to consider, or reconsider, the Christian faith. The Area Superintendent of the Baptist Union told me, 'I do believe that people towards the end of their life should have the opportunity to respond to Christ: some do have roots in the church.' The Archdeacon of Coventry spoke of the benefit of a specific series of meetings for older people, in his previous parish in Nottingham, entitled 'Bonus Years', and how much they had been appreciated. Friendship, listening and sharing personally may be the way (Taylor, 1996a, p.3). A 'Seeker Service' which is non-threatening is what clergy tell me is good. *Reaching Older People with God's Love* (Spriggs, 1998, p.11) is not only a title, but a style.

Healing. 'We need to deal with the problems of pain and suffering,' Bishop Barrington-Ward told me. 'The testimonies of older people to the Gospel, God's help in adversity and healing when they are not physically healed' were issues he wanted addressed. On a wide scale, it may be that the whole ageing process needs healing (Goodman, 1999, p.65; Schachter-Shalomi and Miller, 1995, pp.61–75). At a personal level, there could well be a correlation between religion and well-being (McFadden, 1995), perhaps because of the emotional calm through prayer and meditation and the concerned responses of clergy (Carlson and Seicol, 1990, pp.65–66).

When it comes to specific services of healing, I am aware that most denominations conduct these. It was primarily the Roman Catholics who spoke of them, telling me of the Sacramental System of Penance and Holy Communion and the Anointing of the sick (although none of these is age-related) and, in two cases, an annual Mass for the housebound and sick who are brought to the church and anointed with oil. Certainly older churchgoers spoke of their appreciation for prayers of healing.

Special Services. This is one way in which the Church can share specifically with older people. It may mean a particular style of service. The Precentor of Coventry Cathedral laughed as he told me, 'It has been suggested that we ought to have a Nine O'clock Service for the Classic FM audience!' The answer is, Why not? What about special services to celebrate longevity of life, or of a marriage, or retirement? The other end of life's timescales are thus honoured. Research may be needed to consider church-based services for older people (Sheehan *et al.*, 1988, pp.231–41).

Timing may be of the essence here. The Methodists' Superintendent said that 'We need to make sure events are held at a convenient time.' One of his ministers agreed, saying that 'Traditional churchmanship cannot prevail for the Sunday service because we need to be up-to-date,' and suggesting 'a mid-week fellowship type of thing'. One New Church does just this, with a Thursday afternoon 'special' for older people, with older hymns, and the Sunday for new hymns: their clientele appreciating both. In some churches (especially the Roman Catholics) the Sacrament is taken from the church to the elderly housebound on the Sunday or Monday. All churches could hear what Graham (70), ex-Church of England, told me:

> 'I don't need much persuading to come back. It depends on the time – possibly Saturday morning would be good.

On Sunday morning I go down to the Club to see my friends. My wife would go if I did.'

Here again is the dilemma. To what extent should the church fit in with the wishes of the people? How can a church resolve this combination of passivity and demandingness in those who do not attend? It may be impossible to resolve.

Keep it short. Two lay leaders from a New Church opined, 'In church the services are too long for the elderly,' a point agreed word for word by the head of a residential home. If churches wish to share their spiritual work in the services with older people brevity is the order of the day it seems.

From the spiritual side of what happens in church, I turn to matters which, though more practical, are vital if the church is to share its ministry with older people.

Practicalities

Many of the older people I interviewed asked for churches to provide practical help. In dealing with these briefly, I do not want to diminish their importance. The need was summed up by the head of a residential home: 'We would like the church to be more user-friendly,' she told me. The following are the main needs about which I was told.

Transport. A number of older people need help to get to church. Marjorie (88) said, 'Transport is the greatest need. The church must help older people to get to church and return.' Various suggestions were put to me, such as a co-ordinated bus service for city centre churches or individual churches owning minibuses. A vicar said of his congregation, 'If they can move, they come to church!' His minibus included a disablement facility. A rota for car drivers to bring older people to church was suggested by several.

Access. This was asked for, not only to get wheelchairs into the church building, but also for getting around inside, especially to a Communion rail. Even the simple act of opening a door was requested by Doris (74) at her Baptist church, while a priest admitted that 'The non-step entrance is usually locked'.

Audibility and visibility. 'We could improve the sound system!'

was how one priest replied enthusiastically to, 'How can your church help?' Loop systems for the deaf, good lighting for the poor-sighted, large-print hymn and prayer books, a very visible overhead screen: all these were mentioned in my interviews.

Comfort. 'We could make the church warmer,' a country vicar said. Another minister said that 'We should make the church comfortable for the elderly.' User-friendly seats, non-slip floors and accessible toilets were asked for, too.

To conclude

I was much encouraged by one lay leader's final comment to me after a long chat: 'I realize from this conversation that we could be doing more to reach out to the elderly, and I will have to look into this,' she said. Others echoed her words, with comments like, 'We could do more'. Sadly, some added, 'We don't have the workers,' or 'The people who are willing to do the work are few and far between.'

Without reiterating the many ways detailed in this chapter by which churches can care for the older members of their congregations and also help those who would like to attend, clearly any improvements will impact on personnel, mobilization of human resources and their organization, as well as making demands on money and resources.

The problem of personnel has, to a large extent, been answered in Chapter 9. Churches must look beyond the diminishing numbers of paid employees, especially in the ranks of the clergy, to the many lay people – young and older – who, as Chapter 9 shows clearly, are both willing and able to play their part here. Clergy must look to their young-old, early retired members to organize and mobilize. As to resources, particularly of a financial nature, the adage 'Where there's a will there's a way' was modified by one older lady who told me, 'Where the heart is, the hand will follow'. In other words, if the potential is seen, and the need felt, there are those who will rise to the challenge financially as well as personally.

It is clear that the vast majority of ways in which churches can help do not require vast outlays of money but, rather, a better use of existing facilities and the enthusing of church members to get involved. I am encouraged to believe that, when Chapters 9 and 10 are read together, the aspirations of this chapter are achievable.

11

By Way of Conclusion

The renowned Argentinian preacher Juan Carlos Ortiz will sometimes conclude a talk with the introductory words, 'And now, not because I'm finished, but to finish.' These are my sentiments as this book draws to a close: there is much more to be said, but my current research must end here.

In Chapter 1 I raised a number of questions which needed answering. Although each chapter concludes with a summary of a specific question answered within it, this final chapter enables me to comment on the issues raised and my major findings, together with some of the surprises along the way.

Issues raised

I intend to consider in detail the specific findings of each chapter shortly. However, three key issues seem to me to have been raised.

The need for community

On many occasions throughout this book the question of 'community' has been spoken of as an important issue. It has been acknowledged that, especially for older people, this has disappeared from society on the whole, and is not coming back. Homes have become mini-fortresses, barricaded with security measures, not to be opened except in an emergency, especially after dark.

In this loss of community, the church would still appear to be a 'safe house'. Whether it be a last resort or not, can the church now be where this community feeling can still be found? If it is, do older people want the 'community of the faithful', or to have this 'community' without the 'faith'?

When one considers the findings of Chapter 10, the suggestion comes through that there may be a sedulous secularization of the church's 'fellowship of believers', with far more emphasis on 'community' in the 'community of faith'. The former seems to be somehow contextualized by the latter. Perhaps subconsciously, older people may entertain the hope that their loss of community could socially be compensated for by their local church (or churches, as I shall mention shortly) resurrecting *Gemeinschaft*, this new community within the church as one of 'this world's things', rather than being 'other wordly'.

Churches and their leaders may, deliberately or reactively, exercise a certain disingenuousness in responding to this perceived need by providing such a secularized church community. I have experienced in various parts of my research area the provision of afternoon events for older people. These take the form of a meeting, usually with some spiritual content, which does not last too long. Both before and after this more formal gathering there are much longer periods of informal conversations, which may well take place over tea and biscuits, or a proper meal, whether it be lunch or afternoon tea. There may be games and, depending on the particular church's beliefs, a raffle, a beetle drive, whist or bingo.

Two factors within all this are germane. Firstly, churches in an area co-operate either deliberately or tacitly to ensure they each hold their meetings on different days of the week, enabling an older person to be at the Methodists one afternoon, the Catholics the next, and the Church of England on a third. If there is a Salvation Army and a Baptist Church, every day can be taken up with a 'community' activity, comprising, by and large, the same older people. Secondly, the overtly 'faith' section of each gathering varies according to each church, but rarely takes up the majority of the time. Most older people both expect and enjoy it, but the friendship of the community is paramount.

In itself these provisions can be desirable in wholly secular terms, as they plug the gaps in those convivial provisions (if any) made by social services, giving a sense of warmth in a cold society. This repairing of community is an excellent end in itself, with churches working in tandem with voluntary organizations such as Age Concern to help older people, and give them a sense of being valued. The problem, however, is if the church wishes to regard itself as a 'community of faith', it may nevertheless become almost indistinguishable from those organizations.

Here is the church's dilemma. The concept of a 'faith community' must, by its very name and nature, be something radically different, giving at least equal weight to the words 'faith' and 'community'. Many of those interviewed would be happy to be wooed on their own terms, but the church may be deluding itself in its implied belief that, because it provides some religious input, its faith will be communicated by osmosis. The inherent danger is that the osmosis will work the other way, with the dilution of manifestations of faith resulting in these becoming inoffensive and ineffective. The church is walking a tricky tightrope.

The key issue I see here is a paradigm shift in the source of this secularization. Throughout the theological debates of the late nineteenth and most of the twentieth centuries, it was external factors which affected faith. Even though some of the proponents were from within the church, they argued from outside the accepted orthodoxy. Darwin and his followers questioned the Biblical view of creation. The 1960's 'God is dead' postulate led to a more religio-sociological debate about the 'God of the gaps', making God only of value to explain what science could not. The 'never had it so good' culture (an expression coined by Prime Minister Harold Macmillan (1957–63)) has infiltrated the church, both in affecting its adherents and causing defections, to the extent of a deliberate choice having to be made between church attendance and Sunday shopping. Attitudes like materialism, consumerism and affluence have become a way of life, causing a more spiritual lifestyle to be sidelined (fulfilling Jesus' own story of the sower, when he spoke of the 'deceitfulness of wealth' in Mark 4.19).

David Jenkins, when Bishop of Durham, raised his doubts about aspects of the Resurrection of Jesus. He was not the only person within church life to contribute to the dilution of orthodox beliefs within the church. Don Cupitt was at the forefront of a 'Sea of Faith' movement, seeking to show how virtually no beliefs were necessary in order to assent to some kind of 'faith'. The Church of England (Jenkins and Cupitt) was not alone. John Hick of the United Reformed Church suggested that many matters taken as accepted tenets of belief were open to question. The Methodist Church has seen some of its members leaving membership because of questions over the deity of Jesus proposed by some of its leaders and lecturers. Postmodernist relativism, which encourages religion as long as there are no truth-claims made, has proved a lifeline to be accepted by a number of theologians. But all these matters mentioned thus far were by people speaking from the outside or, at least, putting themselves on the edge of the church's creeds.

What is happening now, and why I use the term 'paradigm shift', is wholly different. All the above largely appeals to those who consider themselves to be 'intellectuals', the academic intelligentsia. But there is now an insidious inside secularization, as the church almost grovels in its attempts not to offend all its members, and those on the outside. There is a growing belief within the church that people do not want faith thrust upon them. Proselytization is a dirty word, banned by the media from the outside, but with non-proselytization embraced from the inside. The church backs away from any possibility of giving offence by sinking to the lowest common denominator of contact with the 'outsider'. Religion becomes inoffensive, with the 'teeth' of Biblical truths being drawn. The message is watered down to exclude any religious demands and any implication that to be a Christian may be difficult. In making its presentation user-friendly, the church may end up perpetrating a dreadful delusion amongst those it seeks to reach, and an even more horrible self-delusion that its methods and message are right.

The church must, therefore, face this key issue: if it is to provide a community for older people, what sort of community will it be? This secularization debate needs to take place, or a drift from faith may be irresistible. I say 'drift', because I do believe this internal shift is unintended. The end result will be, however, that the church in its relationship with older people only fills gaps in community provision for them. It will have swung round completely from the old accusation of being so heavenly-minded as to be of no earthly use, to being so earthly-minded as to exclude heaven. This would be a tragedy of the first order. Older people would, as my research shows, value a genuine spiritual base and basis. Unless the church provides this for them, and see this as of paramount importance, it may become an active accessory to its own demise.

There is, therefore, a paradox. Whilst the churches' largest body of faithful comes from older people, nevertheless, the attempt to minister to yet more older people (or more needs of its older members) represents a new potential force for secularization. Ironically, this could undermine all denominations where they are still strong – among this older age group.

A unity of approach

Throughout this book I have been both surprised and heartened by what I felt was a significant factor, which is the remarkable agreement between churches of all denominations. There is a marked absence of denominational differences throughout, which itself is a most interesting finding. Every denomination has expressed a real concern to help meet the needs of older people, universally agreeing with the school report's perennial observation, 'Could do better'.

Further, the churches are in agreement with the desire of older people that 'something must be done'. The need for community is an agreed objective. What I am not convinced about is that churches are sharing this with each other, or discovering ways in which, individually or collectively, they might respond. Even at a national level, reports by different denominations seem to be instigated and published piecemeal. For me this raised a second key issue: if the meeting of the needs of older people is seen as so vital by all concerned, why are the churches in a particular area all-but ignoring each other? The majority of churches have either admitted to having no specific provisions for older people, or to not doing enough. Is there not a vital need here for dialogue, and an acceptance that both churches of all denominations and the older people within their areas want the same thing?

A need for action

I intend to deal with this in more detail when I look next at my major findings. But here, I want to flag up what I believe is the paramount question: Is there a will for a way forward? Has the church got a real heart's desire to make things happen? It is a truism that 'talk is cheap'. I accept that I am about to point out the difficulties inherent in my research, but the findings I have made represent a trumpet-call to action.

Who will rise to the challenge? Because we are dealing with an older generation, time is not on our side. As the major findings are considered now, what will anyone do about them? Recent history would not smile on this question. National reports are 'received', but are rarely, if ever, acted on. It is crucial that the later section headed 'What can be done?' does not end up with the answer 'Nothing'.

I now proceed to present my major findings in more detail.

Major findings

The difficulty of definitions

Chapter 2, on the subject of what is meant by 'older', proved to be considerably longer and a great deal more fascinating than I would ever have envisaged. The terms 'old', 'old age' and 'older people' evoked an enormous variety of interpretations. There was a marked contrast here between what learned writers said and the 'vox pop'. Writers were much happier to be specific, even though they disagreed with each other. Those interviewed were much more reticent, in particular those 'older' in years. Especially among the 'young-old' there was a marked reluctance to admit to entering an older phase of life.

This is not merely a moot point for academia to pursue as an intellectual exercise: it affects the bearing of this book on the church. If there is no consensual definition of 'old' and of 'older people', how can churches relate to 'older people' without causing offence? One would expect that the church, at least as much as any other group in society, would be extremely anxious to avoid any suggestion of ageism in its approach. But to treat those in their later years as being indistinguishable from those much younger may be doing a disservice to the particular needs, hopes and aspirations of these older ones. Thus it was worth exploring this in detail.

The more I considered this question of ageism, as I did in chapter 3, the more I realized that here was a major – perhaps *the* major – reason for an unwillingness to admit to being 'older'. It became clear that ageism in our society is alive and kicking, causing many wounds when the kicks land on people. A culture of youth often rejects the advice, ideas and attitudes of older people. As a result, few want to be older, for fear of rejection.

One important finding in this area is that ageism does exist, usually passively, within churches and their leaderships. Few admit to it, but many words of denial lead to very few actions to eradicate ageism. In the key area of older people's residential homes there is a feeling of being, at least, ignored, or even forgotten completely. Churches need to take active steps to prevent older people feeling that they are sidelined, as my research showed clearly.

In Chapter 4, it was important to show that there is no simplistic definition of the word 'church'. This may be of particular significance to churches themselves in their approach to those who do not attend. Churches need to have a wide view of how they are perceived, in order to be able to fulfil a breadth of needs as people approach church. Even for older members, churches will want to realize how many different functions they fulfil both in the worship and in the more social and practical aspects of life.

It appeared too easy for the leadership within a church to assume knowledge of what their particular church means to the membership and, even more, to the outsider. To look at 'church' simplistically as 'the building' and 'the people' and then move on, is to forget what nuances people put on these terms, and how many more definitions are possible. As Chapter 4 showed, it was amazing to find over 70 ways of describing the word 'church'. There is a great need for personal pastoring here, to enable a church to fulfil the aspirations of attenders and non attenders alike. This is a need which is universally constrained by the crisis in vocations, but in turn it presents the challenge of utilizing the increasing numbers of young-old, and especially professional lay people who have taken early retirement, as a new 'royal priesthood' to the growing cohorts of the elderly attenders and non attenders alike.

Further, Chapter 5 revealed that there has been a multiplicity of changes in recent years. It may be the cumulative effect of many of these changes which older people find hard either to accept or to understand which gives them a problem. To have over 70 specific changes described in interviews indicates the need for careful explanations, and an understanding of those for whom some change may be a bridge too far.

I had certainly not foreseen this additional diversity. Over 36 per cent of the changes noted were in the church services. This is an important finding. Those who are young either do not know where the church has come from, or are able to see continuity through change. Those who are older, perhaps struggling with great changes in society at large and in their own lives, will need much more help to perceive changes in their church and its services in a positive light. There may well be a need to retain forms of older services for older people, or to explain in a more caring way what is happening.

These difficulties of definitions have been addressed, but it is noteworthy that the problems were much greater than I first envisaged.

Surprises along the way

Although this entire book has been a journey of discovery, three areas in particular have made me ponder.

Saying – and doing

Perhaps it is a universal social factor: people say one thing but do another. I found it interesting to discover this to be true in the context of my research. There was considerable goodwill towards the church from many of those who do not attend, but their fair words did not motivate their renewed attendance. The churches said they cared deeply for older people, yet a number made little or no special provision for them. Ageism was abhorrent, but some older churchgoers felt sidelined or ignored – even disliked.

It is therefore interesting to contrast and compare Chapters 6, 7 and 8. To take Chapter 7 first, the scriptural guidelines for the church's approach to older people are entirely positive. In the Bible, older people are not only treated positively with dignity and respect, but they are encouraged to play an active part in the life of the church while they can, and to be lovingly cared for when they cannot. Examples are given throughout the Old and New Testaments of older people playing a full part in the religious life of their day.

This chapter stood in some contrast with the previous one. Over half of all churches in my survey stated that they had no specific provision for older people, nor any particular policy for their involvement. This was backed up in Chapter 8 by these very same older people agreeing that this was exactly their experience. In the anxiety of churches to attract younger members, the older ones are in danger of being left on one side.

Unspoken words, forgotten people

It is possible I failed to ask specific enough questions on two matters, but I am greatly surprised that I had to rely almost entirely on literature to write about two vital areas relating to older people, and the help needed.

One was dementia. Is it possible that dementia sufferers are either unknown to, or forgotten by, churches? No-one spoke of doing anything with them or for them, either in the church or where they live. Yet, as I showed in Chapter 10, there are very many who struggle with this irreversible problem, and who would value any input from a caring congregation. The other area was that regarding carers. Why were those who care for older people not seen as those who should themselves be pastored and cared for? Many are themselves older, and in need of respite and support. I will mention both these later when looking at possible areas for further research.

Going – and returning

In Chapter 1 I posed the question as to whether secularization was the major cause for older people having left the church. As I have tried to show, the answer is much more complex and, by contrast, some of the reasons given are much more simple. For some, leaving was a crisis. However, for the majority it was a process. Most did not leave for negative reasons: they drifted away because of a romantic relationship, a busy family life, or a move to a new town with no local church of their persuasion.

It is easy for godlessness and a secular society to be blamed for a decline in church attendance. This book may have shown some surprises in why members of older generations have left. It may also have shown what many feared, that recovering these lost older members may be difficult, if not impossible, in many instances. I have been surprised at how many would not now return. Conversely, I have also been surprised how many older people would welcome church involvement where they are, rather than where the church is. Visits to both private and residential homes may not get the people back to the church, but it could get the church back to the people.

What can be done?

I considered this earlier under 'Issues raised', but Chapters 9 and 10 have answered the question 'What can be done?' with a clear answer: a great deal. Older people not only have a lot they can contribute to the life of the church in both practical and spiritual ways, but many of them are willing and able to make their contribution. In the twenty-first century, as society finds it has many more older people, the realization is dawning that the majority of these are young in outlook and fit in body and mind. Among them are considerable numbers – as this book shows – both inside and outside the active life of the church who would willingly get involved, given the chance.

Chapter 8 did show that, of those older people who left church, most did so in their teens and 20's. Bridges would have to be built to reach them, and the church would have to go across those bridges first. During and after World War Two, the sense of obligation to go to church disappeared, new interests replaced church activities, and large numbers left then. Millions of families had had to mark time for as long as six or seven years, and the rebuilding of family life, and the work to support it, became more vital than church-going. The re-establishment of nuclear families also had the impact of slowly excluding the grandparents, particularly with increased population movement because of job-seeking. Despite the move away from church, there is a vestige of goodwill among the majority, and the church could reach out again, with apologies for its own failings, if necessary.

Many older people want to help the local church. They want the church to help them. I believe the findings in these latter three chapters to be crucial.

If only . . .

. . . I could have seen the end from the beginning. After writing a book which evolves, as this one has, certain reflections are inevitable. Let me deal with a few of these briefly.

Qualitative interviewing is, by its very nature, time-consuming. To take just over a year to complete more than 220 interviews was a long time, but felt about right. Movement was bound to take place within that year: as my research ended, the then Archbishop of Birmingham announced his retirement, for example.

I accept the geographical limitations of my research area, even within Great Britain, let alone the world. There will have to be regional adjustments to interpret my findings for the Welsh valleys or the Hebridean islands, let alone in other countries. The worldwide literature from which I have sought to draw comparisons may have helped here.

Pleading lack of resources and manpower is no excuse. Indeed, having one interviewer gives consistency, and money could not have bought the wonderful interviewees. I was delighted that very few people were unwilling to be interviewed (a non-response rate of less than one in every 50), and every church leader gave time and assistance when asked. A postal survey, or a 'tick-box' style, would not have achieved my purposes. A Pilot Study enabled the Questionnaires to be fine-tuned, although, even then, some questions proved slightly superfluous. I do regret starting out with the word 'elderly'. It was too perjorative a term, and that of 'older people' was much to be preferred, and thus was used.

I could (perhaps, should) have visited one or two more non-religious older people's homes and forms of sheltered accommodation to get the views of their staff about church involvement. Seeing a considerable number of residents in these homes did help to deal with this. The church often forgets those hidden away in residential accommodation: I tried not to, but perhaps could have spent more time researching this area. There needs to be further research here – as more older people may well end their days in residential care. In a similar way, I might have explored a little more exactly why people left the church, not just their reasons for not returning. There appear to have been distinctive cut-off points when the church was left and, once the pattern was broken, there was never a re-establishment of the relationship. Again, further research could be pursued here.

Further research

I have referred to one or two matters I have either not covered at all or have dealt with too briefly. Among areas for further research, the following would appear to be of value.

The Black Church. As I have said, there is a problem peculiar to those churches which predominantly cater for those with a West Indian background. Many of their members were immigrants after World War Two. They are now torn between remaining in Britain or returning to their island of birth. Some do the latter, only then to return to Britain. Research needs to be done as to how to help the relationship between these older people and their churches.

Ethnic Minorities. This is another 'if only'. Major research is needed into how the church relates to older members of the many ethnic minorities in Britain.

Older members of other faiths. Here again, a question posed in Chapter 1 has not been answered except by way of silence. Inter-faith relationships is a whole area on its own. Whilst it might have impinged slightly on this book, it was really outside its parameters. Valuable research could be done here.

Carers. As I said earlier in this chapter, there needs to be more research into how the church ought to relate to and help those who care for older people, especially those who are themselves older.

Dementia sufferers. Despite work by people like Petzsch (1984) and Treetops (1996) there is much scope for this whole area to be researched from the church's point of view.

A final thought

An article in *The Gerontologist* entitled 'Religion and Well-being in Later Life' ended with these words:

> The subject of religion and its impact on the older person has only been examined cursorily. In studies in which the correlates of life-satisfaction and well-being have been examined, religion has been given a step-child status, whereas attention has been focused on factors such as social support, socio-economic status and health. (Koenig, Kvale and Ferrel, 1988, p.28)

With all my research, both in literature and through interviews, I feel that the first sentence of these words applies to this book: so little done, so much to do. I have indicated at various points where further research could be carried out. My hope is that this current work may enable the relationship between the church and older people to improve somewhat, and encourage further positive consideration as to how more can be done.

Appendix 1: Questionnaires

Questionnaire 1: General (for everyone)

The Church

1. Your first reaction: What do you understand by the word 'Church'?
2. (Prompt for a Question like this:) Now you've given that answer, would you like to add anything to define 'Church'?

The Elderly

3. Your first reaction: What does 'Elderly' mean?
4. When do people start being elderly? (show chart)
5. When do people start being old? (show chart)
6. To which age-group do you belong? (show chart)
7. Do you think of yourself as being
   – young?
   – midlife?
   – elderly?
   – old?

Under 40
41–45
46–50
51–55
56–60
61–65
66–70
71–75
76–80
81+

Changes

8. What are the main changes in the church worldwide in the last 30 or so years?
9. What do you think the main changes have been in the Church of England/RC/Methodist, etc., church (your denomination) in the last 30 or so years?
10. What have been the main changes in the church you attend (even if rarely) in the last 30 or so years?
11. What are the *best* changes in all 3?
12. What are the *worst* changes in all 3?

Questionnaire 2: Leaders

1. What % do you *estimate* are elderly attenders (65+) in your own church/denomination?
2. How will % change in next 20 years: more/same/less?
3. How do you feel about the elderly in your church? – Good or bad? Too many/too few?
4. Are there any special activities/provisions, etc., made for the elderly by your church/denomination?
5. What do the elderly appreciate most/least in your
   (a) liturgy?
   (b) community?
   (c) pastoral ministry?
6. How do you try and help them?
7. How can the elderly help you and the church?
8. How can the church be more user-friendly for the elderly?

ADDITIONAL QUESTIONNAIRE FOR ANGLICAN AND URC CLERGY

If the clergy are Anglican the question is:

In 1990 the Board of Social Responsibility of the Church of England produced a Report entitled *Ageing* with a workbook entitled 'Happy Birthday Anyway'. Have you seen these? And if so, what have you done about them?

If the clergy are URC the question is:

In January 1998 a Report was made to the Church and Society Committee entitled *Respecting the gift of years.* Have you seen this? And if so, are you doing anything about this?

Questionnaire 3: Elderly

The Church

1. Do you go to church?
2. How often?
3. Did you once go?
4. Have you always belonged to the same denomination?
5. How long have you been in your present pattern?

Attitudes to Church

6. What's good about your church? (a) denomination?
   (b) one you attend?
7. How good is it for *you*?
8. What do you enjoy?
9. What's wrong with your church?
10. What do you most dislike?
11. Do you have any problems with your denomination?

Reasons for going

12. Which of the following is your reason for going to church?
    - Somewhere to go?
    - Framework for your week/day?
    - A safe environment?
    - It doesn't patronize?
    - Social?
    - Spiritual?
    - Sacramental?
    - The age-mix?
    - Or why *don't* you go? What went wrong?

Changes and Needs

13. How do you react to recent changes:
    Since the last minister arrived? *or* In your/your nearest church?
14. What can the church do for you?
15. What can you do for the church?
16. How can the church be more user-friendly for you?
17. What can your church do for the elderly it's not doing now? – and how?
18. What do/did you/husband do work-wise?

Questionnaire 4: Young/mid-age

1. What do you feel about the elderly in the church?
2. Where do the elderly fit into church?
3. Do you feel you have a role to play as far as the elderly are concerned?
4. Can the elderly help the church – and how? (depends on 1–3!)

Appendix 2: Questionnaire for Theological Colleges

1. What percentage of time is spent at College studying Pastoral Care?
2. What training is given for work with children and young people?
3. Is any training given specifically for work with the elderly (65+)?
4. What advice is given regarding the housebound and those in residential homes?
5. What practical ideas are taught concerning attracting the elderly to church?
6. What ideas are suggested for activities for the elderly?
7. What training is given in preaching to the elderly?
8. What advice is given about using the elderly in the work and witness of the church?
9. Do you feel more could be done in all these areas? What?
10. What do you teach about bereavement?

Appendix 3: Questionnaire for Retirement Homes

1. How many residents do you have?
2. What is the age-span?
3. How many are able to get out without/with assistance?
4. Do you, as a management, want church involvement?
5. How many residents would value church involvement?
6. How many denominations are in the Home?
7. Which church are you most associated with?
8. How *is* the church involved *in* the Home/with the residents?
9. How *is* the church involved as a church building?
10. How *could* the church help, spiritually and practically?

Appendix 4: Assistance received

The following people and institutions have given assistance in the preparation of this book, either by allowing themselves to be interviewed, or aiding in the research. The author's thanks are to each and every one.

1. Interviewees **(211)**

(a) Church Leaders

Headquarters (9)

- Board of Mission of the Church of England, London.
- Superintendent Minister for the Coventry Methodist Circuit.
- Warwickshire District Secretary: United Reformed Church.
- General Superintendent West Midlands Area: The Baptist Union of Great Britain.
- Board of Social Witness, Presbyterian Church of Ireland.
- Birmingham Roman Catholic Diocesan Headquarters, Birmingham.
- Coventry Church of England Diocese Headquarters, Coventry.
- Baptist Union of Great Britain, Didcot.
- Board of Social Responsibility (C of E), London.

Clergy and Lay Leaders (46)

Roman Catholic:

- Archbishop of Birmingham (The Most Revd. M. Couve de Murville).
- Auxiliary Bishop of Birmingham (Rt. Revd. P. Pargiter).
- Birmingham Cathedral, Headquarters of RC Diocese (Father P. Daly).
- 4 Town/City Priests.
- 2 Country Priests.
- 3 Lay Leaders.

Church of England:

- Bishop of Coventry (The Rt. Revd. C. Bennetts).
- Bishop of Warwick (The Rt. Revd. A. Priddis).

- Former Bishop of Coventry (The Rt. Revd. S. Barrington-Ward).
- Archdeacon of Coventry (The Ven. I. Russell).
- Precentor of Coventry Cathedral (Canon C. Birch).
- 7 Town/City Priests.
- 3 Country Priests.
- 3 Lay Leaders.

Free Churches:

- 6 Town/City Clergy/Pastors.
- 3 Country Clergy/Pastors.
- 2 Lay Leaders.

Including Baptist, Methodist, United Reformed Church, New Testament Church of God, Church of God of Prophecy, Salvation Army.

New Churches:

- 3 Pastors/Leaders.
- 2 Lay Leaders.

(b) Young(Y)/Middle-Aged(M) Church Members (44)

Town/City/Country

• Roman Catholics:	7(Y)	3(M)
• Church of England:	11(Y)	4(M)
• Free Churches:	11(Y)	2(M)
• New Churches:	4(Y)	2(M)

(c) Elderly Church Attenders (52)

• Roman Catholics:	Town/City:	9 [4 Female(F), 5 Male(M)]
• Roman Catholics:	Country:	2 [1(F), 1(M)]
• Church of England:	Town/City:	16 [7(F), 9(M)]
• Church of England:	Country:	4 [3(F), 1(M)]
• Free Churches:	Town/City:	12 [11(F), 1(M)]
• Free Churches:	Country:	3 [1(F), 2(M)]
• New Churches:		6 [3(F), 3(M)]

(d) Elderly Non Church Attenders (60)
Former connection/persuasion (some recent, some very tenuous):

• Roman Catholics:	Town/City:	8 [6(F), 2(M)]
• Roman Catholics:	Country:	3 [1(F), 2(M)]
• Church of England:	Town/City:	25 [14(F), 11(M)]
• Church of England:	Country:	10 [4(F), 6(M)]
• Free Churches:	Town/City:	9 [9(F)]
• Free Churches:	Country:	5 [1(F), 4(M)]

2. *Theological Colleges (4)*

- St Mary's Seminary, Sutton Coldfield (RC).
- Ridley Hall, Cambridge (C of E).
- Westminster College, Cambridge (URC).
- Wesley House, Cambridge (Methodist).

3. *Retirement Homes (8)*

- Methodist: (2)
- Roman Catholic: (2)
- Church of England: (1)
- Inter-denominational: (1)
- Non-denominational: (1)
- Abbeyfield: (1)

References

Abbott, W. M. ed. (1966) *The Documents of Vatican II*. London: Geoffrey Chapman.

Age Concern (1980) *Claim to be Heard*. Mitcham: Age Concern.

—— (1993a) *How to Avoid becoming an Old Codger*. London: Age Concern.

—— (1993b) *Reflecting our Age: Images, Language and Older People*. London: Age Concern.

—— (1994) *Another Ism*. London: Age Concern.

—— (1997) *Debate of the Age*. London: Age Concern.

Ahuja, A. (1999) 'Age trap: Time to Stop the Tyranny of Ageism' (an interview with Professor Tom Kirkwood), *The Times*, 11 January.

Amis, K. (1988) *One Fat Englishman*. London: Larger Print Edition Oxford: Cleo Press.

An Ageing Population (1988) London: Family Policy Studies Centre.

Andersen, F. I. (1974) *Job (Tyndale Old Testament Commentaries)*. Leicester: Inter-Varsity Press.

Anke, Sister (1993) *Into Another Intensity – Diminishment and Retirement*. Oxford: Fairacres Press.

Apichella, M. (1989) *God's Grey Warriors*. Eastbourne: Monarch.

Appleton, N. (1998) *Respecting the Gift of Years*. A Report to the Church and Society Committee of the United Reformed Church. Witney: URC.

Archbishop of Canterbury's Advisory Group on Urban Priority Areas (1990) *Living Faith in the City*. London: General Synod of the Church of England.

Archbishop of Canterbury's Commission on Urban Priority Areas (1985) *Faith in the City*. London: Church House Publishing.

Ashford, D. (1919) *The Young Visiters*. London: Zodiac Books.

Askham, J., Barry, C., Grundy, E., Hancock, R. and Tinker, A. (1992) *Life after 60: A Profile of Britain's Older Population*. London: Age Concern/Institute of Gerontology.

Atkins, G. G. (1956) *The Interpreter's Bible, Vol. 5*. Abingdon: Cokesbury Press.

Baker, R. (1997) Introduction to The Abbeyfield Lecture. St. Albans: The Abbeyfield Society.

Barrett, C. K. (1973) *A Commentary on The Second Epistle to the Corinthians.* London: Adam and Charles Black.

Baruch, B. (1955) 'Ageless Viewpoint', *Newsweek,* 29 August.

Beasley-Murray, P. (1995) *A Call to Excellence.* London: Hodder and Stoughton.

Beckford, J. A. (1973) 'Religious organisation: a trend report and bibliography', *Current Sociology 21*(2), 7–170.

—— (1985) 'Religious Organisations', in P. E. Hammond, ed. *The Sacred in a Secular Age.* Berkley: University of California Press.

Bell, D. (1980) *What can we do?* Mitcham: Age Concern.

Bellah, R. N., Masden, R., Sullivan, W. M., Swidler, A. and Tipton, S. M. (1985) *Habits of the Heart.* Berkley: University of California Press.

Betjeman, J. (1958) 'Hymn' from *John Betjeman's Collected Poems.* London: John Murray (written 1931).

Biggs, S. (1993) *Understanding Ageing.* Buckingham: Open University Press.

Birren, J. E. (1960) 'Aging: Psychological Aspects', *International Encyclopedia of the Social Sciences,* vol. 1. New York: Macmillan Free Press.

Bishops' Advisory Group on UPAs (1995) *Staying in the City.* London: Church House Publishing.

Blech, B. (1981) 'Judaism and Gerontology', pp.4–20 in Le Fevre, C. and Le Fevre, P. *Aging and the Human Spirit,* Chicago: Exploration Press.

Board for Social Responsibility (1990) *Happy Birthday Anyway!* London: Church House Publishing.

Bond, J., Coleman, P. and Peace S. eds (1993) *Ageing in Society.* London: Sage.

Bone, M. (1996) *Trends in Dependency Among Older People in England.* London: OPCS.

Boote, B. (1994) *Age Potential: Pressures and Responses.* London: The Volunteer Centre.

Bosch, D. J. (1991) *Transforming Mission.* Maryknoll, New York: Orbis.

Boswell, J. (1791). *The Life of Samuel Johnson,* vol. 1 (1934 edn). London: G. B. Hill.

Botting, M. (1986) *Christians in Retirement.* Nottingham: Grove.

Bowrie, W. R. (1952) *The Interpreter's Bible, Vol. 1.* Abingdon: Cokesbury Press.

Brain, P. (1998) 'The United Reformed Church looks at the Year of the Older Person', *Plus 14* (4).
Bray, G. (1991) *Ageing – A sort of Ghetto-Land.* Nottingham: Grove.
Brensinger, T. L. (1996) 'A Brethren in Christ Theology of Aging', *Brethren in Christ History and Life.* 19(3).
Brierley, P. ed. (1991) *Prospects for the Nineties: Results of the English Church Census.* London: MARC Europe.
—— (1999a) *UK Christian Handbook Religious Trends (1998/99) No. 1.* Carlisle: Paternoster.
—— (1999b) Telephone conversation with the author, 11 March.
—— (1999c) *Religious Trends 2000/2001.* London: HarperCollins.
Brierley, P. and Wraight, H. (1997) 'Percentage of Population (Adults and Children) not attending Church', *Factfile* (Christian Research Association), March.
Briscoe, S. (1999) 'The Church where disciples are made.' Eastbourne: International Leaders for Discipleship Conference.
Brodie, I. (1998) 'Walter Cronkite airbourne again', *The Times,* 30 October.
Bromley, D. B. (1988) *Human Ageing.* London: Penguin.
Brooke, S., Barot, T. and Rollin, L. (1998) 'Forever Young', *Sunday Times,* 1 November.
Brookfield, A. (1996) 'Celebrating Old Age', in *Reaching Older People with God's Love.* London: Evangelical Alliance Coalition.
Brown, P. (1982) *The Other Side of Growing Older.* London: Macmillan.
Brown, R. (1998) *Good Retirement Guide.* London: Kogan Page.
Browning, R. *Rabbi ben Ezra,* in *Robert Browning Poems and Plays,* vol. 2, p. 481. London: Dent (published (1906, reprint 1963).
Burns, C. ed. (1991) *Called to be Old.* Leeds: Faith in Elderly People.
Burns, T. and Stalker, G. M. (1966) *The Management of Innovation.* London: Tavistock.
Burton-Jones, J. (1990) *From Generation to Generation.* Basingstoke: Olive Tree Press.
—— (1997) *Now and Forever.* London: Triangle.
Butler, C. (1981) *The Theology of Vatican II.* London: Darton, Longman and Todd.
Butler, M. (1998) 'Spirituality and Growing Older', in *Spiritual Perspectives on Ageing.* Derby: Methodist Homes for the Aged and Christian Council on Ageing.

Buttrick, G. A. ed. (1952) *The Interpreter's Bible.* New York: Abingdon.

Bytheway, B. (1995) *Ageism.* Buckingham: Open University Press.

Cardell, J. (1999) Methodist Headquarters, Birmingham District. Conversation with the author, 18 February.

Carey, G. (1991) 'There'll be a big party going on', *Readers Digest,* March, pp.41–3.

—— (1997) 'Care and Dignity in the next Millennium: will older people have a prayer?', *The Abbeyfield Lecture.* St Albans: The Abbeyfield Society.

—— (1998) Address at a Service for the National Sunday for Older People, Canterbury Cathedral, 27 September.

Caring for the Elderly (1997) London: Care.

Carlson, D. and Seicol, S. (1990) 'Adapting worship to changing needs', *Generations* 14.

Carstensen, R. N. (1983) 'Do We Need a Theology or Hermeneutic of Aging?', *Generations,* 8 (Fall).

Chester, R. and Smith, J. (1996) *Acts of Faith.* London: Counsel and Care.

Christian Council on Ageing (1998) *Age Awareness.* Derby: Methodist Homes for the Aged.

Claim to be heard (1980) The Report of a working party set up by Age Concern England to study the role of religious organisations in the welfare of the elderly. Mitcham: Age Concern.

Clarke, P. (1996) *Britain 1900–1990.* London: Allen Lane.

Clements, W. M. (1979) *Care and Counseling of the Aging.* Philadelphia: Fortress Press.

Coffey, D. (1998) Letter to Author from the General Secretary of the Baptist Union of Great Britain, 9 October.

Coggan, D. (1997) 'Foreword', in *The Fulness Of Time.* London: Counsel and Care.

Cohen, D. and Eisdorfer, C. (1986) *The Loss of Self: A Family Resource for the Care of Alzheimer's Disease and Related Disorders.* New York: Norton.

COHSE (1991) 'Over the hill to new horizons: a discussion document contributing to the changing debate on older people', in *Report by the Confederation of Health Employees.* Banstead, Surrey: COHSE.

Cole, T. (1992) *The Journey of Life: A Cultural History of Aging in America.* Cambridge: Cambridge University Press.

Coleman, P., Bond, J. and Peace, S. (1993) 'Ageing in the

Twentieth Century', in Bond, J. Coleman, P. and Peace, S. eds. *Ageing in Society,* pp.1–18. London: Sage.

Coleman, P., Seiger, C. and Sherbourne, K. (1990) 'Religion, Ageing and Adjustment: Questions for Research', *Generations* 13.

Collins, A. O. (1994) *Holman Bible Dictionary.* London: Parsons Technology (PC for Windows).

Collyer, M. (1997) 'Age does not weary them', *Share It!* (Church Army), Winter.

Congar, Y. (1987) 'Church: Ecclesiology', in Eliade, M. ed. *The Encyclopedia of Religion,* vol. 3. New York: Macmillan.

Cosby, W. H. (1987) *Time Flies.* New York: Bantam.

Crabb, G. (1810) *The Borough.*

Creber, A. (1990) *New Approaches to Ministry with Older People.* Nottingham: Grove.

—— (1994) *Evangelism among Retired People.* Warwick: Church Pastoral Aid Society.

Crompton, S. (2000) 'The Way to Maintain your Brain', *The Times,* 7 March, p.39.

Cross, F. L. ed. (1974) *The Oxford Dictionary of the Christian Church.* London: Oxford University Press.

Cumming, E. and Henry, W. E. (1961) *Growing old: The process of disengagement.* New York: Basic.

Daniels, N. (1988) *Am I my Parents' Keeper?* New York: Oxford University Press.

de Beauvoir, S. (1972a) *Old Age.* London: André Deutsch.

—— (1972b) *The Coming of Age.* New York: Putman.

Dobbins, G. S. (1977) *Zest for living.* Waco: Word.

Douglas, J. D. ed. (1962) *The New Bible Dictionary.* London: Inter-Varsity Fellowship.

Driver, S. R. (1904) *The Book of Genesis.* London: Methuen.

Drucker, P. (1992) 'The New Society of Organisation', *The Harvard Business Review,* 4 September, pp.95–104.

Dulin, R. Z. (1988) *A Crown of Glory: A Biblical View of Aging.* New York: Paulist Press.

Dylan, B. (1964) 'The times they are a-changin'', *Bob Dylan's Greatest Hits,* Colombia CBS Records, BPG 62847.

Edwards, J. (1999) In conversation, Eastbourne, International Leaders for Discipleship Conference, 22 September.

Elliott, E. (1995) 'Forget Me Not: Loving God's Aging Children', *Cross Point* 8 (3).

Elliott, V. (1999) 'Garden where memories grow', *The Times*, 1 June, p.9.

Fahey, C. J. and Lewis, M. A. (1984) 'Catholics', in Palmore, E. B. ed. *Handbook on the Aged in the United States*, pp.145–53. Westport, CT: Greenwood Press.

Faith in the Countryside (1990) Report to the Archbishops of Canterbury and York. Worthing: Churchman Publishing.

'Families and Communities' 1997–8, *Family Policy Bulletin*, Winter, p.16.

Featherstone, M. and Hepworth, M. (1993) 'Images of Ageing', in Bond, J., Coleman, P. and Peace, S., eds *Ageing in Society*, pp. 304–32.

Fennell, J. (1997) Assistant Director: Information, Age Concern, London, letter to the author, 27 November.

Finney, J. (1992) *Finding Faith Today*. Westlea: British and Foreign Bible Society.

Fischer, K. R. (1992) 'Spirituality and the Aging Family: A Systems Perspective', *Journal of Religious Gerontology* 8(4), pp.1–15.

Fletcher, J. (Chair) (1998) *Coventry Community Plan*. Coventry: Coventry City Council.

Frank, A. (1995) *The Wounded Storyteller*. Chicago: University of Chicago Press.

Franklin, A. and Franklin, B. (1990) 'Age and power', in Jeffs and Smith, eds. *Youth, Inequality and Society*. London: Macmillan.

Frean, A. (1999) 'Nursing Home "misery" of the elderly', *The Times*. 16 September, p.16.

Freeman, C. B. (1996) 'Biblical Principles for Senior Adults', *The Theological Educator* 53 (Spring).

Friedman, E. H. (1985) *Generation to Generation – Family Process in Church and Synagogue*. New York: Guildford Press.

Friends of the Elderly (1998) *Annual Review*. London: Friends of the Elderly.

Garner, J. C. (1996) 'Mature Adults: Active, Productive, Alive and Wanting to Stay that Way', *The Theological Educator* 53 (Spring) pp.77–84.

Garrard, Fr. (1999) Secretary to the R.C. Archbishop of Birmingham. Conversation with the author, 19 February.

Gaunt, A. (1998) *The Churches join in the Debate of the Age*. London: Board of Social Responsibility of the Church of England.

General Household Survey, The (1990) London: The Stationery Office.

Gerlach, L. P. and Hine, V. (1979) *People, Power, Change: Movements of Social Transformation*. Indianapolis: Bobbs-Merrill.

Gill, R. (1992) *Moral Communities*. Exeter: University of Exeter Press.

—— (1997) *Modern Leadership in a Post-modern Age*. Edinburgh: T&T Clark.

—— (1999) *Churchgoing and Christian Ethics*. Cambridge: Cambridge University Press.

Gledhill, R. (1999a) 'Faith can keep you healthy into old age', *The Times*, 16 July, p.10.

—— (1999b) 'Pope in plea to respect the old', *The Times*, 27 October, p.5.

Goldman, S. (1997) 'A life in the day of Kirk Douglas.' *The Sunday Times Magazine*, 23 November.

Goldsmith, M. (1996) *Hearing the Voice of people with Dementia*. London: Jessica Kingsley.

Gooding, D. (1990) *True to the Faith*. London: Hodder and Stoughton.

Goodman, J. (1999) 'Harvesting a Lifetime', in Jewell, A., ed. *Spirituality and Ageing*. London: Jessica Kingsley.

Gore, C., Goudge, H. L. and Guillaume, eds (1928) *A New Commentary on Holy Scripture*. London: SPCK.

Grainger, R. (1993) *Change to Life: The Pastoral Care of the Newly Retired*. London: Darton, Longman and Todd.

Gray, R. M. and Moberg, D. O. (1962) *The Church and the Older Person*. Grand Rapids: Eerdmans.

Greeley, A. M. (1972) 'The State of the Priesthood in the United States', *Doctrine and Life* 22(7).

Greengross, S. (1997) *Debate of the Age*. London: Age Concern.

Guillemard, A. M. (1983a) 'Introduction', in Guillemard, A. M., ed. *Old Age and the Welfare State*. London: Sage.

—— (1983b) 'The making of old age policy in France', in Guillemard, A. M., ed. *Old Age and the Welfare State*. London: Sage.

Hacker, S. (1999) 'Wheels: Go granny go', *Guardian*, 18 January, p.14.

Hall, P. (1998) *Coventry Evening Telegraph*, 30 September.

Hammond, G. (n.d.) *Ministry to Older People*. Leeds: Faith in Elderly People.

Handy, C. (1995) *The Age of Unreason*. London: Arrow.

Hannah, L. (1986) *Inventing Retirement: the Development of Occupational Pensions in Britain*. Cambridge: Cambridge University Press.

Harbottle, E. (1998) *Adapting our Lifestyle in Retirement*. Derby: Methodist Homes.

Harris, D. K. and Cole, W. E. (1980) *Sociology of Aging*. Boston: Houghton-Miffin.

Harris, J. (1998a) *The Church's Ministry to Ageing People*. Derby: Methodist Homes.

—— (1998b) *Those Who Care for Others*. Derby: Methodist Homes.

Harris, J. G. (1987) *Biblical Perspectives on Aging: God and the Elderly*. Philadelphia: Fortress.

Harris, L. (1974) In *American Association of Retired Persons News Bulletin Vol. XV*, No. 10, p.8.

Haswell, C. and King, J. (1997) *Life Beyond Sixty*. Training Manual London: Evangelical Alliance.

Heinecken, M. J. (1981) 'Christian Theology and Ageing: Basic Affirmations', in Clements, W. M. ed. *Ministry with the Aging* pp.76–90. San Francisco: Harper and Row.

Heinz, D. (1994) 'Finishing the Story: Aging, Spirituality and the Work of Culture', *Journal of Religious Gerontology* 9(1), pp.3–19.

Henry, M. (1960) (original 1710) *Concise Commentary on the Whole Bible*. Chicago: Moody.

Hess, R. (1996) *Joshua (Tyndale Old Testament Commentaries)*. Leicester: Inter-Varsity Press.

Hiltner, S. (1975) 'Facts and Needs: Present and Future', *Towards a Theology of Aging: Pastoral Psychology Special Issue*, pp.97–101. New York: Henman Sciences Press.

Hird, T. (1995) *Sing With Praise*. London: Fount.

Holmes, U. T. (1981) 'Worship and Aging: Memory and Repentance', in Clements, W. M., ed. *Ministry with the Aging*. San Francisco: Harper and Row.

Holtum, C. (1999) Letter to Author from the Research Officer for the Coventry Diocesan Pastoral Research Group.

Hooker, D. (1998) 'Rochester Older Person's Officer', *Plus 14* (4).

Hore DiFilippo, E. (1982) in 'Foreword' (p.IX) to Tiso, F. V., ed. *Aging: Spiritual Perspectives*. Lake Worth, Florida: Sunday Publications.

Hornsby-Smith, M. P. (1987) *Roman Catholics in England*. Cambridge: Cambridge University Press.

—— (1989) *The Changing Parish: A Study of Parishes, Priests and Parishioners After Vatican II.* London: Routledge.

—— (1991) *Roman Catholic Beliefs in England.* Cambridge: Cambridge University Press.

—— (1999) In discussion at the Sociology of Religion Conference, Durham, April.

Howe, A. (1993) 'Attitudes to Ageing: Views of Older People and the Community', *St Mark's Review* 155 (Spring), pp.3–11.

Howell, B. (1997) 'Mission Impossible and Impossible Living', *Preaching* 12, pp.34–8.

Howse, K. (1999) *Religion, Spirituality and Older People.* London: Centre for Policy on Ageing.

Hubbell, M. W. (1996) 'Am I there yet? Psychological and emotional make-up of senior adults', *The Theological Educator* 53 (Spring).

Hughes, P. (1999) 'Church life in the Year of Older Persons', *Grid 2* (Australia), pp.6–7.

Hunt, A. (1978) *The Elderly at Home: A Study of People Aged Sixty Five and Over Living in the Community in England in 1976.* London: OPCS.

Hunt, T. (1988) *Growing Older, Living Longer.* London: The Bodley Head.

Hutton, W. (1998) *The Life of William Hutton.* Stewdley: Brewin.

Jackson, D., ed. (1998) *Baptist Union Statistics.* Didcot: Baptist Union of Great Britain.

James, R. A. (1996) 'Involving Senior Adults in Missions', *The Theological Educator* 53 (Spring).

Jamieson, P. (1998) *M7 Survey.* Coventry: Kings Church.

Jerrome, D. (1989) 'Age relations in an English Church', *Sociological Review* 37(4), pp.761–84.

Jewell, A. (1998) 'The Challenge of Dementia', *Church Growth Digest* 19(4), Journal of the British Church Growth Association.

—— (1999) *Spirituality and Ageing.* London: Jessica Kingsley.

Johnson, D. P. and Mullins, L. C. (1989) 'Religiosity and Loneliness Among the Elderly', *The Journal of Applied Gerontology,* 8(1).

Johnson, J. and Bytheway, B. (1993) in Johnson, J. and Slater, R., eds. *Ageing and Later Life.* London: Sage.

Johnson, J. and Slater, R., eds (1993) *Ageing and Later Life.* London: Sage.

Johnson, P. and Falkingham, J. (1992) *Ageing and Economic Welfare*. London: Sage.
Jordan, C. F. (1996) 'The Spiritual Dynamics of Aging', *The Theological Educator* 53 (Spring).
Kalish, R. A. and Reynolds, D. K. (1976) *Death and Ethnicity: a Psychocultural Study*. Los Angeles: University of Southern California Press.
Kastenbaum, R. (1979) 'Exist and Existence', in *Aging, Death and the Completion of Being*. Philadelphia: University of Philadelphia Press.
Katz, R. L. (1975) 'Jewish Values and Sociopsychological Perspectives on Aging', *Towards a Theology of Aging: Pastoral Psychology Special Issue,* pp.135–50. New York: Henman Sciences Press.
Kerr, H. (1980) *How to Minister to Senior Adults in Your Church.* Nashville: Broadman Press.
Kidner, D. (1967) *Genesis (Tyndale Old Testament Commentaries).* Leicester: Inter-Varsity Press.
King, J. (1999) *Never Mind the Gap*. London: National Christian Education Council.
Knox, I. (1994) *Bereaved.* Eastbourne: Kingsway.
Koenig, H. G. (1993) 'Religion and Ageing', *Clinical Gerontology* 3(2).
Koenig, H. G., Kvale, J. N. and Ferrel, C. (1988) 'Religion and Well-being in Later Life', *The Gerontologist* 28(1).
Koenig, H. G., Lamar, T. M. and Lamar, B. (1997) *A Gospel for the Mature Years.* New York: Haworth.
Kuhn, T. S. (1970) *The Structure of Scientific Revolutions.* Chicago: University of Chicago Press.
Küng, H. (1968) *The Church.* London: Search.
Lamb, C. (1998) Letter to the author, 10 August.
Lambert, L. (1997) 'Problems of Older People' in *Life Beyond Sixty.* London: Evangelical Alliance.
Lampen, J. (1989) *An Ageing Population: Challenges and Opportunities.* Belfast: The Irish Council of Churches Board of Community Affairs.
Laslett, P. (1989) *A Fresh Map of Life: The Emergence of the Third Age.* London: Weidenfeld and Nicolson.
Lattimore, R. (1982) *Acts and Letters of the Apostles.* New York: Farrar Straus Giroux.
Le Fevre, C. and Le Fevre, P. (1981) *Aging and the Human Spirit.* Chicago: Exploration Press.

Lennon, J. and McCartney, P. (1967) 'When I'm 64', from *Sgt Pepper's Lonely Hearts Club Band.* London: Northern Songs Ltd.

Lesher, E. L. (1996) 'How should the Brethren in Christ Respond to an Aging Society?', *Brethren in Christ History and Life* 19(3).

Lightfoot, R. H. (1956) *St. John's Gospel: A Commentary*. Oxford: Oxford University Press.

Littell, F. (1964) *The Origins of Sectarian Protestantism.* New York: Macmillan.

Litwak, E. (1985) *Helping the Elderly*. New York: Guildford Press.

Longino, C. F. and Kitson, G. C. (1981) 'Parish Clergy and the Aged: Examining Stereotypes', in Le Fevre, C. and P. *Aging and the Human Spirit.* Chicago: Exploration Press.

Lowther Clarke, W. K. (1952) *Concise Bible Commentary*. London: SPCK.

Lyon, K. B. (1985) *Toward a Practical Theology of Aging.* Philadelphia: Fortress Press.

Lyte, H. F. (1933) 'Abide with me.' (1793–1847) *Methodist Hymn Book,* No. 948. London: Methodist Publishing House.

Macdonald, A. M. ed. (1972) *Chambers Twentieth Century Dictionary*. Edinburgh: W & R Chambers.

MacIntyre, S. (1977) 'Old age as a social problem', in Dingwall, R., Heath, C. Reid, M. and Stacey, M., eds *Health Care and Health Knowledge,* pp.41–3. London: Croom Helm.

MacKinlay, E. (1993) 'Spirituality and Ageing: Bringing Meaning to Life', *St Mark's Review* 155 (Spring).

Manley, G. T. (1962) 'Hushai', in Douglas, J. D., ed. *The New Bible Dictionary*. London: Inter-Varsity Fellowship.

Marshall, I. H. (1980) *Acts* (*Tyndale New Testament Commentaries*). Leicester: Inter-Varsity Press.

Marshall, M. (1999) District Secretary of the U.R.C. Conversation with the author, 19 February.

Matheson, J. and Summerfield, C., eds (1999) *Social Focus on Older People.* London: The Stationery Office.

McCreadie, C., Bennett, G. and Tinker, A. (1997) *An exploratory study of general practitioners' knowledge and experience of the abuse/ill treatment of older people in the community*. London: King's College.

McFadden, S. H. (1995) 'Religion and Well-Being in Aging Persons in an Aging Society', *Journal of Social Issues* 51(2), pp.161–75.

McFadyen, D. (1997) *People to People and Focus Areas.* London: Church Army.

Metropolitan Anthony of Sourozh (n.d.) *The Spirituality of Old Age.* Greens Norton: The Christian Council of Ageing.

Midwinter, E. (1991) *The British Gas Report on Attitudes to Ageing 1991.* London: British Gas.

Mills, E. (1999) 'She'll punch your brain into shape', *Sunday Times News Review,* 6 June, p.5.

Minois, G. (1989) *History of Old Age.* Cambridge: Polity Press.

Mission Theological Advisory Group (1996) *The Search for Faith.* London: Church House Publishing.

Moberg, D. (1951) *Religion and Personal Adjustment in Old Age.* Minnesota: University of Minnesota.

—— (1972) 'Religion and the aging family', *Family Co-ordinator,* January.

—— ed. (2001) *Aging and Spirituality.* New York: Haworth Pastoral Press.

Montefiore, C. G. (1909) *The Synoptic Gospels.* London: Macmillan.

Montefiore, S. S. (1997) 'Barnacles on the rock of ages', *The Sunday Times,* 21 December.

Moody, H. (1992) 'Gerontology and critical theory', *The Gerontologist* 32(3), pp.294–5.

Moore, J. (1975) 'The Catholic Priesthood', in Hill, M., ed. *A Sociological Yearbook of Religion in Britain,* 8.

Morrison, M. C. (1998) *Let Evening Come: Reflections on Ageing.* London: Bantam Press.

Moser, C. A. and Kalton, G. (1979) *Survey Methods in Social Investigation.* Aldershot: Dartmouth.

Naish, J. (1999) 'The joy of learning how to remember', *The Times Weekend,* 5 June, p.14.

National Interfaith Coalition on Aging (1975) *Spiritual Well-Being.* Athens, GA: NICA.

National Population Projections (1996) London: Government Actuary's Department.

Neal, M. A. (1970) 'The Relation between Religious Belief and Structural Change in Religious Orders', *Review of Religious Research* 12 (Fall).

Neuberger, J. (1995) *The End or Merely the Beginning.* London: Counsel and Care.

Nissel, M. (1982) *Family Care of the Handicapped Elderly: Who Pays?* London: Policy Studies Institute.

Norman, A. (1987) *Aspects of Ageism: A Discussion Paper.* London: Centre for Policy on Ageing.

Nouwen, H. J. (1995) 'On Death and Aging', *Cross Point* 8(3), pp.1–8.

Nouwen, H. J. and Gaffney, W. J. (1976) *Aging: The Fulfilment of Life.* New York: Image Doubleday.

Nowell, P. (1999) *Mortality Tables.* London: Continuous Mortality Investigation Bureau of the Faculty and Institute of Actuaries.

Office for National Statistics, Government Actuary's Department (1998) *Social Trends 28.*

Office of Population Censuses and Surveys (1991) Population Projections: mid-1989 based, *OPCS Monitor PP2 91/1.* London: OPCS.

Oppenheimer, H. (1999) 'Inner Resources for Growing Older', in A. Jewell, ed. *Spirituality and Ageing,* pp.39–47. London: Jessica Kingsley.

Parkinson, R. (1999) 'Society has to meet Challenge of Elderly', *Church Times,* 28 May.

Pascall, S. (1999) Seminar 'Reaching the Grey Generation', at Past Imperfect Future Tense, Skegness, Spring Harvest Conference.

Patterson, D. (1999) 'A Place for Everyone', *Grid 2,* Australia, p.1.

Patterson, T. V., ed. (n.d.), *Guidelines for the Church's Care of the Elderly.* Belfast: Christian Training Committee of the Presbyterian Church in Ireland.

Paul, S. and Paul, J. (1994) *Humanity comes of Age.* Geneva: World Council of Churches.

Payne, D. F. (1970) *Genesis, Exodus.* London: Scripture Union.

Pearce, L. (1998) 'Anti-Ageing', *The M & S Magazine,* Autumn, p.63.

Peberdy, A. (1993) 'Spiritual Care of Dying People', in D. Dickenson and M. Johnson, eds. *Death, Dying and Bereavement.* London: Sage.

Peifer, J. M. (1996) 'Pastoral Care and Congregational Life with Older Adults', *Brethren in Christ History and Life,* 19(3).

Pereira, J. (1982) 'A Christian Theology of Aging', in F. V. Tiso, ed. *Aging: Spiritual Perspectives,* pp.135–62. Lake Worth, Florida: Sunday Publications.

Persons, T. (1941) 'Things ain't what they used to be' (Song title).

Petzsch, H. M. J. (1984) *Does he know how frightening he is in his strangeness? A Study of Attitudes to Dementing People.* Edinburgh: Centre for Theology and Public Issues.

Phillipson, C. (1993) 'The Sociology of Retirement', in J. Bond, P. Coleman and S. Peace, eds. *Ageing in Society*. London: Sage.

—— (1998) *Reconstructing Old Age*. London: Sage.

Pieper, H. G. and Garrison, T. (1992) 'Knowledge of Social Aspects of Aging Among Pastors', *Journal of Religious Gerontology* 8(4).

Pollak, O. (1948) 'Social Adjustment in Old Age', *Social Science Research Council Bulletin* 59.

Pontificium Consilium pro Laicis (Pontifical Council for the Laity) (1999) 'The Dignity of Older People and their Mission in the Church and in the World', *Briefing* 29(3), pp.11–24.

Pope John Paul II (1982) Sermon in *Ideas for your Special Service* (n.d.) London: Help the Aged.

—— (1984) *Insegnamenti di Giovanni Paolo II*, VIII Rome: Vatican.

—— (1997) 'Encyclical' in *Church Friend Briefing*, Advent (1995) London: Help the Aged.

Pope, A. (1711) *An Essay on Criticism*, lines 342–3.

Population Trends (1998) 'Living arrangements for elderly people in Great Britain, 1995', *Population Trends* 92, p.27.

Pro Mundi Vita (1973) 'Pluralism and Pluriformity in Religious Life: A Case Study,' *Bulletin* 47.

Pruyser, P. W. (1975) 'Aging: Downward, Upward, or Forward?' *Towards a Theology of Aging: Pastoral Psychology Special Issue*. New York: Henman Sciences Press, pp.102–18.

Quoist, M. (1973) *Meet Christ and Live*. Dublin: Gill and MacMillan.

Rainbow, J. (1991) 'Spiritual and Faith Development in the Later Years', *Review and Expositor* 88.

Readers Digest (1997) Vol 151. July. No 903 p.54 (quoting 'Approved Crossword Puzzles').

Reeve, B. (n.d.) *Pastoral Action for Residential Care Homes for the Elderly*. Eastbourne: PARCHE.

Regan, D. and Smith, J., eds (1997) *The Fullness of Time*. London: Counsel and Care.

Regional Trends (1999) 'Prescriptions Dispensed, 1997', *Regional Trends* 34. London: HMSO.

Report of the Social Policy Committee of the Board for Social Responsibility (1990) *Ageing*. London: Church House Publishing.

Report of a Working Party of the Board for Social Responsibility (1995) *Something to Celebrate*. London: Church House Publishing.

Richards, M. and Seicol, S. (1991) 'The Challenge of Maintaining Spiritual Connectedness for Persons Institutionalised with Dementia', *Journal of Religious Gerontology* 7(3).

Richter, P. and Francis, L. J. (1998) *Gone but not Forgotten.* London: Darton, Longman and Todd.

Roberts, N. (1970) *Our Future Selves: Care of the Elderly.* London: Allen and Unwin.

Rosewell, P. (1987) *The Five Silent Years of Corrie ten Boom.* London: Hodder & Stoughton.

Rumbelow, H. (1999) 'Women delight in finding life begins at fifty', *The Times,* 11 June, p.11.

Rumbold, B. (1993) 'Some Reflections on Pastoral Care and Ageing', *St Mark's Review* 155 (Spring).

Runyan, T. H. (1989) 'Aging and a Meaningful Future', *Journal of Religion and Aging* 6.

Ryle, J. C. (1856, 1974 reprint) *Expository Thoughts of the Gospels: Matthew.* Cambridge: James Clarke.

Saunders, C. (1999) 'When you're 81, you don't care about diets', *The Times,* 8 June, p.19.

Sax, S. (1993) 'Public Policy and Ageing', *St Mark's Review* 155 (Spring).

Schachter-Shalomi, Z. and Miller, R. (1995) *From Ageing to Sageing.* New York: Warner Books.

Scrutton, S. (1990) In E. McEwen, ed. *Age: The Unrecognised Discrimination.* London: Age Concern pp.13–14.

Selwyn, E. G. (1947) *The First Epistle of Peter.* London: Macmillan.

Shakespeare, W. (1598) *As you like it,* Act 2, Scene 7, lines 163–6. London: Collins.

—— (1599) *Hamlet,* Act 3, Scene 1, line 65.

—— (c.1600) *Sonnet No. 2.*

Sheehan, N. W., Wilson, R. and Marella, L. M. (1988) 'The Role of the Church in Providing Services for the Aging', *The Journal of Applied Gerontology* 7(2).

Shreeve, M. (1999) 'Uncommon people and the unselfish generations', The Abbeyfield Lecture. St Albans: The Abbeyfield Society.

Sidell, M. (1993) 'Death, Dying and Bereavement,' in J. Bond, P. Coleman and S. Peace, eds. *Ageing in Society,* pp.151–79. London: Sage.

—— (1995) 'Ageing and Death', in J. Neuberger, *The End or Merely the Beginning.* London: Counsel and Care.

Skidmore, D. (1998) Letter to author from the Secretary to the Board for Social Responsibility of the Church of England, 11 August.

Sloan, R. P., Bagiella, E. and Powell, T. (1999) 'Religion, Spirituality and Older People', *Lancet* 353, pp.664–7.

Social Trends 24 (1994) HMSO.

Sparkes, G. R. (1998) Letter to author from the Mission Advisor to the Baptist Union of Great Britain, 21 October.

Spinka, M. (1966) *John Hus' Concept of the Church.* Princeton, NJ: Princeton University Press.

Spriggs, D. (1998) 'Reaching Older People with God's Love', *Church Growth Digest* 19(4), Journal of the British Church Growth Association.

Spurgeon, C. H. (1976) *Selections from the Treasury of David.* London: Marshall, Morgan and Scott.

St Andrew's House, Earlsdon, Coventry 1999 – *Prospectus.*

Stafford, T. (1989) *As Our Years Increase.* Leicester: Inter-Varsity Press.

Stagg, F. (1981) *The Bible Speaks on Aging.* Nashville: Broadman Press.

Strong, J. (c.1970) *Comprehensive Concordance of the Bible.* Iowa Falls, Iowa: World Bible Publishers.

Stroud, P. (1999) Letter to *The Times,* 19 January.

Sutherland, S. (Chair) (1999) 'With Respect to Old Age: Long Term Care – Rights and Responsibilities': *A Report by the Royal Commission on Long Term Care.* London: The Stationery Office.

Talmon, Y. (1968) 'Aging: Social Aspects', in D. L. Sills, ed. *International Encyclopedia of the Social Sciences,* Vol. 1, pp.106–96. USA: Macmillan.

Taylor, J. B. (1970) *The Minor Prophets.* London: Scripture Union.

Taylor, R. (1996a) 'How to lead an older person to Christ', *Reaching Older People with God's Love.* London: Evangelical Alliance Coalition.

—— (1996b) 'Wake up to old age!', *Anglicans for Renewal Magazine* 67, pp.13–14.

—— (1997) *Outlook,* Winter p.1.

—— (1998) *New Christian Herald,* 3 October.

Thomas, M. (1999) 'The Curse of Older Age', *Plus* 15(3), pp.10–11.

Thomson, M. (1998) 'Reaching Older People with God's Love', *Church Growth Digest* 19(4), Journal of the British Church Growth Association.

Tidmarsh, M. (1998) 'The Ageing Process', in *Spiritual Perspectives on Ageing*. Derby: Methodist Homes for the Aged and Christian Council on Ageing.
Tinker, A. (1989) *Why the Sudden Interest in Ageing?* Lecture at King's College. London: King's College, 13 November.
—— (1997) *Older People in Modern Society*. London: Longman.
—— (1999) Lecture, Bawtry Hall, Bawtry (Doncaster).
Tiso, F. V. ed. (1982) *Aging: Spiritual Perspectives*. Lake Worth, Florida: Sunday Publications.
Tobin, S., Ellor, J. and Anderson, R. S. (1986) *Enabling the Elderly: Religious institutions within the community service systems*. Albany: State University Press of New York.
Tongue, R. (1998) 'Breakdown of Church of England Numbers', Conversation with the author, 18 August.
Tournier, P. (1972) *Learning to Grow Old*. London: SCM.
Townsend, P. (1986) 'Ageism and Social Policy', in C. Phillipson and A. Walker, A. eds. *Ageing and Social Policy*, pp.15–44. London: Gower.
Treetops, J. (1992) *A Daisy among the Dandelions*. Leeds: Faith in Elderly People.
—— (1996) *Holy, Holy, Holy*. Leeds: Faith in Elderly People.
Tritschler, J. (1991) 'Vieillir dans l'Amour de la Vie', *Foi et Vie* 90(2).
Troeltsch, E. (1931) *The Social Teaching of the Christian Churches*. London: George Allen and Unwin.
Turgenev, I. (1862) *Fathers and Sons*.
Turner, D. (1983) 'The relevance of Christian values today', *New Life* 39(4).
United Nations (1999) *Principles for Older Persons*. New York: United Nations.
Victor, C. R. (1994) *Old Age in Modern Society*. London: Chapman and Hall.
Wainwright, D. (1999) 'Diminishment in Later Life', *Plus* 15(2).
Wakefield, G. (1998) *Finding a Church*. Unpublished Ph.D. Thesis, Canterbury, University of Kent.
Walker, A. (1993) *Age and Attitudes: main results from a Eurobarometer Survey*. Brussels: Commission of the European Communities.
Ward, R. A. (1984) *The Aging Experience*. New York: Harper and Row.
Warner, R. (1999) 'Too old or too young', *Christian Herald*, 17 July, p.9.

Warren, R. (1995a) *Being Human, Being Church.* London: Marshall Pickering.

—— (1995b) *Building Missionary Congregations.* London: Church House Publishing.

Warren, R., Gerig, J. and Cottone, J. (1997) 'Senior Enlisted Troops', *Leadership* 18(2), pp.103–5.

Watkins, D., ed. (2001) *Religion and Aging.* New York: Haworth Pastoral Press.

Watts, I. (1674–1748) 'O God our help in ages past', *Methodist Hymn Book,* 1933, No. 878. London: Methodist Publishing House.

Webber, A. (1990) *Life later on.* London: Triangle.

Weber, M. (1930) *The Protestant Ethic and the Spirit of Capitalism.* London: Unwin.

—— (1965, first published 1922) *The Sociology of Religion.* London: Methuen.

Weiss, R. (1997) 'Aging – new answers to old questions', *National Geographic,* November, pp.12–18.

White House Conference on Aging: Basic Policy Statements and Recommendations (1961) 87th Congress, 1st Session, prepared for the Special Committee on Aging, US Senate, US Government Printing Office pp.122–5.

Whitehead, E. A. and Whitehead, J. D. (1981) 'Retirement', in W. M. Clements, ed. *Ministry with the Aging.* San Fransisco: Harper and Row.

Whitworth, D. (1998) 'Astronaut legend launches grey pride into public orbit', *The Times,* 30 October.

Wilcock, P. (1999) 'Death and the Spirituality of Ageing' in, A. Jewell, ed. *Spirituality and Ageing,* pp.75–85. London, Jessica Kingsley.

Wilson, B. R. (1968) 'Religious Organisations', in D. Sills, ed. *International Encyclopedia of the Social Sciences,* Vol 13. New York: Macmillan.

Winter, M. (1973) *Mission or Maintenance: A Study in New Pastoral Structures.* London: Darton, Longman and Todd.

Wiseman, D. J. (1962) 'Abraham' in J. D. Douglas ed. *The New Bible Dictionary.* London: Inter-Varsity Fellowship.

World Health Report (1998) Geneva: World Health Organisation.

Yaconelli, M. (1998) 'The gift of growing old', *Aufatmen* (Spring). Witten: Bundes-Verlag.

Yancey, P. (1997) *What's so Amazing about Grace?* Grand Rapids: Zondervan.

259.3
K743
LINCOLN CHRISTIAN COLLEGE AND SEMINARY
104633

Yarbrough, H. L. (1996) 'The Senior Adult Choir', *The Theological Educator* 53 (Spring).

Yeats, W. B. (1956) 'Sailing to Byzantium', *Collected Poems, Definitive Edition*. New York: Macmillan.

Yessick, T. (1995) *The North American Congress on the Church and the Age Wave*. Washington: PAEDIEA.

Yoder, G. (1996) 'The Aging Society: Implications for the Church and Ministry', *Brethren in Christ History and Life* 19(3). pp.417–37.

3 4711 00169 5321